The Smithsonian Guides to Natural America
THE HEARTLAND

WA

The
Pacific
Northwest
OR

MT

The
Northern
Rockies

ND

The
Northern
Plains
SD

ID

WY

Nebraska

NV

The
Far
West

CA

UT

The
Southern
Rockies

CO

Kansas

AZ

The
Southwest

NM

OK

TX

HI

The
Pacific

AK

MN

WI

MI
The
Great
Lakes

Iowa

The
Heartland

Illinois

Missouri

IN

OH

KY

Central
Appalachia

TN

Northern
New
England

ME

VT

NH

NY

The
Mid–Atlantic
States

MA
CT R

Southern
New
England

PA

NJ

MD DE

WV

VA

The
Atlantic
Coast

NC

AR

The
South
Central
States

MS

AL

The
Southeast

GA

SC

LA

FL

THE HEARTLAND
NEBRASKA – IOWA – ILLINOIS
KANSAS – MISSOURI

THE SMITHSONIAN GUIDES TO NATURAL AMERICA

THE HEARTLAND

ILLINOIS, IOWA, NEBRASKA, KANSAS, AND MISSOURI

TEXT
Suzanne Winckler

PHOTOGRAPHY
Willard Clay, Michael Forsberg,
Charles Gurche, and Tom Till

PREFACE
Thomas E. Lovejoy

SMITHSONIAN BOOKS • WASHINGTON, D.C.
RANDOM HOUSE • NEW YORK, N.Y.

Copyright © 1997 by Smithsonian Institution
Maps by Allan Cartography. Raven Maps & Images bases are used by permission.
Cover design by Andy Carpenter.
Permission credits to reproduce previously published photos appear on page 286.
All rights reserved under International and Pan-American Copyright Conventions. Published in the
United States by Random House, Inc., New York, and Smithsonian Books, Washington, D.C., and
simultaneously in Canada by Random House of Canada Limited, Toronto.

Front cover: Rainbow and wildflowers, Cedar Hills Sand Prairie, Iowa
Half-title page: Sandhill crane, Platte River, Nebraska
Frontispiece: Turkey River near El Dorado, Iowa
Back cover: Great horned owl; purple lead plant; black-tailed prairie dog

THE SMITHSONIAN INSTITUTION
SECRETARY I. Michael Heyman
COUNSELOR TO THE SECRETARY FOR
BIODIVERSITY AND ENVIRONMENTAL AFFAIRS Thomas E. Lovejoy
DIRECTOR, SMITHSONIAN PRESS/SMITHSONIAN PRODUCTIONS Daniel H. Goodwin
EDITOR, SMITHSONIAN BOOKS Alexis Doster III

THE SMITHSONIAN GUIDES TO NATURAL AMERICA
SERIES EDITOR Sandra Wilmot
MANAGING EDITOR Ellen Scordato
SERIES PHOTO EDITOR Mary Jenkins
PHOTO EDITOR Sarah Longacre
ART DIRECTOR Mervyn Clay
ASSISTANT PHOTO EDITOR Ferris Cook
ASSISTANT PHOTO EDITOR Rebecca Williams
ASSISTANT EDITOR Seth Ginsberg
COPY EDITORS Helen Dunn, Karen Hammonds
FACT CHECKER Jean Cotterell
PRODUCTION DIRECTOR Katherine Rosenbloom

George Potts, a biologist and environmental writer from Wichita, Kansas,
provided invaluable assistance on the Kansas chapter.

Library of Congress Cataloging-in-Publication Data
Winckler, Suzanne.
    The Smithsonian guides to natural America. The Heartland—
Nebraska, Iowa, Illinois, Missouri, Kansas/text by Suzanne
Winckler; photography by Michael Forsberg . . . [et al.];
preface by Thomas E. Lovejoy.
      p.   cm.
Includes bibliographical references (p. 254) and index.
ISBN 0-679-76481-X (pbk.)
    1. Natural history—Middle West—Guidebooks. 2. Middle West
—Guidebooks. I. Forsberg, Michael. II. Title.
QH104.5.M47W55 1996
508.77—dc20   95-48073
                                              CIP
Manufactured in the United States of America
98765432

HOW TO USE THIS BOOK

The SMITHSONIAN GUIDES TO NATURAL AMERICA explore and celebrate the preserved and protected natural areas of this country that are open for the public to use and enjoy. From world-famous national parks to tiny local preserves, the places featured in these guides offer a splendid panoply of this nation's natural wonders.

Divided by state and region, this book offers suggested itineraries for travelers, briefly describing the high points of each preserve, refuge, park, or wilderness area along the way. Each site was chosen for a specific reason: Some are noted for their botanical, zoological, or geological significance, others simply for their exceptional scenic beauty.

Information pertaining to the area as a whole can be found in the introductory sections to the book and to each chapter. In addition, specialized maps at the beginning of each book and chapter highlight an area's geography and geological features as well as pinpoint the specific locales that the author describes.

For quick reference, places of interest are set in **boldface** type; those set in **boldface** followed by the symbol ❖ are listed in the Site Guide at the back of the book. (This feature begins on page 261, just before the index.) Here noteworthy sites are listed alphabetically by state, and each entry provides practical information that visitors need: telephone numbers, mailing addresses, and specific services available.

Addresses and telephone numbers of national, state, and local agencies and organizations are also listed. Also in appendices are a glossary of pertinent scientific terms and designations used to describe natural areas; the author's recommendations for further reading (both nonfiction and fiction); and a list of sources that can aid travelers planning a guided visit.

The words and images of these guides are meant to help both the active naturalist and the armchair traveler to appreciate more fully the environmental diversity and natural splendor of this country. To ensure a successful visit, always contact a site in advance to obtain detailed maps, updated information on hours and fees, and current weather conditions. Many areas maintain a fragile ecological balance. Remember that their continued vitality depends in part on responsible visitors who tread the land lightly.

C O N T E N T S

PREFACE

The states of the Heartland—Illinois, Iowa, Kansas, Missouri, and Nebraska—possess some of the richest soil in North America. Once monumental grasslands dominated this section of the midcontinent, but today fields of grain stretching unbroken to the horizon are more likely to define this intensely agricultural area. Small pockets of prairie still persist, however, as do mighty springs (including the third largest in the United States), the Western hemisphere's largest sand dunes, networks of scenic rivers, and vast concentrations of snow geese and sandhill cranes.

Among the Heartland's great waterways is the Missouri River, which Meriwether Lewis and William Clark followed north and west as they sought a transcontinental water route to the Pacific in 1804–6. (Because the Smithsonian was not established until 1846, specimens collected on that notable expedition are still housed in Philadelphia's venerable Academy of Natural Sciences.) In the 1830s Swiss artist Karl Bodmer also traveled up the Missouri, accompanying Prince Maximilian of Wied-Neuwied on a North American sequel to their earlier expedition to the Atlantic forests of Brazil. Today along the Missouri, at such places as Iowa's DeSoto National Wildlife Refuge, bits of original riverscape endure, and Bodmer's paintings, so wonderfully evocative of this part of the Heartland in the early nineteenth century, provide an interesting comparison to the fragments of natural landscape that remain as well as a stark contrast to all that has changed.

The Heartland is, in fact, probably the most modified part of natural America. Of the 40 percent of Illinois that was once forest, only 12 percent remains wooded. Wetlands that once covered 30 percent of the state have now dwindled to only 3.5. Nearly 99 percent of the original prairie is gone. In Iowa, prairie has been reduced from 30 million acres to 30,000, of which only 5,000 are formally protected. Prairie is, in fact,

---

PRECEDING PAGES: *Landscapes on the plains are pared to essentials: earth, sky, and clouds. At Nebraska's Agate Fossil Beds, summer grasses spread a green patina over buttes as cloud shadows dance across the ground.*

so diminished that one of the few ways it survives at all is in the protected confines of graveyards, as what are termed "cemetery prairies."
Rivers, their bottomland riverine forests, and other habitats are modified
as well. Nearly 70 percent of the volume of the formerly free-flowing
Platte, for instance, now goes elsewhere, harnessed for other purposes.

Great wildlife migrations were once dramatic elements in this part
of natural America. By the end of the nineteenth century, the vast herds
of bison had been eliminated, and today token herds have been reintroduced in a few places. Wetlands, potholes, and river systems have long
sustained great migrations of ducks, geese, cranes, and other birds.
While much reduced, half a million sandhill cranes (80 percent of the
total world population) still use the Big Bend Reach of the Platte, and
the Heartland continues to support an important flyway for waterfowl.

The geology of the Heartland is of course less altered. The great
midcontinental fossil beds, the amazingly fertile hunting grounds of
such nineteenth-century paleontologists as O. C. Marsh of Yale
University and Edward Drinker Cope of Philadelphia's Academy of
Natural Sciences, still hold great promise. Parts of the region, marked
with glacial moraines, kames, lakes, and ponds, show the heavy im-
print of the ice age. Others areas—the Shawnee Hills in southern
Illinois or the Ozarks in Missouri—escaped the glaciers' flattening reach
and still boast relatively dramatic topography. The Shawnees, in fact,
are part of what is termed the "Driftless Area," a region where glaciers
did not bulldoze sediments, or drift, to produce a fairly featureless terrain. Spectacular karst country, marked by limestone caverns and sinkholes, characterizes the Ozarks region.

More subtle than the Grand Canyon and less dramatic than
Yosemite, the best of the Heartland's preserves and sanctuaries hold
multiple opportunities for glimpses of natural America. A skein of prairie
reserves (the Indian Boundary Prairies) lies near Chicago, Carl Sand-
burg's City of the Big Shoulders. Intensely urban Cook County even has
its own forest preserve. Indeed, in 1963 Illinois became the first state to
set up a system of protected areas based on biological criteria. Wetlands
scattered here and there support major concentrations of shorebirds
such as American avocets, Hudsonian godwits, and white-rumped, buff-
breasted, and Baird's sandpipers (the latter named for the second secretary of the Smithsonian, Spencer Fullerton Baird). Close to half of North

America's shorebirds feed and rest in and around the marshes and mud-flats of the Cheyenne Bottoms in south-central Kansas.

There is still a great deal to be concerned about in the Heartland. This is dust bowl country—a lesson easily forgotten and just as easily repeated. The drawdown of the nonrenewable supply of "fossil" groundwater from the Ogallala aquifer in western Kansas is already affecting springs, streams, and other watercourses. At the same time there is much to celebrate here. A splendid multiplicity of modest but important protected areas dot the Heartland where eastern forest and western grassland meet and dance an ecological conga line back and forth over time in response to many factors, particularly fire.

A variety of formally designated wild and scenic rivers tumble through and glide across the region: the Niobrara, Missouri, and Ozark, among others. Wildflower diversity is spectacular: At the right time of year, landscapes are spattered with the full spectrum of nature's palette. Butterflies abound: The black dash, two-spotted skipper, purplish copper, and aphrodite populate areas near Chicago; the regal fritillary (with all its splendid argent) and other species such as Ottoe's, Pawnee, and dusted skippers flutter across the Loess Hills of Iowa. And in 1996, the United States finally designated the first Tallgrass Prairie National Preserve, in the Flint Hills of Kansas.

So get to the Heartland. Take a walk on the prairie, admire the wildflowers, listen for the songs of the bobolink and the meadowlark. Only here can you enter the souls and see what inspired such quintessentially American writers and artists as Willa Cather, Mark Twain, and Thomas Hart Benton. Only here can you savor the most subtle pleasures that natural America has to offer.

—Thomas E. Lovejoy
Counselor to the Secretary for
Biodiversity and Environmental Affairs,
SMITHSONIAN INSTITUTION

LEFT: *Wildflowers—prairie clovers, black-eyed Susans, daylilies—glimmer in the tall grasses at Illinois's Hetzler Cemetery. Preserved amid the farm fields, undisturbed graveyards often shelter tiny pockets of native prairie.*

THE HEARTLAND

50   0   50 Miles

50   0   50 Kilometers

SOUTH DAKOTA

Pine Ridge Escarpment

Missouri River

Sioux City

NEBRASKA

North Platte River

Platte River

Omaha

LINCOLN

COLORADO

KANSAS

TOPEKA

Wichita

NEW MEXICO

TEXAS

OKLAHOMA

INTRODUCTION

INTRODUCTION:
THE HEARTLAND

From roughly April to October, several hundred different wildflower species bloom in the last prairie pockets scattered across the plains of North America from Illinois and Iowa to Nebraska, Kansas, and Missouri. This show, which lasts half the year but is witnessed by only the most inveterate prairie watchers, is spectacular. It is a constellation of rockets bursting in slow motion.

Amid the fireworks, one wildflower—the purple prairie clover—provides a useful parable about grasslands. Purple prairie clover blooms for a few weeks in midsummer, the exact timing determined by latitude and prevailing quirks of climate. Its vivid thimble-shaped flower spike is shocking: a plush purple-magenta flecked with tiny, glittery blaze-orange stamens. From a strictly botanical perspective, this purple extravaganza is indeed a flower, but it *looks* like a spangle embellishing an article of scanty clothing. After its brief exhibition, the flower fades, and the purple prairie clover settles into obscurity amid the bedlam of other wildflowers and prairie grasses. In its 360 or so days of anonymity, the purple prairie clover distinguishes itself in another way. When touched or crushed, its leaves release a fragrance like no other on the plains: sweet and a little peppery, purple prairie clover is the garam masala of the prairie.

This is the lesson of purple prairie clover: It reveals itself in explosions of clarity but is otherwise subtle and nondescript. It does not beckon and cannot be recognized or appreciated from a distance. These very same traits characterize the vast carpet of grassland and savanna that once unfurled from Illinois to the Rockies and from Canada to Texas, the native prairie lands that are the heart of the Heartland.

Iowa geologist Jean Prior's description of the prairies in her state pertains to all prairies. They are, she says, landscapes "that do not call attention to themselves." Unlike the towering mountain ranges and vast deserts of the West, whose intrinsic beauty is apparent from long distances, the prairie doesn't even meet visitors halfway. They have to go to it. *You have to walk on the prairie.*

Today little is left to walk on. The transformation of North America's mid-continental grasslands and savanna to agricultural uses is one of the most

---

PRECEDING PAGES: *On the High Plains, water defines migration and settlement patterns—of wildlife and humans. With its springs and shady ravines, Lake Scott state park in Kansas has been an oasis for centuries.*

rapid and amazing exploits of human energy and determination on record. Although the dismantling of these natural landscapes has been documented and lamented in many books and articles (see the "Further Reading" section in the back of this guide), there is no substitute for seeing the metamorphosis up-close and firsthand.

October is one of the best and most instructive times to visit the Heartland. First, the remnant prairies are in their glory. The grasses and wild-flowers—especially a number of the tall, brawny species of sunflowers, such as compass plant and prairie dock—have attained full stature and are turning colors of umber, mauve, ocher, and crimson that rival the fall forest vistas of New England. In this last autumn gasp of native prairie flora, the potency of plains soil is dazzlingly apparent.

ABOVE: *Fuchsia petals garnished with orange stamens make the purple prairie clover one of the continent's most ornate prairie wildflowers.*

Second, harvest is in full swing, and fecundity and peril are in the air. Impossibly big pieces of machinery—combines, tractors pulling discs—trundle along at hazardously slow speeds, occupying a lane and a half of roadway. Trucks laden with corn or soybeans (the two major crops on the plains) whiz back and forth from field to grain bins, or elevators, or railheads. Beetle-eyed headlights of combines twinkle down field rows as farmers work well into the night. On the radio, meteorologists predict the first frost, and public service announcements advise how to handle body parts severed in farm accidents to ensure successful reattachment.

In October, the fruitfulness of the plains—whether manifest in an acre of native prairie or in an acre of cultivated corn, soybeans, wheat, or milo—is a thrill and a heartbreak to witness. Of so much capacity for fertility, so little these days occurs in natural landscapes.

The source of this fruitfulness is the soil, which in turn finds its origins in the glacial history of the Northern Hemisphere. During the last million or so years, ice sheets formed in the sub-Arctic four different times. Like frosting on a cake, lobes of ice oozed southward between the Appalachian and Rocky mountains, pulverizing rock and moving tons of soil. When the climate

3

LEFT: *Whether enveloping a broad meadow or growing singly on a rock-strewn hillside, shooting stars typically blossom just as spring shifts into full-blown summer.*

RIGHT: *In a Missouri marsh thick with prairie cordgrass, a protective red-winged blackbird defends its nest. Flashing its scarlet epaulets, the small bird chases away an encroaching great egret.*

warmed, the ice melted, forming great rivers that carried and dropped tremendous cargoes of sediments. Wind often transported and rearranged these loads as well.

The mineral-rich glacial deposits were held fast by the plants that grew in them. Below ground, roots knitted the dirt together; above ground, decaying vegetation was perpetually composting and enriching the soil. In the 1920s, J. E. Weaver and his colleagues and students at the University of Nebraska began an intensive 12-year study of the root systems of prairie plants. Their work, a classic in grassland ecology, revealed the remarkable subterranean life of the prairie.

The roots of prairie plants look like the wild tresses of Rapunzel. Prairie cordgrass can reach depths of 8 to 13 feet; buffalo grass, a pygmy above ground (it grows only a few inches high), boasts a root system 4 feet deep. Just as impressive are the roots of many wildflowers, including compass plant, blazing star, purple prairie clover, and leadplant, which reach down 8 to 12 feet or more. Weaver made the point better than anyone before or since: There is more to the prairie than meets the eye.

This great intimacy of plant and soil, of organic and inorganic, is the *je ne sais quoi* of the prairie. No garden on earth compares to a virgin prairie, which can be experienced only by walking on grassland where the sod has never been broken.

Virtually all of Iowa and Illinois, the northern half of Missouri, and parts of

Kansas and Nebraska owe the character of their landforms to the coming and going of the earthmoving glaciers and to wind and water, which reshaped the soil after the ice retreated. Rumpled and pocked with the telltale imprints of ice, much of the Heartland is a vast atlas of glacial activity. Although most of the natural flora has been stripped away, the landforms are largely intact— and they are glorious. The lakes, bogs, fens, moraines, and kames bordering Chicago form a priceless necklace of glacial remnants around that metropolis. The Sandhills of north-central Nebraska—the largest expanse of sand dunes in the Western Hemisphere—form an exquisite landscape of infinite vistas. Less extensive but just as handsome are the sand dunes along the Illinois River in central Illinois and those on the Arkansas River in south-central Kansas. Iowa is a chaos of undulation, a rolling terrain created almost entirely by glaciers, water, and wind.

A groundswell of interest in grasslands pertains primarily to their conservation. The last remnant prairies are now better preserved and managed. Scattered pockets of savannas (an ecosystem virtually lost and essentially rediscovered in the 1980s) have been resurrected. Grasslands are being re-created on tilled ground.

Yet hardly anybody visits prairies. Perhaps this is good. After just a few groundswells, enthusiasts could easily trample most of the prairies that remain in the Heartland. Only the Sandhills of Nebraska and the Flint Hills of Kansas

5

encompass enough prairie to get lost in.

Prairies remain among the most unpeopled landscapes in this country. Their solitude is immense. Their effect on travelers and immigrants 150 years ago can still be felt. Today many people find these native grasslands unnerving places; others find them boring. A few, however, still agree with Thomas Hart Benton, who wrote, "They make me want to run and shout at the top of my voice."

In *O Pioneers!* noted American author Willa Cather captures a culture that has changed little since the book was published in 1913. Most of her characters view the plains landscape with indifference or consider it an obstacle to be overcome. A few, like Alexandra Bergson and Carl Linstrum, understand its "fierce strength, its peculiar, savage kind of beauty," but are swept up in the inevitability of change. Only Crazy Ivar—Norwegian bachelor, loner, horse doctor, disdainer of shoes, dweller in a cave in the side of a hill—has a different view: "Ivar found contentment in the solitude he had sought out for himself. He disliked the litter of human dwellings: the broken food, the bits of broken china, the old wash-boilers and tea-kettles thrown in the sunflower patch. He preferred the cleanness and tidiness of the wild sod. He always said that the badgers had cleaner houses than people, and that when he took a housekeeper her name would be Mrs. Badger. He best expressed his preference for his wild homestead by saying that his Bible seemed truer to him there. If one stood in the doorway of his cave, and looked off at the rough land, the smiling sky, the curly grass white in the hot sunlight; if one listened to the rapturous song of the lark, the drumming of the quail, the burr of the locust against that vast silence, one understood what Ivar meant."

The landscapes Ivar loved are subtle. Their innate gracefulness becomes apparent only over time and repeated exposure. The Heartland offers visitors much besides plains. Around the edges of the region, where the glaciers never reached, lies terrain of higher drama and more immediate charm. The Driftless Area of northeastern Iowa and adjacent Illinois, the Shawnee Hills at the extreme southern tip of Illinois, and the Ozarks of Missouri are bold, craggy landscapes where geologic forces besides ice prevailed. These places pose great contrast to the sun and wind of the prairie. Here forests and shade, rock-rimmed defiles and crystal-clear rivers—even approximations of mountains—dominate the landscape.

RIGHT: *A limestone bluff towers over Lake of the Ozarks in Missouri's Ha Ha Tonka State Park, where a labyrinth of chasms, caves, and sinkholes offers proof that the Heartland is more than undulating prairie.*

ILLINOIS

ILLINOIS

In the heart of the Heartland, little unadulterated nature has eluded the plow, chain saw, and backhoe. Among the 50 states, only Iowa contains fewer acres of natural landscape than Illinois. People are an intricate part of the terrain in Illinois, which ranks 6th in U.S. population (11,830,000) though it is 24th in area (56,346 square miles). The most sweeping ecological changes in Illinois have occurred where the fewest people live, in the southern sections, because the transformation of natural landscapes is predominantly an agrarian—not an urban—phenomenon.

Today forests, which previously covered almost 40 percent of the state, account for just 12 percent; wetlands, formerly 30 percent, are only 3.5 percent. Also vanished is more than 99 percent of the original tallgrass prairie that once swathed the broad midsection of Illinois. This "wilderness of sky and grass," as John Madson describes it in the classic *Where the Sky Began,* was greeted with indifference or alarm by most Europeans. Gurdon S. Hubbard, newly arrived in Chicago in the fall of 1818, was among the few who were impressed. "I climbed a tree and gazed in admiration on the first prairie I had ever seen. The waving grass intermingled with a rich profusion of wild flowers was the most beautiful sight I had gazed upon." Only a handful of places remain, however, where visitors—even with a prodigious leap of imagination—can picture what Hubbard saw.

To drive across the state's center on Route 136 from Danville to Keokuk today is to journey through the fabled fruited plains of America the Beautiful. The unfolding landscapes are serene, orderly, mostly flat, and immensely productive. They represent an economy built on the temperate and thrifty agrarian values that we Americans as a culture prize. It is not a way of life that places great worth on wild, untamed nature. As Iowa novelist and essayist Jane Smiley has written, "A farmer is not charmed by uncultivated landscape."

For more than a thousand years, the fertile watersheds of the Illinois, Mississippi, and Missouri rivers sustained an emerging culture of farmers. East of present-day Saint Louis arose a metropolis of traders and agrarians.

PRECEDING PAGES: *Near Ottawa, the soft light of sunset illuminates the Illinois River, which slices the state diagonally from Chicago to Saint Louis.*

During its heyday from 1050 to 1250, Cahokia Mounds was the largest prehistoric city north of Mexico, supporting a population of 15,000 people. Today these intensively cultivated lands are a testament to *Homo sapiens*'s remarkable evolution as a farmer.

Glaciers moving across Illinois for half a million years blanketed most of the terrain with deep layers of soils, which were shoved around by sheets of ice, then rearranged by water and wind. Hundreds of streams and rivers worked their way through this glacial cover as they were gently tugged toward the Gulf of Mexico. Illinois is the hub of American rivers, where major river systems—the upper reaches of the Mississippi, the Missouri, Illinois, Ohio, and Wabash—ultimately converge to form the Mississippi, the largest waterway on the continent.

Humans dredged and channelized the rivers and converted floodplain forests and marshes to croplands, towns, barge-docking facilities, and fishing camps. In 1993, the rain-swollen Missouri and Mississippi crested at 10, 20, even 30 feet above flood stage. The rivers breached the levees, depositing trillions of pounds of nutrient-rich sediments throughout a vast ecosystem. It was a reminder that even waterways as domesticated as the Missouri and Mississippi will occasionally consort with their floodplains.

In the north, Chicago contains remarkable examples of the habitats—marshes, wet prairies, savannas, sand ridges, bogs—that once defined this region. Indeed, Chicagoans and their suburban neighbors are among the nation's most active and resourceful conservationists. Far more acres of prairie are protected and restored in highly urban northern Illinois than in areas to the south, where agricultural practices have all but obliterated the native grasslands. Within the six counties that constitute metropolitan Chicago, a quarter of a million acres of publicly owned forests, grasslands, beaches, bogs, marshes, and savannas provide windows on wild Illinois.

George B. Fell, a botanist from Rockford, initiated efforts to protect the last remnants of Illinois's prairies and forests. In 1963 the state became the first to establish a system of nature preserves that shields landscapes for their characteristic biological constituents, not simply for their potential as human recreational terrain. Some 239 sanctuaries across Illinois now safeguard 32,000 acres. From a 1977 volunteer effort to restore North Branch Prairie in Chicago, the Illinois Volunteer Stewardship Network has grown statewide to include more than 6,400 people who support vigorous experiments to restore degraded landscapes. Today Illinois is a major proving ground for innovative methods of habitat restoration and for the notion that nature can not only be protected but also reclaimed.

CHAPTER ONE

NORTHERN ILLINOIS:
NATURE MEETS METROPOLIS

Running between Chicago on Lake Michigan and Rock Island on the Mississippi River, Interstate 80 forms a convenient, if highly unnatural, boundary separating intensely urban northern Illinois from the more rural southern four-fifths of the state. More than 9 million inhabitants make the area north of I-80 the most peopled terrain in the Heartland—and probably the only place where visitors can anticipate getting stuck in traffic on the way to a natural area.

Northern Illinois encompasses three distinct ecological areas with their assortment of terrains, soils, and habitats: lake plains and wetlands in the northeast, the rugged terrain of the Driftless Area in the northwest, and a deep river valley cut clear down to bedrock in between. This geologic montage of dunes and swales, of nooks and canyons supports plants as unlikely on the continent's midriff as white pine, papaw, and prickly pear cactus.

Nature shaped northeastern Illinois as the glaciers advanced and retreated from 75,000 to 13,000 years ago. Human hands then reshaped this same terrain when they built Chicago and its suburbs. Millions of people reside on this crescent shaped plain, once a mosaic of prairies, marshes, and sluggish tree lined rivers. The plain was created as glacial Lake Chicago—now Lake Michigan—began to recede. Sand ridges, rising ten or more feet higher than the lake plain and studded with oaks, marked the old shoreline. Vestiges that have escaped urban development can still be seen at Illinois Beach State Park and Sand Ridge Nature Center.

LEFT: *Golden stalks of little bluestem brighten wintry Nachusa Grasslands, a restored tallgrass prairie. Elaborate tunnel systems under the snow protect small rodents from the cold and from predators overhead.*

Westward beyond the lake plain lay a gently rolling prairie, now largely obscured. Very young in geologic terms, this landscape began to take form about 13,000 years ago as glaciers, like gargantuan earthmoving machines, arranged dirt into countless undulating, sinuous forms. As the climate warmed and the glaciers began to melt, tremendous surges of water assumed the task of rearranging the soil. The northeast corner of Illinois, though largely devoid of prairie, is still a land of serpentine moraines, lakes, bogs, and fens.

The second distinctive northern Illinois natural landscape flanks the 285-mile-long Rock River, which flows diagonally across the northwestern corner of Illinois to join the Mississippi at Rock Island. It might well be called the Bedrock River. Cutting through cakelike layers of glacial till, the Rock has exposed ancient sedimentary beds of limestone, dolomite, sandstone, and shale deposited 500 million years ago, when much of the Midwest was covered by an inland sea. In the process, the river has etched scenic ravines and gorges and created cool, shadowy niches where pockets of Ice Age plants persist.

The third natural division of northern Illinois is the Driftless Area, so named because it escaped, for the most part, the earth-altering effects of drift, which is the material carried by glaciers. Lacking a blanket of glacial soil, this landscape of rugged river and stream canyons is markedly different in aspect from the gentle, somnolent terrain that characterizes so much of Illinois. This diminutive area covers parts of two counties in extreme northwestern Illinois and extends into the similarly modest corners of Iowa, Minnesota, and Wisconsin. But the myriad ups and downs of its terrain make up for the Driftless Area's small size.

Many sites in this chapter—the Mississippi Palisades, Nachusa Grasslands, even Chicago's Ryerson Woods—offer an opportunity to disengage from the material world. However, the natural areas in this part of Illinois are irrevocably tied to the demographic and economic palpitations of the third largest city in the United States. Cities have not been kind to nature, and the natural lands that persist in northern Illinois have escaped the double whammy of agricultural *and* urban development.

Nevertheless, conservationists have enthusiastically taken up the ecological challenges of metropolitan Chicago. Stories abound of nail-biting

---

OVERLEAF: *In late summer, the prairie palette shifts from greens to an autumnal rainbow of golds, purples, browns, and reds. Here false boneset, an aster, tints a broad swath of Nachusa Grasslands a creamy yellow.*

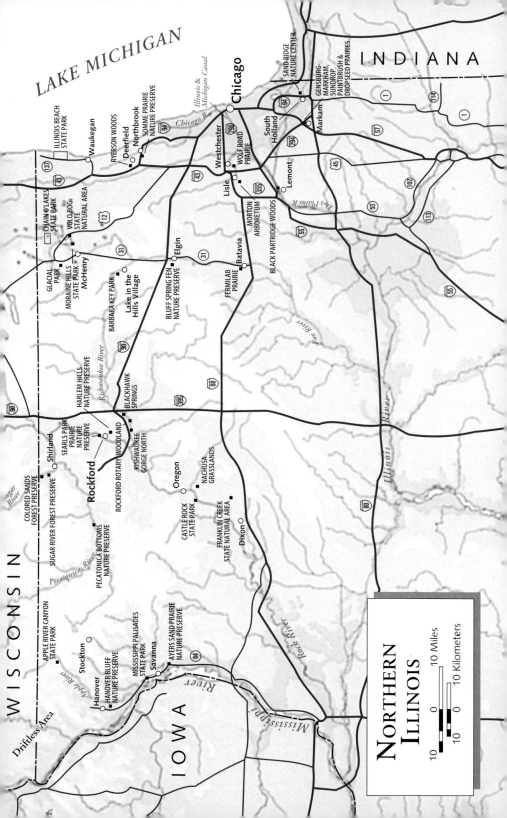

last-minute saves and complicated, creative orchestrations. In 1986 the Nature Conservancy purchased the core of Nachusa Grasslands near Dixon just 15 minutes before an auction of the land as five-acre homesites was to begin. In 1990, when a prairie near Elgin was slated to disappear under a new road, 400 volunteers rolled up grasses, wildflowers, and 18 inches of topsoil and transported the prairie "carpet" to Bluff Spring Fen, where it now thrives.

After exploring the old lake plain along the shores of Lake Michigan, this chapter moves to the last bogs, fens, and prairies in and around metropolitan Chicago. Next the itinerary travels west to the Rock River valley and concludes in the Driftless Area and palisades along the Mississippi River. Because space does not permit the inclusion of every natural area in Chicago, the chapter focuses on the most informative and accessible examples of surviving glacial terrain. Among the ways to study the last natural remnants around Chicago are trips sponsored by the Field Museum. A year-round curriculum of nature classes and field trips are also offered by Prairie University, a consortium of nature centers, county conservation districts, universities, and museums coordinated by the Nature Conservancy.

ABOVE: *With dappled plumage providing camouflage, red-shouldered hawks haunt the mature riverine forests near Lake Michigan.*

LEFT: *Lake Michigan waves deposit drift-wood on the pebbly shore of Illinois Beach State Park.*

THE NORTHEAST CORNER: GLACIAL LAKES AND FENS

At **Illinois Beach State Park❖**, the blues of Lake Michigan meet the pearly shore along one of the last unadulterated stretches of lakefront in the state. Almost in Wisconsin, the park lies north of Wau-kegan and east of Route 137 about 50 miles from downtown Chicago. Despite its simple appearance, this exquisite place is an intricate tiering of beach, dune, sand prairie, savanna, marsh, oak woodland, and old beach terraces. The profusion of different habitats—ecologists have identified 13 high-quality natural communities within the park—sustains one of the richest conjunctions of plant life in Illinois.

The dunescapes are an elegant introduction to the glacial history of the region and to the sculpting power of wind and water. Lake Michigan was a

LEFT: *In late summer fringed gentian blooms at Illinois Beach State Park. One of the loveliest native wildflowers, this gentian thrives only on unsullied wet prairies.*

RIGHT: *Each spring a constellation of starry false solomon seal and scattered yellow bouquets of hoary puccoon flower on the sandy terraces at Illinois Beach State Park.*

big chunk of ice 12,000 years ago, and the melting glacier formed a mammoth lake 50 feet higher than current levels. Water levels have continued to fluctuate; the beach terraces along the western flank of the park mark a period of higher water. Sand unanchored by vegetation is constantly being rearranged by shifting wind patterns, longshore currents, and wave action. At Illinois Beach, waves pushed across the lake by northeasterly winds are shoving the dunes southward.

Within the 4,160-acre park, the **Illinois Beach Nature Preserve❖** encompasses a 170-acre northern unit and a 1,081-acre southern unit. The preserve is crisscrossed with trails (the longest 2.3 miles), which lead over old beach ridges through sand prairie, woods, and along the well-named Dead River. Only in times of high water does the sluggish waterway breach the sand dunes and drain into Lake Michigan.

In midsummer, the prairiescapes are a riot of wildflowers—blazing star, black-eyed Susan, lobelia, butterfly milkweed, *Calapogon* orchid, prairie clover, Saint-John's-wort, and prickly pear cactus. From mid-September to mid-October, impressive numbers of hawks—including red-tailed, northern harriers, goshawks, and various accipiters—migrate southward along the shoreline of Illinois Beach.

To the west of Illinois Beach State Park lies the lake country, where melting chunks of glacial ice left a landscape pocked with aquamarine pools. Many are now snarled with boat traffic, their shorelines clotted with houses and docks. **Chain O'Lakes State Park,** reached from Wilmot Road north of Route 12, is one of these invaded places. But a spin through the 2,793-acre park, which borders three glacial lakes, provides a glimpse of the power of ice in shaping land.

More serene examples of the glaciers' handiwork are nearby. Seven

miles north of the town of McHenry and just west of Route 31 is **Glacial Park❖,** where the land speaks for itself. In a succession of ups and downs shaped first by ice and then by meltwater, moraines (levee-shaped bulwarks of earth) and kames (conical piles of gravelly soil) intermingle with marshes, sloughs, sedge meadows, fens, and bogs.

The 2,905-acre natural area spreads across tranquil hills that slip into the valley of Nippersink Creek. This beautiful pastoral landscape is also a blunt demographic boundary. At the end of the twentieth century, greater Chicago is vigorously chomping at its rural edges. Acquisition of land for Glacial Park, which began in 1975, anticipated the urban onslaught in the nick of time.

ABOVE: *A yellow-throated Blanding's turtle wallows in bright green duckweed. This classic but threatened wetland reptile is now protected at Glacial Park.*

RIGHT: *Duckweed and iris edge a boardwalk at Volo Bog State Natural Area. Ringed by metropolitan Chicago, this preserve is a priceless remnant of the region's ancient glacial landscape.*

In the mid-1970s, Glacial Park was a patchwork of old fields and pasture, and its terrain, while incorporating the classic glacial landforms, was hardly pristine. Today its prairies, savannas, meadows, and wetlands, traversed by more than eight miles of trails, are being gradually restored in an effort that illustrates a significant trend toward reclaiming nature.

Glacial Park provides sanctuary for many plants and animals that have been squeezed between farm and city, including a number of orchids and sedges, round-leaved sundews, and such compromised prairie birds as the upland sandpiper and bobolink. The endangered Blanding's turtle, a marsh- and bog-loving species, lives at Glacial Park but is menaced by raccoon, which prey on the newly hatched young. A program is now under way to incubate, hatch, and rear young Blanding's turtles, then release them when they are too big to be raccoon snacks. Glacial Park is also a paradise for butterflies, including the black dash, purplish copper, Baltimore checkerspot, Acadian hairstreak, and silver-bordered fritillary.

Volo Bog State Natural Area❖, about ten miles east of McHenry on

the west side of Route 12, contains a glacial lake in its final death throes, and considered from another point of view, a forest in its infancy. Over the last 6,000 or so years, a 50-foot-deep lake has slowly filled with vegetation. The last of the lake is a limpid pool, 10 feet deep and barely 100 feet wide, winking from a jumble of black willow, deadly nightshade, tamarack, cattails, sedges, sphagnum moss, pitcher plants, and other marsh- and bog-loving plants.

A half-mile-long floating boardwalk, at some spots practically engulfed in vegetation, loops through the heart of the bog. Midway along the boardwalk is the pool, where bullfrogs drift, eyeballs bulging on the surface and limbs lazily dangling. A virtual gumbo of tadpoles and small aquatic life, the pond is a perfect hunting ground for green herons and other birds that eat fish and amphibious creatures. In summer, the marsh is noisy with the songs and chatter of red-winged blackbirds, sedge wrens, yellowthroats, catbirds, and occasionally veeries. A 2.8-mile trail skirts the perimeter of the marsh.

Nearby 1,690-acre **Moraine Hills State Park❖,** just southwest of Volo Bog and about three miles south of McHenry, straddles a glacier-shaped landscape of gravelly hills and kettle holes. The cooler northerly faces of

*LEFT: At Moraine Hills State Park, water
lilies flourish on Lake Defiance, one of the
glacial lakes that dot the northern and
western fringes of metropolitan Chicago.
RIGHT: Bloodroot, a member of the poppy
family, appears in early spring among the
forest leaf litter. The plant exudes a red
fluid, which explains its sanguinary name.*

the hills are cloaked in trees, such as bur oak,
white oak, and shagbark hickory, while the
warmer southerly faces tend toward prairie.
The kettle-hole pools, thumbprints left in the
earth by melting shards of ice, are wetlands
in various stages of filling in.

Two of these kettle holes—115-acre Pike
Marsh and 120-acre Leatherleaf Bog—are pro-
tected as Illinois nature preserves because they harbor numerous rare wetland plants, including false asphodel, white lady's slipper, and one of the
state's largest populations of carnivorous pitcher plants. In **Pike Marsh,** in
the southeast corner of the park, a .7-mile trail and boardwalk traverse
sedge meadow, alkaline bog, cattail marsh, fen, hill prairie, and upland oak-
hickory forest. **Leatherleaf Bog,** in the northwest part of the park, is a floating mat of sphagnum moss and leatherleaf encircled by a 3.2-mile trail.

At the center of the park is 48-acre **Lake Defiance,** one of the last
largely undeveloped glacial lakes remaining in Illinois. Its spongy, precari-
ous shoreline of peat is just one indication that Lake Defiance, like the
surrounding kettle holes, is slowly losing its lake identity. A half-mile interpretative trail on the northwest tip of the lake explains how a body of
water becomes terra firma.

Fens are wetlands where extreme aquatic conditions prevail. Depending on the chemistry of the surrounding soil, the water that feeds fens is
either harshly basic or acidic. Although these conditions are not favorable
to most plants, fens often shelter species that have developed tolerances
for such severe pH levels. Fenologists can expound on the many nuances
of these bizarre wetlands—each fen seems to have its own peculiarity—
but most beholders can distinguish fens by their pockets of bonsai-like
plants. Amid lush vegetation—stands of cattails, shrubby cinquefoil, and
prairie dock—are barren little moonscapes where stunted ground-hugging
plants such as beaked spike rush grow.

ABOVE: *Midsummer at Bluff Spring Fen brings on a riot of colorful wild-flowers, including the mauve powder-puff blossoms of wild bergamot (an aromatic mint) and the droopy yellow blooms of gray-headed coneflower.*

Scattered like a broken strand of pearls, fens punctuate the middle of the continent along the lowland margins of glacial activity. Always uncommon, they are now extremely rare because like other wetlands they have not been preserved. They are also fragile places, easy to trample and hard to repair. Ten thousand years ago, conditions in northern Illinois were ideal for creating fens. They have now dwindled to a few, of which fewer still are open to the public.

One that welcomes visitors is **Lake-in-the-Hills Fen** just north of Lake in the Hills village in **Barbara Key Park❖,** on the west side of Pyott Road. The fen here is throttled on all sides by development, which makes the view from the valley rim, where the trail begins, all the more beguiling. From this vantage point, a broad sweep of grass-covered hills descends to a serpentine wetland where cattails and the spindly flower stalks of prairie dock nod. This vista is particularly striking in mid-October, when big and little bluestem and other prairie grasses have turned many shades of gold, rust, umber, and mauve—a reminder that grasslands rival forests for autumn color.

A portion of Crystal Creek, a tributary of the Fox River, runs through the 231-acre preserve. A .3-mile trail winds across a dry hillside prairie

ABOVE: *A former trash dump, Bluff Spring Fen preserve is now a blue-ribbon prairie restoration. A crystalline stream winds through grasses and wildflowers, including prairie dock with its platter-sized leaves.*

down into the valley, which shelters a lethargic creek, sedge meadows, and pockets of bona fide fen. Lake-in-the-Hills protects several rare wetland plants, including bog valerian and woolly milkweed.

About ten miles farther south in the Fox River valley, another beautiful fen enjoys a setting less beset by rampant development. **Bluff Spring Fen Nature Preserve❖,** in the town of Elgin, is tucked behind the peaceful oak-shaded grounds of Bluff City Cemetery. Once the 90-acre expanse of prairie, fen, and oak savanna was a trash dump and speedway for all-terrain vehicles. Since 1979, when restoration work began, parts of the preserve have been returned to near-pristine conditions.

The undulating landscape provides a primer in glacial terminology. The kames at Bluff Spring Fen, for instance, are right out of a textbook—tidy tapered hills of gravel that ancient rivers deposited in the gaping cracks of glaciers. Because gravelly soils do not retain moisture, kames are patchy hillocks of drought-loving plants, including such grasses as little bluestem and side-oats grama. The kames rise in marked contrast to the low, moist fen and its tangle of vegetation.

In the fen, water that has seeped down through the kames burbles up from the ground. Rich in dissolved limestone, these seeps create an alka-

line condition that sustains only certain kinds of plants and retards decay. Fen flora includes a number of orchid species, beaked spike rush, and shrubby cinquefoil. The trail through the fen—spanning the accumulation of eons of partially decayed plants—bounces underfoot.

In midsummer, when flowering plants such as the tall, robust spikes of deep pink blazing star and yellow prairie dock form giant candelabras, Bluff Spring Fen becomes a haven for butterflies. Monarchs and the more common species reach peak numbers from August through early September. Some of the more restricted species, including the Baltimore checkerspot, appear on the wing from mid-June through early July.

CHICAGO AND ITS LAKE PLAIN: WOODS AND PRAIRIES

Chicago and its suburbs straddle the meandering Chicago and Des Plaines rivers, which drain the lake plain and have been greatly altered. The Chicago River, which once emptied into Lake Michigan, has been engineered to flow in the opposite direction. Completed in 1848, the Illinois and Michigan Canal, often called the I&M, connects the Chicago and Des Plaines with the Illinois River, creating a transportation link to the Mississippi River.

LEFT: *Throughout the summer, Illinois's grasslands are jewel boxes for butterflies, which feast on the nectar of native wildflowers. At far left, a giant swallowtail (top) feeds on a common ironweed, and a tiger swallowtail (bottom) on a coneflower. The orange and black Baltimore checkerspot (near left) is a nymphalid, a member of the largest family of butterflies.*

RIGHT: *Two monarch butterflies mate among yellow bur marigolds. Monarch larvae, however, feed only on species of milkweed, which makes the adults distasteful to predators.*

Deep and dark, the forests along the Des Plaines River in 550-acre **Ryerson Woods✥** are an ecological flashback to a time when majestic trees growing in rich soil stretched like emerald ribbons across the lake plain. The former summer home of Chicago industrialist and philanthropist Edward L. Ryerson, the woods are in Deerfield, one mile east of Interstate 94 and about 30 miles north of downtown Chicago. In 1966 the Ryerson family donated the property to the Lake County Forest Preserve.

The old-growth floodplain forest here supports some very big trees—bur, white, and black oaks, shagbark hickory, and black walnut—and extravagantly gnarled black willows flank the banks of the Des Plaines River. An abundance of sugar maples makes Ryerson Woods the place to see foliage colors in mid-October. In spring impressive numbers of warblers migrate through, usually peaking during the first two weeks of May.

Ryerson Woods also still harbors a few massasauga rattlesnakes, whose future is clouded because the population is small and presumably genetically isolated. Known also as swamp rattlers, these classic snakes of floodplains, bogs, and wet prairies have fared as poorly as their requisite habitat. A management program started in 1989 to control the urban deer population has greatly benefited the understory vegetation in Ryerson Woods, as attested by thriving colonies of ferns, jack-in-the-pulpits, ramps, wild gin-

ger, mayapples, and other low-growing, shade-loving plants.

A crown jewel of Chicago, **Somme Prairie Nature Preserve**❖ is tucked away (north of Dundee Road, east of Pfingsten Road, and west of the Chicago, Milwaukee, Saint Paul and Pacific Railroad) in the village of Northbrook. Somme Prairie is one of the last, best wet prairies in the state. Although long suppression of natural fires has allowed thickets to invade the grassland, restoration work, which began in 1977, is returning this 70-acre prairie to peak condition. It is most appealing from midsummer to fall, when the grasses reach full stature and wave their spangled seed heads, and wildflowers such as blazing star, prairie dock, Culver's root, rattlesnake master, and various milkweeds are in bloom.

Fermilab covers 6,800 acres of old fields on the edge of Batavia, about 40 miles west of downtown Chicago. Although its primary mission is to explore the secrets of atomic particles, the laboratory has devoted some energy to examining the mysteries of prairies. In 1975, ecologists began restoring 9 acres of prairie at Fermilab; by 1996, the restored prairie totaled more than 1,000 acres. Most easily reached by the lab's west entrance on Kirk Road a few miles north of Route 88, a 50-acre portion of the **Fermilab Prairie**❖ is open to the public. Two trails (.5-mile and 1.2-mile) meander through stands of Indian grass, big bluestem, and other grasses, some reaching heights of five and six feet. The site supports a healthy mix of wildflowers—compass plant, rattlesnake master, milk-

LEFT: A short, thick-bodied rattlesnake, the now-rare massasauga is synonymous with the wetlands that once laced northern Illinois. An isolated massasauga population persists in Ryerson Woods on the Des Plaines River in the heart of Chicago.

RIGHT: One of the first harbingers of spring, the song sparrow has a smudge on its breast, a long, rounded tail, and a rollicking song. This bird is not bashful: Individuals often sing from an exposed perch, tirelessly and with head thrown back.

weeds, yellow coneflower—always a good indication of successful prairie restoration. Many of the original plants in the Fermilab prairie grew from seeds collected at the nearby Gensburg-Markham Prairie, 25 miles southwest of Chicago. The well-written interpretative signs along the half-mile trail provide a concise overview of prairies and the patience required to restore them. On a warm summer day, the silence here is broken by the various clicks, *witchety* calls, wheezes, and trills of sedge wrens, yellowthroats, song sparrows, and field sparrows.

On Route 53 in the town of Lisle, about 25 miles west of downtown Chicago and just north of Route 88, **Morton Arboretum❖** is a lovely place, partly because the native landscape has not been eclipsed by incessant horticulture. A happy coincidence of a family's wealth and passion for trees, the arboretum is the legacy of Joy Morton, founder of Morton Salt Company and son of J. Sterling Morton, the Nebraska politician who indefatigably promoted the idea of Arbor Day.

The auto route that traverses the 1,700-acre arboretum offers frequent parking turnouts so that visitors can examine pockets of the botanical garden more closely on foot. In addition, more than 12 miles of walking trails lace the property. A short loop near the visitor center, called the Illinois Trees Nature Trail, supplies a brief course in the trees typically encountered in the state. At the west end of the arboretum is the **Schulenberg Prairie,** a 200-acre reconstructed grassland and savanna that features a

ABOVE: *Fluffy white spikes of wild hyacinth, a spring-blooming lily, and pink wild geraniums are part of a colorful succession of flowers that*

.7-mile trail and provides a basic introduction to the classic landscape on which Chicago stands. The east end of the arboretum is largely native woodlands, including some of the best surviving oak-maple forest in the region, where fall colors usually peak between October 10 and 15.

Two dozen species of warblers—from the common yellow-rumped and Blackburnian to the less frequent cerulean and northern water-thrush—appear at Morton Arboretum during spring migration, a sign that this island of green in the urban ocean is a haven for birds and birders. The first week of May is generally the height of warbler migration.

Some 18 miles from downtown Chicago just east of Route 294 in the western suburb of Westchester, at the busy intersection of Wolf Road and 31st Street, is a spectacle akin to a mirage. It is a vacant lot, also known as **Wolf Road Prairie❖**. Since 1975 a group of Chicagoans has been working, in and out of court, to save this 80-acre plot from development because it is one of the best examples of tallgrass prairie in Illinois and by far the largest remaining in metropolitan Chicago.

Part of the Salt Creek watershed, the land at Wolf Road Prairie was never farmed because it was too low and wet. In the 1920s it was platted for a subdivision, but its developers were stymied by the Great Depression. Today a grid of sidewalks, a slightly surreal reminder of the prairie's near fate, serves as a trail system.

32

blossom all summer and into autumn at the 80-acre Wolf Road Prairie, the largest tallgrass prairie remnant in the metropolitan Chicago area.

Harboring impressive diversity, the site encompasses bur oak savanna, prairie, and marsh. The wildflower display, which begins rather modestly in spring with shooting star and Indian paintbrush, is positively exuberant by mid-July, when yellow coneflower, prairie dock, and compass plant bloom yellow, blazing star shoots up purple wands, Culver's root adds a touch of white, and bergamot brings a lavender accent. By fall, the stands of big bluestem and Indian grass reach heights of five and six feet and exemplify the true meaning of tallgrass.

Named for an influential leader of the Potawatomi people in the early 1800s, **Black Partridge Woods❖** (just west of the town of Lemont off Bluff Road) occupies 80 acres of bluffs and ravines on the north bank of the Illinois and Michigan Canal. Completed in 1848, the canal became an important commercial artery because it linked Lake Michigan with the Illinois and Mississippi rivers and ultimately the Gulf of Mexico. History confirms an inverse correlation between commerce and nature—when the former increases, the latter decreases—and this remnant woodland near one of Chicago's early efforts to extend its commercial reach across the continent is a potent reminder of that trend.

Part of the Cook County Forest Preserve, Black Partridge Woods is characterized by its old stands of white oak, red oak, basswood, and sugar maple—a mixture that promises brilliant colors in October. Steep

ravines shelter seep springs, shadowy, moist places favored by skunk cabbage, marsh marigolds, and other spring wildflowers.

The 235-acre **Sand Ridge Nature Center❖,** near the town of South Holland east of Route 94, lies on sand and clay deposited by the retreating waters of glacial Lake Chicago, a precursor of Lake Michigan. Because clay holds water and sand does not, Sand Ridge is a landscape rippled with old beach ridges where marsh and sedge meadow intermingle with dry sand prairie and savanna. The nature center offers interpretative exhibits and four miles of well-marked trails.

Clustered around Interstate 57 in the town of Markam, about 25 miles southwest of downtown Chicago, is an archipelago of remnant grasslands called the **Indian Boundary Prairies❖.** The name refers to the boundary, now followed roughly by I-57, of land that the Potawatomi relinquished to the United States in 1795. The four prairies in the group are the 150-acre **Gensburg-Markham Prairie,** the 100-acre **Sundrop Prairie,** the 60-acre **Paintbrush Prairie,** and the 13-acre **Dropseed Prairie.**

Like nearby Sand Ridge, the Indian Boundary Prairies rest upon swirls of different soils—from acidic sand to rich black loam—that sustain a complex habitat of prairie plants, birds, and insects. Together, these prairie sites har-

LEFT: *Late summer at Gensburg-Markham Prairie brings goldenrods and fuchsia blazing stars.*
RIGHT: *Yellow marsh marigolds provide the first color of spring in fens, marshes, and muddy seeps.*

bor a remarkable number of restricted or compromised grassland denizens, including an outstanding array of butterflies that require specific prairie plants to complete their life cycles. Among these are the bunchgrass skipper, two-spotted skipper, purplish copper, and aphrodite. The most conspicuous constituents of the Indian Boundary Prairies are the showy and abundant wildflowers, which include shooting star, blazing star, rattlesnake master, gentian, Indian paintbrush, and compass plant. Throughout the long blooming season from April to October, the palette changes to give each prairie its own distinctive beauty.

The largest of the four sites, **Gensburg-Markham Prairie** is a last nesting stronghold for several grassland birds, including the bobolink, the fastest-declining bird in Illinois. This quintessential prairie species has experienced a 93 percent decline in its northern Illinois breeding population in the last 25 years, primarily because of the conversion of prairie, pasture, hay fields, and oats to row crops such as soybeans.

THE ROCK RIVER VALLEY

The Rock River dramatically cleaves the glacial fabric of northern Illinois. Along with its scenic tributaries—including the Sugar and Kishwaukee rivers and Franklin Creek—the Rock has cut through to bedrock and in the process created many steep, craggy ravines. Although these places look sturdy, soils are thin and easily eroded, and the most scenic of the Rock River areas suffer from too much visitation. Agriculture and urban develop-

OVERLEAF: *The Rock River flows by Castle Rock State Park, where grasses colonize crevices of sunny cliffs and white pines grow in shady woods.*

LEFT: *On hot summer days, Illinois prairies buzz with the insectlike song of the grasshopper sparrow. Shy and plainly plumaged, this quintessential prairie bird is more often heard than seen.*

RIGHT: *The Nature Conservancy's Nachusa Grasslands, a mosaic of prairie, pasture, and cropland, is endowed with a fine population of rough blazing star, a showy wildflower of late summer.*

ment have also taken their toll. For instance, Winnebago County—the city of Rockford now dominates its southeast corner—was once 30 percent forest and 70 percent prairie. Now the figures are 6 percent and .1 percent.

A number of forest and prairie remnants near Rockford are managed by the **Winnebago County Forest Preserve District.** These include the floodplain forest at **Pecatonica Bottoms Nature Preserve❖** (13 miles west of downtown Rockford on the Pecatonica River); the sand forest, sand savanna, sand prairie, and wetlands along the **Sugar River** at the **Sugar River Forest Preserve❖** and **Colored Sands Forest Preserve❖** (about five miles northwest of Shirland); and the upland and floodplain forests in string-of-pearls parks on the **Kishwaukee River** (**Kishwaukee Gorge North, Rockford Rotary Woodland,** and **Blackhawk Springs**), which flows along the southern rim of Rockford.

Two fragments in Rockford feature prairies of very different sorts. The 66-acre **Searls Park Prairie Nature Preserve❖,** in Searls Memorial Park on Central Avenue, is a moist black-soil prairie. The much drier 53-acre **Harlem Hills Nature Preserve❖,** the state's largest and best remaining example of a gravel hill prairie, is renowned for such showy wildflowers as pale purple coneflower. Both, especially Harlem Hills, are fragile places at risk because of their proximity to Rockford.

Three miles south of the town of Oregon, along the crenellated west bank of the Rock River, is **Castle Rock State Park❖.** Within the 2,000-acre park, the 700-acre **George B. Fell Nature Preserve** is a refugium of boreal plants—white pine, aspen, wild sarsaparilla, bunchberry, ground pine—that have persisted in cool crannies such as this since the retreat of the last glaciers.

Studded with sandstone outcrops that made parts of the area too rocky

to plow, the 1,020-acre **Nachusa Grasslands**❖ encompasses one of the largest prairie restoration projects in Illinois. The Nature Conservancy owns and manages the grassland, which is about ten miles east of Dixon, just north of **Franklin Creek State Natural Area.** Contradicting the notion that prairies are flat and featureless places, Nachusa Grasslands unfolds across a rolling landscape that varies from upland tallgrass prairie and sand savanna to sedge meadow and fen. A succession of flower species blooms from May to October, and birdsong in spring and early summer includes the insect buzzes of grasshopper sparrows, the flutings of meadowlarks, the whispering lisps of Henslow's sparrows, and the tootling of upland sandpipers. By October, the big bluestem and Indian grass—tallest of the prairie grasses—have reached heights of five to six feet and turned shades of gold, copper, and umber.

When first protected in 1986, the preserve contained pockets of prairie amid fields of corn and soybeans. Only about 20 percent of the land was still high-quality remnant prairie and wetland; 80 percent was cropland, woodland, and degraded prairie pasture. Thanks to the reseeding of old fields and pastures with native plant species and the reintroduction of controlled fires to the prairie, the fabric of the grassland is becoming whole again. Because of its large size, Nachusa Grasslands is also proving

an important site for the reintroduction of endangered invertebrates, especially butterflies.

Just to the south, intimate, cloistered 572-acre **Franklin Creek State Natural Area❖** offers a perfect counterpoint to the wide-open spaces of Nachusa Grasslands. The creek for which the area is named has cut deeply through eons of bedrock to 500-million-year-old Ordovician sandstone, the oldest exposed rock in Illinois. The excavation produced dramatic cliffs lined with maples, basswood, oaks, hickories, hop hornbeam, and papaw, whose autumnal foliage casts golden light into the gorge in mid-October.

Four and a half miles of trails wind along Franklin Creek. Pioneer Pass, a two-mile section of trail, is the most scenic portion of the valley. The rugged cliffs afford footholds for an array of ferns and wildflowers, and skunk cabbage and swamp rose grow in the seeps and springs along the banks of the creek. The Franklin Creek gorge creates microclimates that accommodate surprising conjunctions: Here papaw, an understory tree of southern persuasion, grows near Canada yew, an evergreen shrub of northern woodlands.

THE DRIFTLESS AREA:
PALISADES AND SAND DUNES OF THE MISSISSIPPI

With impressive cleavages cut by the river, **Apple River Canyon State Park❖** is a quintessential Driftless Area site. The 297-acre park is eight miles northwest of Stockton on Route 10. Six miles of trails traverse a variety of terrain, including cliffs of dolomite along the river. Black willow, sycamore, box elder, and silver maple grow at the water's edge, while basswood, black walnut, shagbark hickory, and bur oak climb the slopes. The cool north-facing slopes sustain white pine, rare in Illinois. In early spring the forest floor is spangled with hepatica, bloodroot, trillium, and wild ginger.

Farther downstream, near the Apple's confluence with the Mississippi and about two miles southeast of Hanover, **Hanover Bluff Nature Preserve❖** stands on dolomite cliffs wedged between the two rivers. (The preserve is on Whitton Road about two miles south of its intersection with Hanover Hill Road.) Noted for its display of spring wildflowers and fall colors, the 360-acre preserve is mainly an upland forest of oaks and basswood. Microhabitats, ranging from spring seeps in the ravines to sunny arid

---

LEFT: *Snow softens the jagged edges of Apple River Canyon State Park. Enclosing a valley of dolomite cliffs, the park is part of the Driftless Area, a region of rocky, rugged terrain never touched by glaciers.*

ABOVE: *Prickly pear cactus grows in sunny landscapes where the soil is sandy. Hill prairies along the Mississippi make perfect perches.*
BELOW: *The yellow lady's slipper, a native orchid, appears in woodlands, wetlands, and even on open prairies. Nowhere, however, is it common.*

dolomite prairies, make for a diverse botanical roster. Rarely do northern orchids and prickly pear cactus occur so close together.

Among Hanover Bluff's distinctive eco-pockets are sand hill prairies, sometimes called perched dunes. These unusual sandy places are scattered along the Mississippi River where it arcs eastward between Dubuque, Iowa, and the Quad Cities (Davenport, Bettendorf, Rock Island, and Moline). Deposited by glacial meltwater, the sand was then wind-whipped into dunes along the river's floodplain and bluffs. Unable to retain much moisture, the sand prairies of Illinois bear striking resemblances to short-grass prairies farther west. Little bluestem and hairy grama, both scruffy low-growing plants that thrive in dry conditions, are the dominant grasses on the sandhill prairies at Hanover. Overgrazing and suppression of fire have diminished the extent of sand prairies in Illinois, but where grazing can be controlled and fire reintroduced, remnants are being preserved.

Another example—this one in the Mississippi floodplain—lies about 20 miles south of Hanover Bluff. **Ayers Sand Prairie Nature Preserve**❖ (2.5 miles south of the town of Savanna, half a mile east of the intersection of Airport Road and Route 84) contains about a hundred acres of rolling dunes (some 20 feet high), flatter sand prairie, and blowouts. The latter, as the name implies, are craterlike pockets in the sand created by wind and generally barren of vegetation. In summer, upland sandpipers and loggerhead shrikes, prairie birds that are increasingly rare in Illinois, occasionally appear amid the dunescapes at Ayers Sand Prairie, but western meadowlarks, grasshopper sparrows, and

ABOVE: *Below the limestone bluffs at Mississippi Palisades State Park, the continent's greatest river wends its way south toward the Gulf of Mexico. Maple, box elder, willow, and cottonwood trees line the banks.*

dickcissels are the birds that are more frequently encountered.

Three miles north of Savanna, 2,500-acre **Mississippi Palisades State Park❖** is a fortress of forested limestone bluffs fronting the mightiest river on the continent, and views from the cliff tops are stunning in any season. By late September, the emerald forest of summer has shifted into brilliant crimsons, ochers, golds, and siennas. Against this autumn backdrop, southward-bound turkey vultures and hawks glide on thermals. In January and February, bald eagles often congregate along unfrozen stretches of the river.

The southern portion of the park is noted for impressive geologic formations and a rich forest of oaks, basswood, and sugar maple. The park's 14 miles of trails cover precipitous terrain and can be challenging, especially those in the South Trail System.

CENTRAL AND SOUTHERN ILLINOIS:
PRAIRIE AND FOREST, SAVANNA AND SWAMP

Central and southern Illinois were once overwhelmingly prairie. Today the original grassland landscape survives only in places too sandy, too precipitous, or too wet for farming; sites where pioneers buried their dead; and plots whose non-conforming owners withheld their property from wholesale development. Perhaps the most famous and lamented lost grassland of Illinois is the Grand Prairie, where rich velvet-black soil nourished the tallest of the tall grasses, and marshes and sloughs swarmed with cranes, geese, ducks, swans, muskrat, and massasauga rattlesnakes.

An immense bulge of flat to rolling terrain east of the Illinois River, the Grand Prairie covered an area 80 miles wide and 100 miles long. Its boundaries outline the bulldozing consequences of the most recent glacial activity in North America (the Wisconsin stage, active from 75,000 to 13,000 years ago). Its five million acres of prairie are all but gone. The 2,600-acre Goose Lake Prairie is the last best example of the low, slough-laced grasslands of the Grand Prairie. The only remnants of black-soil prairie are preserved in three tiny rural cemeteries near Bloomington and Champaign-Urbana, with the exciting 1996 addition of the 19,000-acre Midewin National Tallgrass Prairie on the former site of the Joliet Arsenal.

Although stripped of their native vegetation, the landforms of central Illinois still speak of a dramatic past. Some 10,000 years ago, as the climate warmed and the glaciers began to melt, huge lakes near present-day

LEFT: *In Shawnee National Forest, mist shrouds the Ohio River as sunrise warms the flanking cliffs. The craggy terrain of Illinois's southern tip is a far cry from the prairiescapes that define so much of the state.*

Kankakee rose behind glacial dams. The waters eventually overflowed, cutting a wide swath in the Kankakee Basin. For thousands of years, the diminished river has meandered across this shallow, very broad valley, which in places was an almost impenetrable muck of wet prairie, marsh, and swamp forest. Called variously the Great Kankakee Swamp and the Grand Marsh, it encompassed at least 400,000 acres that were a paradise for waterfowl ("duck, brant, geese, and swans in countless millions," noted a writer in 1904) and other wildlife (bears, foxes, beavers, bison, elk, cougars, wolves, and otters). All but a few hundred acres of the wetlands are now gone, and the river is a vestige of its serpentine self. The Indiana portion of the Kankakee, which once made 2,000 bends in 75 miles, is a straight ditch.

Rivers animate landscapes. As bearers of nutrients, they are terra firma's vascular system, nourishing extensive wetlands and forests. The region's grand watercourses—the Missouri, the Mississippi, the Ohio—are magnificent to behold; but their many tributaries—the Kankakee, Illinois, Mackinaw, Sangamon, Vermilion, Wabash, and Cache—harbor some of the best natural areas in central and southern Illinois. And although the region's wetland corridors have been greatly diminished, glimmers of the original landscape still survive in the Momence Wetlands on the Kankakee, Beall Woods on the Wabash, and Heron Pond on the Cache.

For the last 10,000 years, the eastern deciduous forests and the mid-continental grasslands have played an ecological tug-of-war in a zone stretching from the Great Lakes to Texas. Along this line, rainfall is sufficient to support large trees, but the climate is dry enough to provide tinder for fires. Caused by lightning or set by Native Americans to drive game and nourish perennial grasses, fires were once a shaping force on the Great Plains.

Begotten by fire, a hybrid landscape flourished along the border where forest met prairie. In parklike settings, carpets of prairie grasses and flowers grew amid scattered oaks that often attained grand proportions. Called the Midwest oak savanna (or parkland or barrens), this forest-cum-prairie is estimated to have covered 30 million acres down the middle of the continent. Very little oak savanna—perhaps .02 percent—remains. Among the various assaults on this habitat, the suppression of fire has probably

---

OVERLEAF: *The tracery of surging waters has shaped the glacial landscape of central and southern Illinois. Edged by hardwoods—maples, oaks, hickories—Rock Creek etches through limestone to join the Kankakee.*

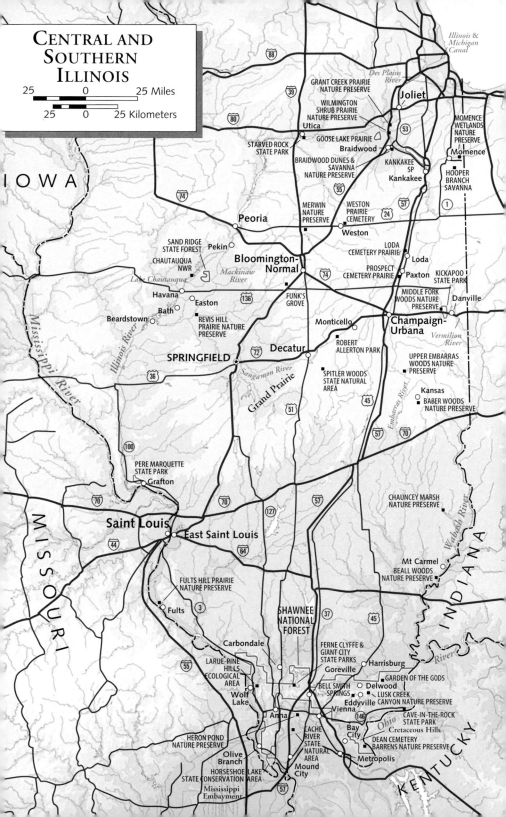

CENTRAL AND SOUTHERN ILLINOIS

25　0　25 Miles
25　0　25 Kilometers

IOWA

MISSOURI

INDIANA

KENTUCKY

Illinois & Michigan Canal

Des Plaines River

GRANT CREEK PRAIRIE
NATURE PRESERVE

WILMINGTON
SHRUB PRAIRIE
NATURE PRESERVE

Joliet

Utica

STARVED ROCK
STATE PARK

GOOSE LAKE PRAIRIE

Braidwood

BRAIDWOOD DUNES &
SAVANNA
NATURE PRESERVE

MOMENCE
WETLANDS
NATURE
PRESERVE

Momence

KANKAKEE
SP

Kankakee

HOOPER
BRANCH
SAVANNA

MERWIN
NATURE
PRESERVE

WESTON
PRAIRIE
CEMETERY

Peoria

Weston

SAND RIDGE
STATE FOREST

Pekin

CHAUTAUQUA
NWR

Lake Chautauqua

Mackinaw River

Bloomington-
Normal

LODA
CEMETERY PRAIRIE

Loda

PROSPECT
CEMETERY PRAIRIE

Paxton

KICKAPOO
STATE PARK

Havana

Bath

Easton

REVIS HILL
PRAIRIE NATURE
PRESERVE

FUNK'S
GROVE

MIDDLE FORK
WOODS NATURE
PRESERVE

Danville

Beardstown

Illinois River

Monticello

Champaign-
Urbana

Vermilion River

SPRINGFIELD

Decatur

ROBERT
ALLERTON PARK

UPPER EMBARRAS
WOODS NATURE
PRESERVE

Sangamon River

SPITLER WOODS
STATE NATURAL
AREA

Kansas

BABER WOODS
NATURE PRESERVE

Grand Prairie

Embarras River

PERE MARQUETTE
STATE PARK

Grafton

CHAUNCEY MARSH
NATURE PRESERVE

Wabash River

Saint Louis

East Saint Louis

FULTS HILL PRAIRIE
NATURE PRESERVE

Mt Carmel

BEALL WOODS
NATURE PRESERVE

Fults

Mississippi River

SHAWNEE
NATIONAL
FOREST

Carbondale

LARUE-PINE
HILLS
ECOLOGICAL
AREA

FERNE CLYFFE &
GIANT CITY
STATE PARKS

Goreville

Harrisburg

GARDEN OF THE GODS

Wolf
Lake

BELL SMITH
SPRINGS

Delwood

LUSK CREEK

EDDYVILLE
CANYON NATURE PRESERVE

Anna

Vienna

Bay
City

CAVE-IN-THE-ROCK
STATE PARK

Cretaceous Hills

HERON POND
NATURE PRESERVE

CACHE
RIVER
STATE
NATURAL
AREA

DEAN CEMETERY
BARRENS NATURE PRESERVE

Ohio River

Olive
Branch

Mound
City

Metropolis

HORSESHOE LAKE
STATE CONSERVATION AREA

Mississippi Embayment

been the most ruinous. In the absence of fire, oaks formed denser stands, other species of trees invaded, and the ensuing shade snuffed out native prairie grasses and flowers. Illinois lies along the savanna border, and thanks to aggressive restoration efforts—which include the reintroduction of fire—a number of thriving outdoor monuments to an almost lost ecosystem are scattered across the state.

Extreme southern Illinois is bounded on the north by the Shawnee Hills and on the other three sides by the Mississippi, Ohio, and Wabash rivers. Because glaciers never scoured this part of the continent, the land bears little resemblance to the rest of the state. Here the open, undulating, no-place-to-hide terrain that characterizes so much of Illinois gives way abruptly to cliffs, cloisters, and shade.

And what a difference trees make. Shawnee National Forest sprawls across 270,000 acres of southern Illinois. Along with many private lands, the Shawnee is now blanketed with second-growth forest, much of which has regenerated since the 1930s, when willy-nilly cutting for farming and pasturing livestock left great swaths of the hills denuded.

Vistas abound. Unlike the prairie, which demands close inspection to appreciate fully, the hills and hollows of southern Illinois make an immediate impression. In spring and summer, overlapping ranges recede to the horizon in a multitude of greens and shadowy blues. In fall—mid-October is the peak—the colors change to brilliant reds, umbers, and golds.

This chapter begins amid the sand dunes and primeval swamp forests along the Kankakee River and travels onto the Grand Prairie. It then follows the mostly southward-flowing lattice of rivers to the extreme southern tip of the state, where the prairie becomes a jumble of rocky forest-covered hills.

NORTH-CENTRAL ILLINOIS: THE KANKAKEE BASIN

The Kankakee River rises in swamps near South Bend, Indiana, and flows generally westward 140 miles, eventually joining the Des Plaines to form the Illinois. The Potawatomi, who inhabited the region when the first French explorers arrived in the seventeenth century, called the river Ti-yar-ac-ke, or "wonderful land." The French gave it various names, including Quin-que-que; Kankakee appears to be an English rendering of the French.

Although small, the Kankakee once had many twists (before most of it was ditched), and its history is a dramatic one. Tracing its saga requires, ideally, two people—one to drive and one to read the map—with a tolerance for each other and for undivided, congested highways because the remnants of this once vast landscape are scattered and inconspicuously marked.

The place to start is the easiest to find: **Kankakee River State Park❖** lies between Routes 113 and 102 about six miles northwest of the city of Kankakee. Although relentlessly manicured, the 4,000-acre park skirts 12 miles of river, enabling visitors to imagine this landscape 13,000–10,000 years ago, during the peak of glacial meltdown, when the Kankakee was *really* a river.

As the climate warmed and the glaciers began to melt, huge lakes formed behind the earthen moraines that were piled up ahead of the ice sheets. The lakes eventually breached these dams in a torrential flood called the Kankakee Torrent. Water carrying tremendous loads of gravel, sand, and silt surged down the Kankakee and into the Illinois River. As the deluge subsided, the water dropped its freight of soils along the route. Today piles of sand along the Kankakee and Illinois are natural worlds unto themselves—semiarid pockets that bear affinities to more westerly parts of the continent and shelter some of the most serene and bizarrely beautiful places in the Heartland.

Two small remnants and an impressively large one are currently maintained in a natural state. **Braidwood Dunes and Savanna Nature Preserve❖** is on the southeast edge of Braidwood, south of Route 113 not quite a mile east of its junction with Route 53. The 288-acre preserve is a wild tangle of Indian grass and big and little bluestem amid scattered oaks.

The 146-acre **Wilmington Shrub Prairie Nature Preserve❖** lies near the west bank of the Kankakee River about three and a half miles northeast of Braidwood Dunes. The preserve is on the west side of County Road 1317 (Wilmington Road), which connects Routes 53 and 113, about a mile and a half north of 113. Despite its small size, Wilmington is crammed with biotic diversity, a composite of marsh, sedge meadow, and various shades of prairie. Its shrub prairie, for example, displays such standard elements as Indian grass and big bluestem, but is remarkably bushy because such plants as bristly blackberry and hardhack (a native *Spiraea*) also grow there. Wilmington is one of the best examples of surviving shrub prairie in Illinois.

The largest protected zone of Kankakee sand is in **Hooper Branch Savanna Nature Preserve❖,** located within the **Iroquois County Conservation Area,** about 20 miles southeast of Kankakee. Here almost 2,500 acres of dunes and swales undulate across the landscape. Sand

ABOVE: *The pink wild pasture rose often hides amid the welter of tallgrass prairie vegetation. Its bright red fruits, called rose hips, are rich in vitamin C.*

LEFT: *A feisty songbird, the loggerhead shrike was once a common prairie sentinel. Biologists tie the bird's recent decline to habitat loss and pesticides.*

prairie, on the higher elevations, and sand savannas (or barrens) give way to wet sedge meadows in the low spots. Barrens may require an adjustment of expectations because gnarly trees (predominantly black and white oaks) and scruffy vegetation often make them seem rough around the edges. Throughout summer, however, the sand savanna and prairie are bejeweled with flowers—spiderwort, wild pasture rose, black-eyed Susan, blazing star. And in fall the wine and copper colors of the oaks, big bluestem, little bluestem, and Indian grass appear.

Red squirrels, typically found in boreal coniferous forests much farther north, reside in the conservation area, one of the few places where this species occurs in Illinois. And the site is also one of only three areas in the state where Henslow's sparrows, a declining prairie species, still breed in fair numbers.

The only stretch of the Kankakee still reminiscent of its natural state runs from the town of Momence (pronounced mo-MENCE) six and a half miles east to the Illinois-Indiana line. A drive along any of the numerous back roads heading north from Route 114 leads into a shadowy primeval landscape of forested swamp. Because the topography is flat, the river and

ABOVE: *Red squirrels, usually found in coniferous forests, prosper at Hooper Branch Savanna, an expanse of prairie and oaks that blankets barren-looking sand dunes.*

RIGHT: *The moist swales at Hooper Branch Savanna perfectly suit marsh blazing star, which likes wet feet. This prolific plant spreads in great drifts of Day-Glo purple.*

its floodplain share virtually the same altitude—about 625 feet above sea level. Places where the river and the road seem ominously proximate illustrate the Kankakee's fidelity to its floodplain and the preposterousness of trying to separate the two.

The 72-acre **Momence Wetlands Nature Preserve❖** lies within this last quasi-wild stretch of the Kankakee about six miles east of Momence, between County Roads E1639N (Lively Boulevard) on the west and E1700N on the east. The floodplain forest is composed of silver maple, pin oak, swamp white oak, river birch, and American elm. Visitors should be forewarned that Route 114 is a busy thoroughfare and intersecting roads are poorly marked.

THE GRAND PRAIRIE

The Grand Prairie, which once covered thousands of square miles in central and eastern Illinois, is gone. Among the few places where modern visitors can conjure it up is **Goose Lake Prairie❖**, about 25 miles southwest of Joliet, a 2,600-acre state park and nature preserve that contains the largest remnant of native prairie east of the Mississippi River. Wedged

LEFT: *Among the natural and restored tall-grass prairie plots at Goose Lake Prairie, an old farm field filled with weedy golden-rod slowly reverts to native prairie plants.* RIGHT: *The yellow ear tufts and glowing eyes of a great horned owl are complemented by native goldenrod; this nocturnal hunter is seldom seen but often heard at dusk or dawn.*

among industrial sites on the banks of the Illinois River, the site is a presettlement throwback in a distinctly surreal setting. Goose Lake Prairie was preserved primarily because its low, often wet, and very rocky terrain diminished its agricultural worth. Farming was attempted on some parts of the site, and because livestock overgrazed the prairie, Goose Lake still lacks the requisite diversity of wildflowers—even after almost 30 years of nurturing. Magnificent stands of tall grasses—big bluestem, Indian grass, switchgrass, and cordgrass—ripple in the breeze. Cattails, bulrushes, and sedges border the marshlands.

Goose Lake Prairie is a nesting stronghold for a number of declining grassland bird species, including Henslow's sparrow. From late winter through summer, it is also a great place to hear the distinctive and varied bird sounds of marsh and prairie—the whinnying of common snipes, the basso profundo hoot of great horned owls, the buzz of woodcocks, the enthusiastic clatter of sedge wrens, and the lovely flutings of eastern meadowlarks, to name a few. This small grassland is a potent reminder that the Grand Prairie must have been a wonderfully musical landscape. Dusk, a splendid hour to be out on the prairie, is the time to listen for great-horned owls, snipes, and woodcocks.

Goose Lake Prairie is one of the last places in the state—Nachusa Grasslands and Sand Prairie–Scrub Oak Nature Preserve are two others—where visitors can stand in the encompassing grass and begin to understand the immensity of the prairie, to feel what writer John Madson describes as "a land of excess—of blazing sun and great weathers."

Although much smaller than Goose Lake, nearby **Grant Creek Prairie Nature Preserve❖** is a superb grassland remnant. The 78-acre parcel is in the **Des Plaines Conservation Area,** east of Interstate 55 just off the Wilmington exit. Here the predominant grasses—prairie dropseed, Indian grass, big bluestem, and switchgrass—are intermingled with a fine collection of wildflowers, including leadplant, purple prairie clover, blazing star, goldenrod, rattlesnake master, and bottle, or closed, gentian.

Three cemetery prairies in the heart of the Grand Prairie harbor fewer than 15 acres of an ecosystem that once encompassed 5 million acres. All

across the Great Plains, rural cemeteries are often the last repositories of native prairie. Because cemeteries are small and throttled on all sides by pasture or row crops, conservation biologists consider them dead-end places, their flora and fauna vulnerable to disease, climate stresses, and inbreeding. Nonetheless, cemetery prairies are priceless ecological and cultural templates. They are sources of native seeds needed by prairie restorationists, their soil profiles yield insights into the natural history of the Great Plains grassland ecosystems, and they offer intimations of a vast and lost landscape.

ABOVE: *The Omaha and Ponca peoples called the native leadplant "buffalo bellow plant" because it blooms during the rut of the bison in late spring.*

The five-acre **Prospect Cemetery Prairie Nature Preserve**❖ is 27 miles north of Champaign-Urbana, east of Route 45 on the south side of Paxton. **Loda Cemetery Prairie Nature Preserve**❖ lies four miles farther north on Route 45, a 3.5-acre site on the northwest edge of Loda village. The five-acre **Weston Cemetery Prairie**❖ is just north of Route 24, one-half mile east of Weston and about 25 miles northeast of Bloomington-Normal. Resting on the moist black soil that has made this part of Illinois such rich agricultural terrain, all three prairies share such characteristic flora of the tallgrass prairie as big bluestem, compass plant, rattlesnake master, and prairie clover. Yet each has its own tenor. Visiting all three is a reminder that considerable nuance and variety exist under the rubric of prairie. Of the three, Weston Cemetery best conveys the high lonesome of the Grand Prairie. Here, amid a welter of grasses and wildflowers, the big sky meets the flat earth. It is a perfect place to watch a Great Plains sunset.

Paradoxically, in the Grand Prairie region the natural element that perseveres is not grass but trees, which tend to grow in untillable places. The suppression of fire has favored the growth of trees on the prairie and also changed the character of Illinois's woodlands. Admittedly beautiful, the Grand Prairie's contemporary forests bear little resemblance to presettlement woodlands.

Some of the oldest trees in the state grow in the steep canyons of **Starved Rock State Park❖,** a scenic and historic site on the south bank of the Illinois River a mile south of Utica, just south and east of the conjunction of Interstates 80 and 39. In the 1680s, French explorer La Salle and his lieutenant Henri de Tonti built Fort Saint Louis at Starved Rock in an effort to strengthen ties with the native populations. The park is named for a dramatic 130-foot sandstone butte where a group of Illini Indians reportedly starved to death during a siege by the Ottawa in the 1770s. The 3,000-acre park's more than 15 miles of hiking trails traverse many of the canyons and bluffs. A 582-acre dedicated nature preserve within the park contains a sampling of upland hardwood forest.

ABOVE: *Many birds eat the seeds, flowers, and leaves of the blue violet, Illinois's state flower; wild turkeys prefer to feed on its tuberous roots.*

At the 700-acre **Merwin Nature Preserve❖,** about 18 miles north of Bloomington, a mosaic of hardwood forests grows along the bluffs and floodplain of the scenic Mackinaw River. A swath of savanna is being reclaimed here, and a restored prairie lies at the southwest corner of the site. At Merwin the forest shifts from white oak and shagbark hickory, dominant trees on the uplands, to sycamore, cottonwood, hackberry, silver maple, and green ash in the floodplain. Eastern hop hornbeam (*Ostrya*)—distinguished by its elmlike leaves and finely fissured, scaly bark—commonly grows in the understory, and purple-flowered redbuds, which bloom in mid-May, thrive along the drier rims of the bluffs.

OVERLEAF: *More than a dozen streams cascade through forested gorges in Starved Rock State Park. In Wildcat Canyon, American elm, American basswood, and red oak shade a creviced cliff face and wispy waterfall.*

Merwin Preserve stages an impressive display of spring wildflowers, which begins with hepatica in late March; continues through April with Virginia bluebells, bloodroot, Dutchman's-breeches, and marsh marigolds (uncommon flowers in the region); and extends into May, with red trillium, mayapple, and columbine. Also peaking in early to mid-May are delicate

shooting stars, very rare in Illinois, which grow along the bluff north of the river. Singers accompanying the show of flowers include house wrens, rose-breasted grosbeaks, wood thrushes, eastern wood-pewees, and great crested flycatchers in the forest and field sparrows, brown thrashers, and catbirds in the thickety old fields interspersing the woodlands. Migrant birds reach peak numbers about mid-May.

ABOVE: *Its dark maroon flower poised amid three mottled leaves, red trillium, or toadshade, blooms in Illinois Canyon at Starved Rock State Park.*

RIGHT: *A cathedral of trees among the tallgrass, Funk's Grove glimmers in autumn when maples and mulberries turn gold. Now rare, such groves persist along streams and glacial ridges.*

Running through the preserve, the Mackinaw River, a tributary of the Illinois, is a limpid, riffling stream. Seven species of clams—mollusks requiring clear, oxygen-rich water—have been recorded in the area. Wood ducks, which nest in cavities in large trees or boxes provided for them by humans, are common along the Mackinaw, as are beavers. River otters were introduced in 1996. In spring and early summer, the Mackinaw is a fine river to canoe.

Prairie groves, discrete islands of hardwood forest scattered across the tallgrass prairie, typically occurred downwind from natural firebreaks such as streams or glacial ridges. In the nineteenth century, prairie groves were settled first because they provided what pioneers needed—shade, fuel, and building material. By the early 1900s most of these emerald bastions had been cleared. One of the last and largest old-growth forests in Illinois is **Funk's Grove,** near the village of Funk's Grove west of I-55, about 15 miles south of Bloomington-Normal. Travelers may call Moraine View

LEFT: *Prairie marshes, sloughs, and potholes are the preferred habitat of the blue-winged teal. A dabbling duck, the teal feeds by skimming the water's surface or by tipping bottom up to eat vegetation submerged in the shallows.*

RIGHT: *The green-winged teal is the smallest of the North American puddle ducks. In breeding season the drake is distinctive, with his rust head and green stripe; female plumage remains protectively drab throughout the year.*

Recreation Area for more information about visiting the grove.

Funk's Grove has survived thanks to a tradition of stewardship engendered by the original settlers, Isaac Funk and his brother-in-law Robert Stubblefield. More than a thousand acres of forest, savanna, and prairie are now protected and managed by family heirs, state agencies, and private conservation organizations; additional acres of pasture or cropland are also being restored to presettlement conditions.

Funk's Grove contains glorious trees. Solitary specimens, generally bur or red oaks, dominate the savanna on the **Ewing Tract** amid prairie grasses and wildflowers. Blessed with bountiful space and light, these oaks support immense spreading crowns and branches that droop almost to the ground. In the cathedral-like forest at **Stubblefield Grove,** stately white oaks, sugar maples, and basswood grow to heights of 120 feet. Underneath, forest wildflowers—trout lilies, phlox, and trillium—blossom in late April and early May, and on the sunnier savanna, different species of prairie flowers bloom throughout the summer and into October. Funk descendants still maintain a sugar camp at Funk's Grove, where they tap sugar maples in the winter to make maple syrup, a business in operation since 1891.

CENTRAL ILLINOIS: HILL PRAIRIES AND RIVER FORESTS

From Funk's Grove, Route 136 heads west, arrow-straight and pancake-flat, toward the Illinois River, traversing 50 miles of continuous corn and

soybean fields. Tucked away down roads with no names, four natural fragments are worth seeking. **Revis Springs Hill Nature Preserve❖**, south of 136 about five miles beyond Easton, provides some verticality in an otherwise horizontal landscape. One of the finest remaining examples of a loess hill prairie in Illinois, it unfolds across a steep south-facing bluff overlooking the Sangamon Valley. The dusty, parched look of the 53-acre prairie is caused by the floury texture of its loess soil and by the incessant baking that the southern slope receives from the sun. The hill is tufted with little bluestem, side-oats grama, leadplant, and ladies' tresses (*Spiranthes*), and an upland forest of oaks and hickories fringes the summit. A splendid panorama unfolds from the top of Revis Hill.

A magnificent pile of sand that originated with the Kankakee Torrent, **Sand Prairie–Scrub Oak Nature Preserve❖** is a 1,460-acre expanse of savanna, oak-hickory forest, and sand prairie about ten miles west of Revis Hill prairie and four miles east of Bath. Mottes (mounds) of dwarfish trees lie scattered amid sand dunes bunched with little bluestem, porcupine grass, and prickly pear cactus. The preserve is large and remote enough to afford visitors an inkling of how Illinois (along with much of the Midwest) looked—and sounded—before it was peopled over and plowed up. Standing in Sand Prairie–Scrub Oak Preserve, only the most impervious observer will not be struck by the pervasive sound of silence, a stillness broken only occasionally by the wind or by the songs of birds.

ABOVE: *John J. Audubon sketched the American beaver, a remarkable dam-building rodent, from life. This color lithograph appeared in* The Quadrupeds of North America, *published after the artist died in 1851.*

Six miles north of Havana, the 4,500-acre **Chautauqua National Wildlife Refuge❖** perches on the east bank of the Illinois and slips into its floodplain. Starting around the middle of October, until the blue waters of Lake Chautauqua freeze, thousands of ducks, Canada geese, and snow geese congregate at the refuge. Mallard are by far the most numerous, joined by lesser numbers of pintail, wigeon, blue-winged teal, green-winged teal, gadwalls, mergansers, and wood ducks (which also nest on the refuge). Gatherings of waterfowl are generally attended by bald eagles, raptors noted for their vulturelike habit of feeding on dead waterfowl. In winter dozens of bald eagles hunker down in the leafless trees or cruise above the shoreline of the lake.

Along a half-mile self-guided nature trail, which winds through a mature upland woodland of mockernut hickory and black oak, three overlooks provide views of the floodplain forest and Lake Chautauqua.

Reached via an assortment of bucolic back roads, **Sand Ridge State Forest❖** lies 12 miles northeast of Havana. The forest straddles large swells of sand deposited by subsiding glacial waters during the Kankakee Torrent and then whipped into dunes by prevailing westerly winds. Crouching on the plain east of the Illinois River, these dunes stretch from Pekin (just south of Peoria) about 80 miles southwest to Beardstown. Some of the largest dunes along this ridge occur in the state forest, where the porous sand— unlike the dark, moist soil on much of the Grand Prairie—was poorly suited for agriculture. As a result, the 7,500-acre site contains about 4,000 acres of native oaks and hickories and 2,500 acres that have been planted, primarily in red and white pines. Traversed by 44 miles of marked hiking trails, Sand Ridge State Forest accommodates a full slate of recreational activities, from snowmobiling to camping, hunting to trapshooting.

Like Funk's Grove, the 202-acre **Spitler Woods State Natural Area❖**, eight miles southeast of Decatur, is an outstanding remnant forest that was safeguarded by a vigilant steward. Its namesake, Ida B. Spitler, allowed no timber harvesting, grazing, or hunting in her forest, which she owned from 1892 to 1937, when she donated it to the state. Spitler Woods is a roller coaster of uplands and ravines. White, red, and black oaks and shagbark hickory rule the uplands, and red oak, basswood, sugar maple, and black walnut grow on the slopes. In the wetter ravine bottoms are sycamore, hackberry, and American elm. Diameter at breast height, or DBH, is a standard measure of girth and grandeur in trees. In Spitler Woods, numerous individual trees—white oak, bur oak, black walnut, sycamore—boast impressive breast-height diameters of 30 to 40 inches.

Although not virgin prairie, 1,500-acre **Robert Allerton Park❖** is large and intact, encompassing expanses of old second-growth forest along the Sangamon River. The park is just south of I-72 about midway between Decatur and Champaign-Urbana and four miles southwest of Monticello. Chicago livestock baron Samuel Waters Allerton began purchasing the land in 1863, and his son, Robert Henry, managed the estate and developed the fertile uplands for livestock and crop production. In 1946 Robert Allerton donated the Farms, as the estate was called, to the University of Illinois, and at the park's core is his Georgian mansion, now a conference center, and about 90 acres of formal European-inspired sculpture gardens. A 20-mile network of trails leads into the wildwood. Skirting approximately 600 acres of the river is an exceptional floodplain forest of silver maple, cottonwood, and sycamore. Another 400 acres of upland oak-hickory forest, primarily south of the Sangamon, constitutes one of the oldest forest remnants in the Grand Prairie.

Around the city of Danville, the several arms of the Vermilion River slip off the Illinois map to join the Wabash River in Indiana. A vast hardwood forest once traced the floodplains and uplands of the Wabash and its tributaries. Most of that forest is gone, but a swatch survives along the Vermilion in **Middle Fork Woods Nature Preserve❖** in **Kickapoo State Park,** about ten miles west of Danville.

The Middle Fork of the Vermilion is a sweet river, shallow and clear. Although modest by most standard definitions, it boasts fine flat-water canoeing in spring; a 17.1-mile portion forms the **Middle Fork of the Vermilion National Scenic River,** the only waterway so designated in the Indiana-Illinois-Iowa region. In the preserve, the forest slopes from flat uplands down steep ravines to the river. Here a profusion of oak species flourish above an understory of redbud, dogwood, hornbeam (*Carpinus*), eastern hop hornbeam (*Ostrya*), and sassafras. American beech, scattered on the ravine slopes, is at the western limits of its range. In the upland forests, the endangered silvery salamander breeds in ephemeral ponds.

In **Walnut Point State Park,** about 50 miles southeast of Champaign-Urbana, the **Upper Embarras Woods Nature Preserve❖** protects a small (65 acres) but outstanding forest of oaks, hickories, sugar maple, and basswood. The park straddles the Embarras (Em-ba-RA) River, a tributary of the Wabash.

MARSHES AND FORESTS OF THE WABASH

Vestiges of the power and influence of rivers abound throughout southern Illinois. The last large marsh in the Wabash River basin, **Chauncey Marsh Nature Preserve❖** lies in an ancient oxbow lake formed when the Embarras River carried a much larger volume of water than it does today. Chauncey (pronounced Chance-y) Marsh is about 25 miles west of Vincennes, Indiana, and about 3 miles east of the village of Chauncey, Illinois. This 155-acre expanse of cordgrass and bulrush is interspersed with thickets of willow and a lowland forest of oaks, hickories, black walnut, and sweet gum.

Of all the prairie grasses, cordgrass made perhaps the biggest impression on westward-bound explorers and settlers. It came to be called ripgut, a precise description of what it did to the bellies of horses. To empathize, visitors to Chauncey Marsh can run a finger cautiously down a rasping blade of cordgrass. A classic plant of the wetter areas of tallgrass prairie, this robust grass can reach heights of five to seven feet, compara-

---

RIGHT: *Mauve redbud flowers and lime-green maple blossoms brighten springtime vistas at Kickapoo State Park. The park's clear lakes appeared when water filled the pits left from coal strip mining in 1939.*

ABOVE: *Beall Woods Nature Preserve still harbors a wonderful fragment of the impenetrable forest that once lined the Wabash River. Here an impressive oak rises among sugar maple, black gum, and tulip trees.*

ble to big bluestem and Indian grass, and in late summer it produces spectacular spangly golden seed heads.

Within Beall Woods State Park, the 329-acre **Beall Woods Nature Preserve❖** occupies the west bank of the Wabash about six miles south of Mount Carmel. The park is named for the Beall (pronounced Bell) family, who owned the property from 1861 to 1962, a century when they did little to alter one of the last great examples of eastern deciduous forest east of the Mississippi. The terrain ranges from rolling well-drained upland woods to floodplain forest, which, not surprisingly, is often carpeted with standing water. One of the most venerable natural areas in Illinois, Beall Woods, also called the Forest of the Wabash and the University of Trees, harbors specimens of great size and height.

Oak and hickory grow in the upland forest, where yellow poplar, sweet gum, sugar maple, American elm, and hackberry are also common. The bottomlands and sloughs sustain sycamore, silver maple, pecan, cottonwood, willows, and oaks. The nature preserve contains five self-guided trails from one to two miles long. The Ridgeway Trail was named in honor of the great twentieth-century ornithologist Robert Ridgeway, who spent his boyhood in the Mount Carmel area.

MISSISSIPPI BOTTOMLANDS AND BLUFFS

Pere Marquette State Park❖, northwest of Saint Louis and five miles west of Grafton on Route 100, is named for the seventeenth-century explorer priest. In 1673, he and his partner Louis Jolliet, guided by Native Americans, became the first Europeans to travel the Mississippi River. The 8,050-acre park overlooks the Illinois River near its confluence with the Mississippi; 12 miles of trails offer numerous views of the river and its backwaters. Within the park, a 300-acre nature preserve harbors oak forests in the uplands, sugar maple and sassafras in the wetter ravines, and a wide variety of wildflowers and prairie grasses on its loess hill prairies. Limestone outcrops provide toeholds for a number of fern species.

About 35 miles south of East Saint Louis near the town of Fults, the 532-acre **Fults Hill Prairie Nature Preserve❖** occupies a high bluff overlooking the Mississippi River. Along with Revis Hill near Havana, Fults Hill is one of the finest loess hill prairies remaining in Illinois. The precipitous west-facing site is steep, well drained, and parched by sun and prevailing westerly winds. The preserve's arid conditions foster prickly pear cactus and plains scorpions, which typically occur farther west. Plumed with little bluestem, big bluestem, Indian grass, and side-oats grama, Fults Hill Prairie is renowned for its vistas and its summer-long display of wildflowers.

THE SOUTHERN TIP: FORESTED HILLS

The far-flung **Shawnee National Forest❖** dominates this part of Illinois, and any number of roads—including north-south Routes 3, 127, 37, 45, and 147—offer overviews of this beautiful and complicated terrain. One particularly rewarding route, the 70-mile **Shawnee Hills on the Ohio National Forest Scenic Byway❖,** begins in Mitchellsville and follows Routes 34 and 1 southeast toward the Ohio River; it then meanders southwest on Route 146 to the Smithland Locks and Dam Visitor Center. For those who have time to see the world on foot, a 57-mile section of the **River-to-River Trail** travels between Camp Cadiz, a national forest campground just west of Route 1, to Route 45 just north of Vienna. Veteran hikers consider this path one of the more challenging treks in Illinois, and it traverses fascinating terrain, including some of the mammoth sandstone formations in the Garden of the Gods Wilderness Area. For traveling deep

---

OVERLEAF: *Framed by ash, dogwood, and eastern red cedar, a vista of the Illinois River stretches west from Pere Marquette park. Nearby, three great waterways—the Illinois, Mississippi, and Missouri—converge.*

69

into the backcountry, get a map of the Shawnee National Forest (Third Principal Meridian), available at the Shawnee National Forest Supervisor's Office in Harrisburg.

This relatively unknown southern extremity of the state harbors an impressive assembly of landscapes, which in turn spawn a rich and complex flora. One site alone—LaRue–Pine Hills—contains a whopping 35 percent of the plant species found in Illinois. The most dramatic of these converging landscapes is the system of sandstone ridges called the Shawnee Hills, which twist like the Great Wall of China across the tip of the state between the Ohio River and the Mississippi. The hills rise over a coastal plain of gravelly hillocks, sluggish streams, and wetlands, now largely ditched and drained for farming. Called the Mississippi Embayment, this plain was a bulge of the Gulf of Mexico several times—the latest, 23 to 34 million years ago—and its bald cypress and tupelo swamps are still reminiscent of pockets of the Deep South along the present-day Gulf. Add to the hills and coastal plain a piece of Mississippi River bottomlands (of which little natural remains) and a sliver of the Ozarks, which hug the western edge of the floodplain, and the complexity of the terrain becomes apparent.

Because the Shawnee Hills encompass extremes of cool forest and hot, exposed rock, rue anemone and mayapple—exemplars of shady forests—often grow within a stone's throw of rare species of lichens baking on sun-drenched sandstone outcrops. Much of the Shawnee Hills' botanical diversity is determined by which direction the land happens to face and the chemistry of the soil. In the forest, the seldom-seen wood thrush sings its melancholy minor-key song on spring and summer days, while the wild, loopy whistles of whippoorwills and chuck-will's-widows fill the dark of night.

Scattered across 270,000 acres of southern Illinois, the **Shawnee National Forest**❖ offers short and long forays that lead to waterfalls, quiet pools, boulder-strewn creeks, and austere sandstone ledges. A number of recreation and wilderness areas enfold distinctive trademarks of the Shawnee Hills such as **Bell Smith Springs Recreation Area**❖, near Eddyville. At Bell Smith, a system of spring-fed creeks has etched a convolution of gorges through the sandstone. Twelve miles of trails meander through upland forests of American beech and yellow poplar (which create a golden blaze in October) and then down to the sandstone pavements that form the creekbeds. Rocks (some as big as ship prows) dislodged from the cliff faces lie collapsed in and along the creeks. The scant soil supports an array of

ABOVE: *In Shawnee National Forest, angular sandstone boulders repose in Bay Creek. This clear, placid stream flows through Bell Smith Springs, a dappled realm of sun and shade that nurtures a gamut of wildflowers.*

flowering plants. June—and plenty of sun—bring on the satin-ribbon-like yellow flowers of prickly pear cactus, following the May show of delicate white flares of shooting star blooming in the shade of cliff overhangs.

About two miles north of Bell Smith Springs is **Burden Falls,** found along Forest Road 402 three miles west of the village of Delwood. The falls comprise an impressive pile of rocks over which water cascades only intermittently, usually in early spring or after torrential downpours. A three-mile trail runs above the waterfall, and in the absence of water one can traverse the waterfall to access the trail. The 3,671-acre **Burden Falls Wilderness❖** lies immediately to the north, and the 2,866-acre **Bay Creek Wilderness❖** just to the south.

Embedded within the national forest like hidden jewels are a number of state nature preserves, which harbor distinctive landforms, flora, and fauna. These areas are well worth seeking out. About three miles east of Bell Smith Springs is the **Lusk Creek Canyon Nature Preserve❖,** another chasm etched in sandstone. The preserve is reached via a 1.5-mile hike in upland forest through the southern edge of the 4,796-acre **Lusk Creek Canyon Wilderness Area.** The gateway to the preserve is a sunbaked sandstone glade, a stark contrast to the cool, shadowy habitat a quarter-

mile below. The short, steep trail terminates at **Indian Kitchen,** which can also be reached by canoe. The focal point of the preserve, Indian Kitchen is an echoing amphitheater where Lusk Creek has cut a hairpin turn through the sandstone. The cliffs provide toeholds for ferns and mosses and nest sites for swallows.

On the eastern edge of Shawnee National Forest, about 15 miles southeast of Harrisburg, is **Garden of the Gods❖.** In this recreation area, five miles of trails wind through 300-million-year-old rock formations with epithets such as Camel Rock, Devil's Smoke Stack, Noah's Ark, and Mushroom Rock.

Ferne Clyffe State Park, one mile south of Goreville and easily accessible from Interstates 57 and 24, and Giant City State Park, east of Route 51 about five miles south of Carbondale, contain small but lovely nature preserves that are emphatic examples of Shawnee Hills natural history. In **Ferne Clyffe State Park❖** the **Round Bluff Nature Preserve** is an island of sandstone separate from other bluffs in the park. A 1.3-mile loop trail wanders around and over this gigantic rock, through a woodland of white oak, yellow poplar, and shagbark hickory and across sunny south-facing glades

LEFT: *The lichen-encrusted sandstone out-crops at Garden of the Gods offer splendid views of the Shawnee Hills that ebb to the horizon in shades of green and blue.* RIGHT: *A game animal with a seesaw history, the white-tailed deer was decimated by hunters. Now too abundant, hungry deer scour woodlands of native vegetation.*

that support prairie grasses, prickly pear cactus, fire pink, and other sun-loving plants. In shady pockets, Christmas, rattlesnake, and hay-scented ferns cling to the rock or grow on the forest floor amid sassafras and papaw. Giant fissures in the bluff emit cool and eerie breaths.

Under the influence of sun and shadow, **Fern Rocks Nature Preserve** in **Giant City State Park❖** is an equally impressive and mammoth rock garden. In early May the two-mile loop trail begins in dappled woods of maple, hickory, and oak amid a mother lode of trillium and climbs to a remnant ridgetop prairie. Along the way, Fern Rocks provides one of the best displays of spring wildflowers in Illinois.

ALONG THE OHIO: THE COASTAL PLAIN

Swamps, marshes, floodplain forests, ancient oxbows, prairie barrens, and mineral-laden seeps characterize the swath of land along the Ohio River. Less obviously beautiful than the Shawnee Hills, the coastal plain is rich in the biological nuances characteristic of wetlands. The **Cache River** is the first prize of the coastal plain. Short and languid, the cocoa-brown Cache is an old channel of the Ohio that rises in the Shawnee Hills. The Upper Cache River begins near the town of Anna and meanders 60 miles before reaching the Post Creek cutoff, which hastens drainage into the Ohio River. The Lower Cache stretches 55 to 60 miles before it is diverted into the Mississippi River. This classic southern swamp river is at the northern limit of a lush and historically exploited habitat. The bottomlands of the Cache, like its southern counterparts, have long been logged for prime timber and ditched and drained for farming. The last fragments

ABOVE: *Large boulders flank the forest trails in Giant City State Park, which is renowned for its rock formations and wildflowers. In spring redbuds brighten the wooded landscape.*

RIGHT: *Looking more like a swamp than part of a river, Heron Pond on the low-lying Cache River is punctuated with flaring bald cypress trees and glazed with bright green duckweed.*

of its forest and swamps are being protected and restored at **Cypress Creek National Wildlife Refuge❖,** within the Cache River Wetlands.

The **Cache River State Natural Area❖** contains 11,499 acres of swamp and bottomland forest; many of the remote areas are only accessible by foot along 18 miles of trails. Another recommended way to see this primeval landscape is by canoe or johnboat. Winding through a beautiful oak-hickory forest, a 1.5-mile round-trip trail gains access to **Heron Pond** (south of Vienna and west off Route 45), one of the stellar attractions of Illinois. The path intersects the slow-moving Cache, then circles a magnificent swamp of bald cypress and lesser numbers of water tupelo. For a closer inspection, a 6-foot wide floating boardwalk extends 381 feet into the celadon-green swamp between flaring buttresses of bald cypress. In spring and early summer, the plaintive calls of eastern wood-pewees, great crested flycatchers, and wood thrushes are interspersed among the more enthusiastic endorsements of prothonotary warblers and Carolina wrens.

Skirting the north bank of the Cache River at this point is **Wildcat Bluff–Little Black Slough Nature Preserve❖,** an altogether different place where steep limestone cliffs rise suddenly out of the swamp. The trail leads through an unbroken oak-hickory upland forest and is one of

the places in southern Illinois where visitors can observe migrant warblers and other small songbirds in late April and early May. Within the woodland are limestone barrens saturated with southern light, which support a prairie realm of little and big bluestem, side-oats grama, Indian grass, and prairie wildflowers. The trailhead for Wildcat Bluff is six miles southwest of the town of Vienna off Route 146; access to Heron Pond is seven miles southwest via Route 45 and the road to Belknap.

The 1,500-acre **Limekiln Springs Preserve❖,** owned by the Nature Conservancy, has a tupelo and bald cypress swamp on its northern border. The beauty of this place is enhanced by a peculiar hydrologic feature: A limestone outcrop at the edge of the swamp is the source of springs that continually refresh the wetland. The super-fresh waters here harbor a number of rare invertebrates and fish, including the cypress minnow. A mile-long trail and a boardwalk traverse the natural area.

About a mile south of the town of Olive Branch, a giant loop of water encircles an island of old-growth timber. **Horseshoe Lake State Conservation Area❖,** an ancient oxbow of the Mississippi River, is perhaps best known as wintering grounds for a quarter of a million Canada geese and an attendant battery of bald eagles. Natural attrition among the former

affords easy pickings for the latter. The forests at Horseshoe Lake are magnificent, although the 1993 floods destroyed many trees. When floodwaters inundated portions of the oxbow and dropped massive amounts of sand along this part of the Mississippi floodplain, 70 percent of the trees in the lower-lying areas of Horseshoe Lake were killed. Hardest hit were the tupelos and several species of white oak.

The other endowment of the Illinois coastal plain is the **Cretaceous Hills,** roly-poly mounds of reddish gravel in the **Shawnee National Forest❖** that lie along the Ohio River just south of Bay City. Crisscrossed by roads where vehicles raise reddish dust on all but the wettest days, the hills are named for the ocean that churned up the area in the Cretaceous period, 100 or so million years ago.

Located on the southern flank of the Cretaceous Hills about eight miles northeast of Metropolis, two preserves are ideal, if somewhat hard-to-find, introductions to this peculiar gravelly landscape. Inquire at the Forest Service's office in Harrisburg for exact directions before proceeding. **Dean Cemetery Barrens Preserve❖** appears rather mangy and unkempt to an unappreciative eye, but in late summer it presents a spectacular display of prairie wildflowers. The 237-acre **Cretaceous Hills Nature Preserve❖,** about one mile north

ABOVE: *A resident of swamps and bottomland forests, the wood duck nests in trees. The vividly colored drake is probably the most gorgeous waterfowl in North America.*

LEFT: *In the soft light of an early fall evening, bald cypress and tupelo trees are mirrored in the still waters of Horseshoe Lake, an ancient oxbow of the Mississippi floodplain.*

of Dean Cemetery, spreads over hill and hollow, enveloping prairie barrens, upland forests, and acid seeps. White, scarlet, and Spanish red oaks are common here, as are hickories and yellow poplar, and the dogwood show in May is the best in southern Illinois. Occasional loblolly pines, which are not native to these hills, recall the Dust Bowl era, when the U.S. Forest Service began buying exhausted farm sites and planting pines to stop erosion. The seeps, hidden in ravines, are fed by mineral-laden water percolating through extremely acid gravel deposits. These boggy places are fern heaven. Amid carpets of sphagnum moss, a procession of ferns—cinnamon, royal, sensitive, and bracken—unfurl their lacy fronds in a display

LEFT: *The acidic soils in the fens and seeps at the Cretaceous Hills Nature Preserve are ideal for cinnamon ferns, whose distinctive reddish-brown fertile fronds produce the plants' reproductive spores.*

RIGHT: *A bastion of botanical diversity, La Rue–Pine Hills natural area encompasses a swamp in the Mississippi River bottoms and a forest of oaks, hickories, and shortleaf pine atop 350-foot limestone bluffs.*

worthy of a Victorian funeral parlor.

On the state's western border near the town of Wolf Lake, **La Rue–Pine Hills/Otter Pond Research Natural Area**❖ is one of the most remarkable and poignant natural areas in the Heartland. In a wedlock of opposites, a last fragment of bottomland swamp and forest conjoins a soaring fortress of limestone, which is clad with oaks and hickories and in its highest, driest reaches with shortleaf pine, the only *Pinus* native to southern Illinois. Seldom do such diametric habitats occur in such close proximity.

In dark and humid **La Rue Swamp,** titan oaks, hickories, honey locust, yellow poplar, sycamore, and biceps-size grapevines suggest the former magnificence of the Mississippi bottomland forests. Rising abruptly 350 feet above the floodplain, the serpentine ridges of the Pine Hills are, by contrast, brisk with breezes and lavished in light. A number of west-facing ridgetop vantages (including one midway along the three-quarter-mile Inspiration Point Forest Trail) offer dramatic views of the broad and much-altered valley of the Mississippi below. A drive through La Rue–Pine Hills can be accessed from Route 3 three miles north of the town of Wolf Lake. A portion of this route, Forest Road 345, which follows the base of the limestone bluff, is closed to vehicular traffic twice a year (March 15 to May 15 and September 1 to October 31) to protect migrating cottonmouths and other water snakes, king and rat snakes, and state-threatened timber rattlesnakes.

IOWA

CHAPTER THREE

IOWA:
TRACES OF GLACIERS IN THE
HEART OF THE TALLGRASS

I owa is voluptuous, its landscapes all gentle angles of thighs, elbows, scapulas, vertebrae, and big round buttocks. These seductive contours were created by glaciers grinding over the terrain for 2.5 million years. Only the northeastern corner of the state, known as the Paleozoic Plateau or Driftless Area, largely escaped the sculpting influence of moving ice. Across the endless fields of corn and soybeans that now so define most of Iowa, its glacial topography remains quite distinct. The natural fabric of tallgrass prairie that once cloaked this gorgeous body, however, has been reduced to tatters. Iowa is the most reworked piece of property in this country.

Over the last 30,000 years, as the climate cycled through periods that were cold and wet, then warm and dry, the Great Plains were a vast stage where forest and prairie performed an elaborate botanical minuet. The forest advanced; the prairie stepped back; their strides reversed; then they embraced. Between 30,000 and 20,000 years ago, when weather was cool and moist, spruce and pine forests dominated. The period between 9,000 and 8,000 years ago, when prairie vegetation overtook the forests as the plains began to parch, marked the ascendancy of the tallgrass prairie, the vast grasslands that stretched south from Manitoba and Saskatchewan to Texas and east from Nebraska to Ohio.

Iowa was the heart of the tallgrass belt. For centuries roughly 30 mil-

PRECEDING PAGES: *Wild prairie roses, Iowa's state flower, ramble over Mississippi River bluffs at Pikes Peak State Park during the 1993 floods.*
LEFT: *On the roller-coaster terrain of the Loess Hills, a red oak stands amid black-eyed Susans—a classic scene in this semiarid grassland.*

lion acres—85 percent of the state—were covered in billowing grasses and rainbows of wildflowers. Although climatically the tallgrass should still reign, humans obliterated it with astounding speed. Virtually the entire 30 million acres of tallgrass were plowed up in just 80 years—from the 1850s, when the steel moldboard plow was invented, to the 1930s, when widespread drought and the Great Depression gripped the state.

Biologists estimate that about 30,000 acres of prairie remain in Iowa, of which only 5,000 acres are open to the public. Scattered in small, disjunct parcels, most tallgrass remnants in Iowa are no bigger than 200 acres. The state's largest remaining swath of native prairie, about 1,500 acres, is actually two contiguous sites—Five Ridges and Broken Kettle—just north of Sioux City in the Loess Hills.

Visiting these places is both a joy and a heartbreak. Compared to the monocultures skulking on their edges, the native grasslands are riotous with life. In their isolation, however, these remnants have become genetic cages for many plants, invertebrates, small reptiles (herps), and mammals. Some sites are too small to attract larger prairie fauna, such as badgers and northern harriers, that need space to roam. Today conservationists are working to improve the situation. In a grand experiment begun none too soon, the U.S. Fish and Wildlife Service in 1991 embarked on an ambitious project at Walnut Creek to restore about 8,600 contiguous acres southeast of Des Moines to tallgrass prairie.

With its tidy farms and endlessly undulating fields of corn, soybeans, and alfalfa, the great middle of Iowa is a Grant Wood painting. The state lies between the major stems of the continent's largest river system, bordered on the east by the Mississippi, which traverses a craggy landscape that defies most preconceived notions about Iowa, and on the west by the Missouri, which churns through a broad valley fluted by handsome ridges of windblown loess.

Along the Mississippi, the state's northeastern corner is a jewel of ancient fractured bedrock. Curving from the Minnesota border to just south of Dubuque, the arc of land that borders Wisconsin is the only section of the state not inundated by glacial deposits, or drift. This sliver of Iowa and adjacent parts of Wisconsin, Illinois, and Minnesota have long been called the Driftless Area, a wonderfully descriptive and poetic term seeming to suggest that a shroud has been lifted from the landscape. "In no other region of the state," writes geologist Jean Prior, "is bedrock in such complete control of the shape of the land surface."

The woods here are deep, the terrain rugged. The dominant trees are

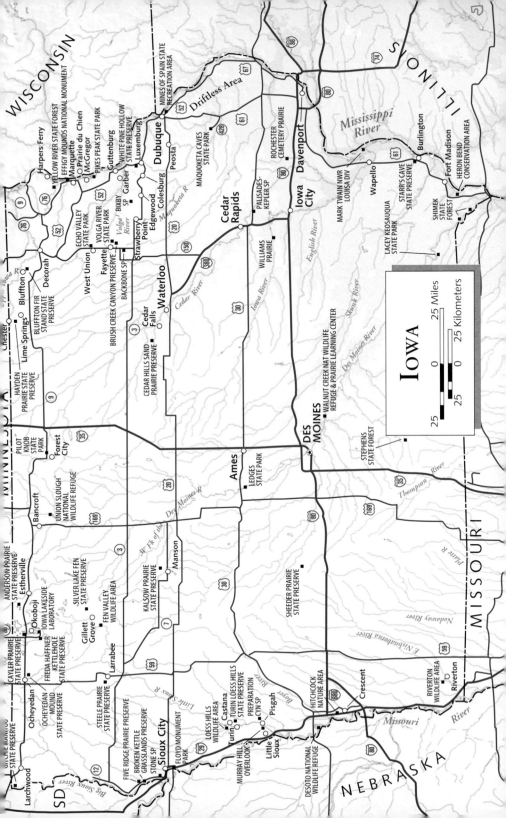

ABOVE: *Two races of rufous-sided towhee occur in Iowa: spotted, or western, towhees, seen here, and eastern towhees, which breed in southern Iowa.*

oaks, hickories, basswood, and maples. In spring, such ephemeral flowers as bloodroot, anemone, and mayapple spangle the woodland understory. In June and July, nesting forest birds reign—catbirds, rufous-sided towhees, ovenbirds, blue-winged warblers, redstarts, yellowthroats, cardinals, rose-breasted grosbeaks, scarlet tanagers, and house wrens. In fall, changing colors splash the river bluffs; late September brings migrating hawks that drift and glide down the Mississippi Valley on thermal air currents.

The western edge of Iowa lacks the obvious splendor of the east, partly because the once-daunting Missouri River is so diminished. The striking landscapes described by Lewis and Clark now appear only in the mind's eye. What has survived is the Loess Hills, a geological gem unlike any other landform on the continent. Composed of deep windblown silt from the Wisconsin-stage glaciers, this shadowy, rippling ridge of soil curves along the eastern margin of the Missouri River, from Sioux City south to Mound City in northwestern Missouri. Great swaths of the central Great Plains are mantled in loess, but nowhere else did the loess pile up so dramatically.

ABOVE: *A sunburst of yellow stripes decorates the carapace of the ornate box turtle, a reptile that flourishes on the semi-arid slopes of the Loess Hills.*

Over time water has eroded the Loess Hills, giving them an elephantine aspect. They are hulking and wrinkled. Although their ruggedness has largely protected them from farming, their scenic charm now attracts the suburban sprawl of Sioux City, Council Bluffs, and Omaha. Large parts of the Loess Hills remain a mosaic of prairie and woodland, but the suppression of fire has fostered an increase in trees, especially eastern redcedar. The porous soil and steep

ABOVE: *Native son Grant Wood (1892–1941) captured the essence of Iowa in his paintings. In* Young Corn *(1931), the state's voluptuous landforms and the fertility of its glacial soils are splendidly apparent.*

sunbaked slopes of the Loess Hills insert a digit of desertlike prairie into Iowa. The tallgrass is sparser and yucca conspicuous in this dryland habitat, which shelters such wildlife as the ornate box turtle, prairie pocket mouse, and prairie race runner.

The very best specimens of Iowa's natural landscapes are protected within a far-flung system of state preserves. An invaluable aid to finding them expeditiously is the *Iowa State Preserves Guide,* available free from the Iowa Department of Natural Resources. Because glacial sculpting is often subtle, Iowa's landscapes will test visitors' powers of observation. Persistence and a copy of Jean Cutter Prior's *Landforms of Iowa,* however, should enable travelers to distinguish between a young 12,000-year-old glacial landscape and ancient 2-million-year-old terrain. If possessing this skill sounds appealing, then Iowa is for you.

In exploring Iowa, this chapter follows a counterclockwise route beginning on the spectacular bluffs along the Mississippi River north of Dubuque. It then moves west to the Driftless Area and continues west across the

northern half of the state. Next the itinerary visits the Loess Hills and follows the Missouri River south along the state's western border. Finally it travels across the southern drift plain to conclude in southeastern Iowa.

NORTHEASTERN IOWA: ALONG THE MISSISSIPPI

One of the best introductions to the Driftless Area is Route 52 from Luxemburg (about 25 miles northwest of Dubuque) to Guttenberg. Heading north, the road crosses a high, broad tableland, then drops suddenly, like a collapsing soufflé, into the valley of the Mississippi River. On the horizon dense forests and rocky precipices create landscapes of enduring pleasure to the human eye, and the archaeological record confirms that people have long been drawn to this area.

Farther north along the Mississippi, stunning vistas are only part of the

ABOVE: *In this 1974 photo, limestone traces the Great Bear Mound Group at Effigy Mounds. Today the park service lets the forms remain unoutlined, leaving more to the imagination.*

LEFT: *A blaze of autumn on the trees and a hint of dawn on the horizon create a gorgeous vista at Effigy Mounds National Monument, which overlooks part of the 200,000-acre Upper Mississippi River national wildlife refuge.*

appeal of **Effigy Mounds National Monument❖,** three miles north of Marquette on Route 76. Among the trove of prehistoric archaeological sites in the 2,300-mile Mississippi Valley, few are as accessible, informative, and haunting as Effigy Mounds. Surrounded by scenic vistas, the 1,475-acre national monument stands atop forested bluffs fronting the west bank of the Mississippi River.

Close to 200 known mounds are protected within the preserve, the largest collection of prehistoric earthworks in the country open to the public. They were constructed by a variety of Woodland cultures over a span of some 1,800 years—from 500 B.C. to A.D. 1300. Although most are conical or linear, 29 mounds are effigies of bears and birds, a type of ceremonial earthwork seen only in northeastern Iowa and adjacent areas of Minnesota, Illinois, and Wisconsin. Some of the graceful, tranquil effigies

91

display grand proportions: Great Bear Mound measures 70 feet across the shoulders and is 137 feet long and 3.5 feet high.

The visitor center offers excellent exhibits on the history and natural history of the area, and a 6.5-mile trail winds past many of the mounds and through a deep forest. In summer, evening hikes through the monument are conducted on Saturdays of the full moon, when guides expound on the area's venerable history. In the fall, the bluffs make excellent vantages for watching migrating hawks; raptor numbers usually peak in late September. Autumn colors are spectacular through October, but be warned: A quarter of the monument's annual visitation occurs in that month.

Six miles south along the bluffs on the edge of the town of McGregor, the 970-acre **Pikes Peak State Park❖** perches atop 500-foot embankments that constitute the highest point along this stretch of the Mississippi. Some 12 miles of trails traverse the up-and-down bluffs, wandering through handsome oak-hickory forests and around dozens of effigy, conical, and linear mounds.

Near the park's concession area, a dramatic overlook shaped like a ship's prow juts above the bluffs, offering vertiginous views of the broad valley beyond. The vista is historic as well as scenic. On the far bank, at the confluence of the Wisconsin River and the Mississippi, explorer-adventurer Louis Jolliet and Jesuit priest Jacques Marquette first saw the Mississippi in 1673. The park is named for Zebulon Pike, who was dispatched in 1805 to find suitable locations for military installations along the Mississippi. The government selected the broad terraces on the river's eastern bank adjacent to the bluffs at Prairie du Chien, the second-oldest settlement in Wisconsin.

About 12 miles north of the Effigy Mounds–Pikes Peak area, in **Yellow River State Forest❖,** the hills are as rough as terrain in Iowa gets. Besides trout fishing on Big Paint and Little Paint creeks, the 4,500-acre **Paint Creek Unit,** accessible off Route 76, features 25 miles of hiking trails and another 13 of bridle paths.

In the 1920s, pollution, siltation, and habitat destruction along the upper Mississippi River inspired some of the earliest scrutiny of the nation's unfettered commerce. The navigational channel in the upper Mississippi, for instance, has been dredged progressively deeper, from 4.5 feet

---

RIGHT: *Iowa, like the rest of the Heartland, has a continental climate with humid summers and harsh winters. Here at Pikes Peak State Park, a snowy mantle softens the prospect of the Mississippi below.*

in 1878 to 6 feet in 1907 to 9 feet by 1930. As part of a compromise between commercial and environmental interests, the **Upper Mississippi River National Wildlife and Fish Refuge**❖ was established in 1924. A leader of this effort was Will Dilg, cofounder of the Izaak Walton League. Stretching 260 miles along the Mississippi between Wabasha, Minnesota, and Rock Island, Illinois, the preserve encompasses some 200,000 acres of river, forests, marshes, prairies, and floodplain.

Some of the most spectacular scenery on the Mississippi River occurs in

ABOVE: *Handsome, uncommon waterfowl, canvasbacks migrate through Mississippi's McGregor District in unusual numbers.*

northeastern Iowa and adjacent parts of Wisconsin within the refuge's 78,000-acre **McGregor District.** The district manages Pools 9, 10, and 11, segments of the river subdivided by locks and dams of corresponding numbers. Lock and Dam 10, in the river town of Guttenberg, demonstrates the forces of water and human ingenuity. Pool 9, stretching behind Lock and Dam 9 just north of Harpers Ferry, is a noted fall staging area for canvasback ducks. Some 100,000 canvasbacks have been known to converge on Pool 9, an astounding number for a species that is uncommon and in decline. From late October to mid-November, these svelte and beautiful diving ducks funnel south down the Mississippi Valley, more or less turning east at Pool 9 toward their wintering grounds on Chesapeake Bay.

Waterfowl follow shifting food resources. Historically, canvasbacks have been attracted to the wild celery in Pool 8, but in the last decade this aquatic plant has mysteriously waned along this stretch of the river. Since 1993, however, Pool 9 has enjoyed a blossoming of invertebrate life, which now sustains the canvasbacks. In winter, the McGregor District is also home to bald eagles, which are attracted to any unfrozen patches of water. More than 200 eagles have been counted in a mile and a half of river in Pool 11, which lies between Guttenberg and Dubuque.

On the southern edge of Dubuque, the 1,380-acre **Mines of Spain State Recreation Area**❖ explores the intertwining narratives of human and natural history along the bluffs of the Mississippi, where sheltering cliffs, oak-hickory woodlands, and easily excavated veins of lead have attracted a variety of cultures since at least 5000 B.C. The **E. B. Lyons Nature Center**, the interpretative arm of the recreation area, offers displays in a nineteenth-century farmstead setting and maintains a self-guided nature trail; restoration of a prairie is in progress.

Rivers in northeastern Iowa afford fine opportunities for canoeing, fishing (for smallmouth bass, trout, walleye, sauger, northern pike), and studying the bedrock of the Driftless Area. Near the Minnesota border, the 16-mile trip on the **Upper Iowa River** from Lime Springs to French Creek Bridge begins on the prairie but soon digs deep into limestone and dolomite to form a tight, twisting passage to the Mississippi. Farther south, a 14-mile stretch of the **Volga River,** from Langeman's Ford to Garber, offers similar flora, fauna, and geology. The Iowa Department of Natural Resources provides brochures on canoeing the Upper Iowa and Volga, as well as for two dozen other rivers in the state.

ABOVE: *Bald eagles follow waterfowl flocks south along the Mississippi Flyway, feeding on the dead and dying en route.*

THE DRIFTLESS AREA: ON THE WESTERN ESCARPMENT

The Driftless Area is crisscrossed with gravel county roads, which dictate slower speeds and thus offer more intimate views of this craggy region. County Road W20, for instance, heads north from Decorah (a charming town whose Vesterheim Museum is chock-full of Norwegian-American artifacts) to the village of Bluffton on the Upper Iowa River. Here, on the south bank of the river, the **Bluffton Fir Stand State Preserve❖** presents its exquisite cliff face where a tangle of old-growth trees includes the largest known population of balsam fir in the state. The far-flung pocket of boreal forest persists here because the north-facing bluff is cool and shady. Although the forest is virtually inaccessible, the sight of it is worth a pilgrimage. Bluffton Fir Stand is typical of the rare and fragile landscapes hidden in gorges and ravines along the western rim of the Driftless Area. One logical and scenic approach to the region is to wander along this escarpment, which forms a rough northwest-to-southeast arc connecting the small rural communities of West Union, Fayette, Strawberry Point, Edgewood, Colesburg, and Peosta.

95

Compared to Iowa's sunny, forthright prairiescapes, places along the western rim seem shadowy and mysterious, even slightly eerie. A classic enigma of the Driftless Area, **Bixby State Park**❖ lies in a chasm about two miles north of Edgewood. The 184-acre preserve harbors an unusual and extremely delicate ice cave, which emits cool air in spring and summer. The drafts, caused by slowly melting ice wedged in fissures in the bedrock, are a a welcome relief on muggy July days. A restricted and peculiar microhabitat of plants and invertebrates thrives amid these exhalations. Encircled by deep green clumps of Canada yew, mosses, and ferns, and shaded by a gnarled yellow birch, the cave presents a striking boreal tableau.

Four miles southwest of Strawberry Point, 1,750-acre **Backbone State Park**❖ occupies the narrow rock-rimmed valley of the Maquoketa River, which has cut a path through the glacial plains along the southern rim of the Driftless Area.

One spot in Iowa that retains a real semblance of wildness—a place where visitors could get turned around—is **White Pine Hollow State Preserve**❖ (on a road heading west off Route 52 about a mile and a half north of Luxemburg). The 712-acre forest, predominantly oaks and hickories, is named for its stands of majestic white pines. Because the preserve has no trails, the best way to cover ground—and not get lost—is to follow the major watercourses.

About 30 miles south of Dubuque, on Route 428 6 miles west of the junction with Route 61, **Maquoketa Caves State Park**❖ lies outside the official bounds of the Driftless Area. Its jagged terrain, where water removed tons of glacial overburden, is nonetheless reminiscent of Driftless landscapes. In the gorge of Raccoon Creek, a tributary of the Maquoketa River (pronounced Ma-KO-ke-ta), the park contains dozens of features characteristic of karst topography—cliffs, caves, sinkholes, a picture-perfect natural bridge, streams, and springs.

NORTHERN IOWA:
GLACIAL FOOTPRINTS, REMNANT PRAIRIES

Less than a dozen miles as the crow flies from the western escarpment of the Driftless Area, the **Hayden Prairie State Preserve**❖ occupies a glaciat-

RIGHT: *Like the vertebrae of ancient serpents, outcrops of dolomite trace the maple-shaded gorge of the Maquoketa River at Backbone State Park.*

OVERLEAF: *Earth meets sky unequivocally at Hayden Prairie, where oxeye daisies and pink showy tick trefoil contribute to the wildflower display.*

ABOVE: *Sumac splashes its swath of scarlet across the glacial formations at Pilot Knob. Breathtaking in autumn, sumac gets mixed reviews from prairie managers because it dominates grasslands in the absence of fire.*

ed plain about three miles south of the town of Chester. At 240 acres, Hayden Prairie comprises the largest remnant of black-soil prairie in Iowa and is a potent reminder that the state was once a vast undulating plain of tallgrass. Iowa's first protected prairie was purchased by the state in 1945 and named for Dr. Ada Hayden, a botanist who catalogued and worked to save Iowa's last prairies in the 1940s.

Hayden Prairie is a jewel. From April to October the site presents a changing show of colorful wildflowers and gorgeous grasses that inch taller and taller. In years following prescribed burns, clumps of big bluestem, Indian grass, and prairie cordgrass reach heights of five or six feet. Bobolinks, the birds considered the heart and soul of tallgrass prairie, still nest at Hayden.

In north-central Iowa, a huge glacial tongue called the Des Moines Lobe licks into the state from the north. Its U-shaped outline can be visualized by drawing a line down Interstate 35, looping west around Des Moines, and then heading diagonally northwest toward Okoboji and the cluster of other glacial lakes on the Minnesota border. The icy vise of the Wisconsin-stage glaciers released this geologically young landscape, still in

100

ABOVE: *Grassy marshes and prairie potholes carpeted with bright green duckweed punctuate the landscape at Union Slough National Wildlife Refuge, which protects wetlands critical to migratory and nesting waterfowl.*

its formative stages, just 14,000 to 12,000 years ago. Water, which tends to stand in potholes and swales, has yet to erode substantial drainageways off this terrain.

Because the area contains some of the richest soil in America, agriculture has imposed a green uniformity on the land. During the floods of 1993, however, the landscape fleetingly assumed a presettlement aspect. As rains reclaimed the low spots, water-filled swales, like thousands of eyes, once again blinked and glittered across the rolling plains.

The Des Moines Lobe presents a veritable primer on glacial landforms. About eight miles west of I-35 off Route 9 near Forest City, **Pilot Knob State Park**❖ features a kame, an isolated conical hill that slowly accumulated as sediment was deposited in a depression in the overlying glacial ice sheet. The park lies among the rumpled ridges of an end moraine, an earthen bulwark that formed along the edge of a stalled ice front. Perched on a slope of Pilot Knob, Dead Man's Lake is a classic kettle hole that formed when a chunk of glacial ice slowly disintegrated. From a 35-foot round stone tower on the ridge of the moraine, visitors can see the washboard topography of minor moraines left by the succession of glaciers as they receded northward. At 1,450 feet, Pilot Knob is the second-highest point in Iowa; the highest, at 1,670 feet, is in a hog lot on County Road L44 north of the town of Sibley on the far western side of the Des Moines Lobe.

About 30 miles due west of Pilot Knob via county roads, **Union Slough National Wildlife Refuge❖,** off Route 169 about six miles east of Bancroft, is a marshland restoration project begun in 1937. Relatively small

ABOVE: *The goldfinch, state bird of Iowa, uses its bill with tweezerlike precision to extract tiny seeds from plants such as cattails.*

at about 2,975 acres, the refuge is nonetheless a critical wetland way station for migratory waterfowl crossing the Great Plains. April is usually the best time to see a diversity of ducks—including mallard, blue-winged teal, and in good years thousands of canvasbacks. Wood ducks and pied-billed grebes nest here.

Farther west via Route 9, Dickinson County on the Minnesota border offers an abundance of glacially influenced landforms, including the resplendent **West and East Okoboji Lakes** and **Spirit Lake.** These gorgeous aquamarine bodies of water occupy basins formed by massive hunks of melting glacial ice. Unfortunately such manifest beauty in an otherwise subtle landscape suffers the consequences. For a century, Okoboji, as the area is collectively called, has been a summer destination for folks from Minneapolis, Omaha, Des Moines, and other surrounding midwestern cities. As a result, all the edifices and devices associated with humans in pursuit of recreation have accreted around the lakes.

One of the last stretches of natural shoreline lies within the 148-acre **Iowa Lakeside Laboratory❖** on Miller's Bay at West Okoboji Lake. This research and teaching station is maintained by Iowa's three state universities. It was established in 1909 by a group of scientists and naturalists, including Thomas Macbride and Bohumil Shimek, who realized that this little swatch of Iowa represents much that is beautiful and curious in glacial landscapes. The grounds of the laboratory encompass a 40-acre virgin prairie; the income from another 27 acres, planted with rotating crops of corn, soybeans, and alfalfa, provides scholarships for students. The laboratory conducts summer classes, supports research, and offers public lecture series and nature-study weekends.

Surrounding Okoboji are several splendid glacial artifacts that attract less traffic than the lakes. The 200-acre **Anderson Prairie State Preserve❖**, on the west bank of the West Fork of the Des Moines River about four miles northwest of Estherville, and the 160-acre **Cayler Prairie State Preserve❖**, a few miles west of West Okoboji Lake and two and a half miles south of Route 9, stretch across morainal landscapes that rise and fall like ocean swells. Thanks to these undulations, the two preserves contain considerable botanical variation. The well-drained, gravelly crests of the moraines support dry prairie plants such as little bluestem and side-oats grama; the swales, which tend to be damp or marshy, sustain sedges, cattails, and prairie cordgrass. The fauna here reflects the diversity of landscapes and flora: 72 species of terrestrial vertebrates have been recorded at Cayler Prairie, an impressive roster for a 160-acre parcel.

ABOVE: *If one song captures the wild abandon of the prairie, it is the bobolink's, whose habitat is declining throughout the hemisphere.*

Partly because it is only a few miles from the Iowa Lakeside Laboratory, Cayler Prairie has been the subject of much scientific investigation. Here, for example, grassland ecologist William J. Platt determined the significant role that badgers play in shaping prairies. As they dig holes in pursuit of prey such as ground squirrels, badgers excavate mounds of dirt that provide pockets of habitat for small mammals and herps (reptiles) and form islands of soil ready to be colonized by windblown or vertebrate-deposited seeds of prairie plants.

Two miles west of Route 86, where the road jogs around the southern end of West Okoboji Lake, the 110-acre **Freda Haffner Kettlehole State Preserve❖** protects a prairie that occupies two thumbprints left by glacial ice. The larger impression, 200 feet wide and 80 feet deep, is a nearly perfect example of a kettle hole. The smaller kettle has partially washed out and slumped into the nearby Little Sioux River. A north-facing slope in the northern portion of the preserve supports a rich diversity of prairie plants.

In the early 1980s, researchers swept across Iowa seeking fens, boggy wetland peat deposits fed by groundwater seeping through mineral-rich

ABOVE: *Nature's backhoe, the badger continually excavates the prairie searching for underground prey such as ground squirrels and pocket gophers. Wind-borne wildflower seeds then take hold in the disturbed soil.*

subsurface layers. Because they are either acidic or basic, fens often harbor rare plants adapted to extreme water conditions. The researchers documented about 100 fens of botanical significance, of which some 25 were prime ("intact sites with high species richness"). About a third of these enjoy conservation protection, and fewer still are open to the public. Among those that are is Silver Lake Fen, about three-quarters of a mile north of Route 9 on the western edge of Silver Lake, and **Fen Valley Wildlife Area❖,** about 50 miles southeast just beyond the village of Gillett Grove.

Fragile and full of nuance, fens can seem a bit opaque, causing some visitors to wonder why they took the time to explore one. Fens, however, are beloved by botanists because they are rich in flora. In Iowa this watery habitat constitutes a mere .01 percent of the landscape but harbors 10 percent of the state's native flora. Only ten acres, **Silver Lake Fen State Preserve❖** is a spongy zone of peat deposits where the dominant vegetation is sedges, prairie cordgrass, sunflowers, beakrush, and cattails. Because foot traffic can compact the soil in fens, visitors should walk with concern and caution.

Farther west on Route 9, a hundred-foot pile of sand and gravel rises from the landscape like an Egyptian pyramid. This kame, about a mile and a half south of the village of Ocheyedan on County Road A22, is the **Ocheyedan Mound State Preserve❖;** a walk to the summit affords splendid views of this part of the Des Moines Lobe.

ABOVE: *Hot air rising off Cayler Prairie and the surrounding plain produces towering thunderheads—the hallmarks of a classic Iowa summer. The prairie's undulating terrain attests to its glacial heritage.*

In the far northwest corner of Iowa along the Big Sioux River, 144-acre **Gitchie Manitou State Preserve❖** (11 miles west of Larchwood on County Road K10) contains a glimpse of ancient bedrock. The 1.6-billion-year-old outcrop of lustrous pink quartzite here is the oldest exposed rock in Iowa. Since the late nineteenth century, the combination of prehistoric rocks, prairie, and woodland has attracted geologists and botanists to this remote corner of the state.

Southeast of Gitchie Manitou on the lonesome grid of country roads that portion the endless, hypnotic fields of Iowa corn and soybeans, two more protected pockets shelter tallgrass prairies. Two parcels—one 40 acres, the other 160—form **Steele Prairie State Preserve❖,** west of Route 59 about three miles from Larabee. Here big bluestem is the dominant tallgrass, sedges and prairie cordgrass punctuate the wetter spots, and cattail marsh spreads along the drainages. This part of Iowa was last glaciated 30,000 to 20,000 years ago, and the gently rolling terrain at Steele Prairie indicates that water has had time to make an impression on the land.

By contrast, the 160-acre **Kalsow Prairie State Preserve❖,** about 70 miles southeast near Manson—and back in the geologically younger province of the Des Moines Lobe—is pancake flat. In the spring of a wet year, one of the best times to visit Kalsow, visitors shod in rubber boots squish through this lovely prairie and gain an intimate understanding of stranded water on the Des Moines Lobe. In spring and early summer,

105

Left: Clustered with vivid orange flowers, butterfly milkweed grows on a drier portion of Kalsow Prairie, a rich, moist mosaic of wet prairie and pothole wetlands. Right: Butterflies of the Loess Hills prairies, rare Ottoe skippers are partial to the pale purple coneflower. Skippers are named for their erratic flight.

these prairie islands are raucous with birds—bobolinks, sedge wrens, brown thrashers, yellowthroats, meadowlarks, goldfinches, red-winged blackbirds, and various sparrows (including grasshopper, song, swamp, clay-colored, and Henslow's).

THE WESTERN BORDER: THE LOESS HILLS AND MISSOURI RIVER

Venerable, rumpled, and magnificent, the Loess Hills snake more than 200 miles along the western border of Iowa and into the northwestern tip of Missouri. At the northern end, the hills are broad, high, and round; farther south, they begin to taper, becoming more angular and losing their loftiness.

An overview from the Nebraska side of the Missouri River can provide a splendid introduction to the hills, especially at sunset when the play of light accents their wrinkled hide. (For flatlanders, this vista is as close as it gets to purple mountain majesties.) Airline passengers flying to or from Omaha, which is tucked next to the southern end of the Loess Hills, also get a splendid bird's-eye view of the serpentine ridge. The best introduction, of course, is on foot, accompanied by Cornelia Mutel's *Fragile Giants: A Natural History of the Loess Hills*. As she asserts, only by walking up and down the steep slopes can visitors truly appreciate these peculiar landforms.

Route 12, which leads north from Sioux City, is a fine route for exploring the lunarlike landscapes of the northern reaches of the hills. The 1,069-acre **Stone State Park❖**, on the northwest edge of Sioux City between Route 12 and Talbot Road, provides one of the most accessible introductions to the Loess Hills via the **Loess Ridge Nature Center** and two self-guided nature trails affording panoramic ridgetop vistas.

About 15 miles north of Sioux City off Route 12, the 1,187-acre **Broken Kettle Grassland Preserve❖** (east of Route 12) and nearby 790-acre **Five Ridge Prairie Preserve❖** (access from County Road K18) protect two of

107

ABOVE: *In Stone State Park, the brawny shoulders of the Loess Hills provide a perfect perch for sky watching, a popular plains diversion. Thunderstorms typically roll in from the west, often with high drama.*

the largest prairie remnants in Iowa. On such preserves, where prescribed burning is controlling the encroachment of trees and sumac, visitors can appreciate the vastness and spareness of these hills. Both Broken Kettle and Five Ridge present grand landscapes. Walking on these giant mounds of loess graphically conveys the immense proportions of eons of windblown silt. These grasslands also provide refuge for several increasingly rare butterflies, including the regal fritillary and three skippers (Ottoe, Pawnee, and dusted). The butterflies are on the wing during the hottest days of summer.

On the south side of Sioux City, the obelisk poking skyward in **Floyd Monument Park❖** marks the gravesite of Sergeant Charles Floyd, who died in August 1804 on the outward-bound journey of the Lewis and Clark expedition. On July 31, Floyd wrote in his journal, "I am verry sick and has ben for Somtime. . . ." Although it remains a mystery, the cause of his death may have been peritonitis from a ruptured appendix. He was, miraculously, the only person to die on the two-year trek through unknown and treacherous terrain. The 23-acre park also contains a small remnant of bluff prairie.

The Loess Hills are at their most jagged around the towns of Castana, Turin, Pisgah, and Little Sioux. Just a few miles north of Turin, the 2,700-acre **Loess Hills Wildlife Area❖** and nearby 220-acre **Turin Loess Hills**

108

ABOVE: *Hoary vervain, with its rich purple flower spikes, is a robust wildflower, in part because livestock avoid its bitter flavor. It blooms throughout the summer in old fields, roadside ditches, and prairies.*

State Preserve❖ combine to form a large swath of prairie and woodland. The **Loess Hills Prairie Seminar,** held every June at the Loess Hills Wildlife Area, began in 1976 and is one of the longest-running outdoor learning experiences in Iowa.

About five miles southwest of Moorhead, **Preparation Canyon State Park❖** feels like a fortress; unlike the wide-open sunbaked prairiescapes that typically define loess hills, these rises are dominated by woodlands. Although only three acres, the **Murray Hill Overlook,** midway between Pisgah and Little Sioux at the junction of County Roads F20 and L14, is a hike not to be missed. Climbing the precariously narrow ridge is like scaling the spinal plates of a stegosaurus. The hill is fringed in prairie, and the view across the wide Missouri seems to extend forever. Although lugging along an oversize art book might seem ludicrous, Murray Hill is the place to have a copy of *Karl Bodmer's America* to compare the Swiss artist's 1830s paintings and sketches of the Missouri River with the contemporary vista.

Today the floodplain is an agricultural landscape through which the much-

OVERLEAF: *Festooned with creamy bell-shaped flowers, a yucca plant clings to an abrupt slope in the Loess Hills, where porous, well-drained silt favors plants and wildlife that prefer arid environments.*

tempered Missouri flows. Upstream, seven major dams restrict the volume of water and nutrient-rich sediment, and almost 70 percent of the river has been impounded or channelized. The Missouri has lost nearly all its sandbars, sloughs, backwaters, forests, and marshes, once home to myriad wildlife.

A last piece of Bodmer's river survives on a seven-mile-long oxbow of the Missouri at **DeSoto National Wildlife Refuge**❖ (just off Route 30 west of Missouri Valley), a 7,823-acre sanctuary designed and managed to accommodate migratory waterfowl. In November, more than 500,000 snow geese stop to rest on the oxbow lake and feed in the fallow fields where residue grain has been left for them. Following the geese, bald eagles perch high in the cottonwoods along the lakeshore. The visitor center contains an astounding display of 200,000 Civil War–era artifacts retrieved from the *Bertrand,* a stern-wheeler that sank in the river in 1865.

The 661-acre **Hitchcock Nature Area**❖ is a serene and lovely gathering of loess hills enhanced by the knowledge that in the mid-1980s a group of concerned citizens halted a plan to turn it into a landfill. On the fringes of greater Council Bluffs–Omaha, five miles north of Crescent and a mile west of Route 183, Hitchcock offers urbanites a quick tutorial in loess hills geology and natural history. A deck overlooking the Missouri Valley has become

ABOVE: *A flower of quiet water, American lotus blooms at the DeSoto refuge, home to one of the last oxbow lakes in the Missouri valley.*

LEFT: *In the 1830s Swiss artist Karl Bodmer accompanied the pioneering Maximilian expedition up the Missouri. This 1833 watercolor,* **Mouth of the Big Sioux River,** *was executed near present-day Sioux City.*

a popular hawk-watching perch for birders in September and October.

In extreme southwestern Iowa, the **Riverton Wildlife Area**❖ occupies the floodplain of the East and West Nishnabotna River, just northwest of the town of Riverton. A managed wetland where water levels are controlled to manipulate food and cover for waterfowl, the 2,721-acre area includes lake, swamp, marsh, mudflats, woods, and upland fields. This convergence of different habitats makes it one of the hottest birding spots in the state, especially for shorebirds. In late April and early May, Riverton's lakeshore mudflat hosts one of the best gatherings of shorebirds in the upper Midwest, including American avocets, Hudsonian godwits, and white-rumped, buff-breasted, and Baird's sandpipers. In late summer, as water sources elsewhere shrink, herons, egrets, and terns often congregate at Riverton. Ducks and geese appear in the fall, and by Thanksgiving, 80,000 to 200,000 snow geese blanket the lake.

THE SOUTHERN DRIFT PLAIN:
AN ANCIENT GLACIAL LANDSCAPE

The southern half of Iowa is an endless series of buxom cleavages created over the last half-million years when the region's many rivers—the Boyer,

Nishnabotna, Nodaway, Platte, Thompson, Chariton, Des Moines, Skunk, and English—and their tributaries eroded the deep overlying glacial drift. Because Interstate 80 runs straight through this stunning landscape, most of the world sees only this part of Iowa. That people still describe the state as flat and featureless is further proof that interstate driving is a form of sensory deprivation.

Just 11 miles north of I-80 about 50 miles west of Des Moines, **Sheeder Prairie State Preserve**❖ (4 miles west of Guthrie Center) is one of a handful of native grasslands surviving on this plain of rolling grassland. At 25 acres, Sheeder is small but spectacular, a last gasp of biodiversity in a sea of monoculture. To find such complexity in a small space is always a surprise and a joy. Noted for its wildflowers, this prairie features a succession of blooms that last all summer: leadplant, anemone, purple coneflower, butterfly weed, coreopsis, delphinium, lobelia, rattlesnake master, compass plant and other sunflowers, and various species of blazing star.

Just 20 miles west of Ames off Route 30, **Ledges State Park**❖ is virtually a city park for Ames and for only slightly more distant Des Moines. Jammed on weekends and holidays, the park is large (1,200 acres), old (it was dedicated in 1924), and rugged compared to the gentle farmlands that surround it. On its way to the Des Moines River, Pease Creek has cut a serpentine valley through sandstone here. The north- and south-facing aspects of its cliffs create specialized worlds for different species, making Ledges one of the state's more botanically rich areas. Because the steep slopes have discouraged logging, some of the oldest and biggest trees in Iowa grow here. A number of oaks in the park are estimated to be more than 300 years old.

Walnut Creek National Wildlife Refuge and Prairie Learning Center❖, about 20 miles east of Des Moines, is a cooperative endeavor to restore a tallgrass prairie and create a savanna ecosystem large enough to sustain a thriving genetic pool of grassland flora and fauna. Rather than a cage of genetic information—like the small, isolated prairie remnants—Walnut Creek will be a bank. The effort, begun in 1991, will ultimately encompass 8,654 acres of magnificent rolling terrain—originally slated for a nuclear power plant—about three miles wide extending some five miles along Walnut Creek, a tributary of the Des Moines River.

RIGHT: *Tiny white pinwheels of daisy fleabane and five-foot-high tassels of burnt-red grasses signal autumn's arrival at Walnut Creek, site of an ambitious effort to reclaim some 8,000 acres of tallgrass prairie.*

ABOVE: *The sunrise highlights the dolomite bluffs at Palisades-Kepler State Park. Here the Cedar River has exposed ancient marine deposits.*

Although tallgrass prairie remnants of this size and larger still exist in Kansas (Konza Prairie in the Flint Hills) and Oklahoma (Tallgrass Prairie Preserve in the Osage Hills), those preserves harbor near-virgin grasslands that have never been plowed. In a massive undertaking never before attempted, biologists and volunteers at Walnut Creek are starting from scratch—on fallow farm ground. By late 1995, 5,000 acres had been purchased, and more than 1,100 acres seeded with native prairie grasses and wildflowers. Based on the twin notions that most people know little about prairie and savanna landscapes and do not value what they do not know, Walnut Creek has developed a vigorous educational agenda, including talks, demonstrations, and hands-on programs for children and adults.

SOUTHEAST IOWA:
FORESTS, WETLANDS, PRAIRIES

Scattered over 12,000 acres across southern Iowa, the six units of **Stephens State Forest❖** stretch along the slopes and bottoms of streams; oak-hickory forest covers the uplands, and cottonwood, hackberry, green ash, silver maple, and black walnut flourish along the watercourses. Be-

Acadian flycatchers, yellow-throated vireos, and blue-gray gnatcatchers nest in the nearby woodlands; at dusk bats patrol the river for insects.

cause it was envisioned as a demonstration forest, Stephens also includes plantings of nonnative pines, spruce, Douglas fir, and yellow poplar. The 1,100-acre **Lucas Unit** and 2,800-acre **Whitebreast Unit,** both just south of the town of Lucas, are the easiest to access and the most congenial for hiking, backpacking, and camping.

About 75 miles southwest of Lucas, 1,653-acre **Lacey Keosauqua State Park❖** stands on bluffs overlooking a large horseshoe bend in the Des Moines. The venerable old park, dedicated in 1921, is known for its river vistas and oak-hickory forests. It is a popular destination for birders and botanizers (especially April through June) and for lovers of fall foliage (color peaks in October). The name Lacey commemorates John Fletcher Lacey, a Civil War veteran, Iowa politician, and late-nineteenth-century advocate of conservation, while Keosauqua (pronounced Kee-o-SOCK-wa) is traceable to the Native Americans who inhabited the area. (Probably of Sauk-Mesquakie derivation, the word refers either to the bend in the river or to ice and snow jams that occur here in spring.)

Adjoining Lacey Keosauqua on its western flank is the 918-acre Keosauqua unit of **Shimek State Forest❖.** Four other parcels of the 9,209-

117

ABOVE: *At Cedar Hills sand prairie, the vivid colors of an overarching prairie rainbow compete with more earthy rivals: hot-purple blazing star, buttery-yellow goldenrod, and snow-white flowering spurge.*

acre state forest are scattered along the Des Moines River as well. Two of these—the 2,207-acre **Farmington** unit and the 1,223-acre **Donnellson** unit—lie along Route 2 about 20 miles east of Lacey Keosauqua State Park. Shimek State Forest, the oldest and largest woodland reserve in Iowa, is named for the much revered Bohumil Shimek, a botanist, naturalist, and early twentieth-century conservationist in Iowa.

At the tip of southeastern Iowa near the city of Keokuk is the 302-acre **Heron Bend Conservation Area❖.** The reserve, two miles north of the junction of Routes 61 and 404 in Montrose, overlooks Pool 19 on the Mississippi River. With trails and a viewing blind, Heron Bend is an accommodating place to observe migrating ducks, which gather by the tens of thousands in spring (mid-February to mid-March) and fall (mid-November). White pelicans visit from mid-March to June and late August to mid-October. Bald eagles winter in the area, and in summer more than two dozen skinny, gawky great blue herons, looking improbable in their treetop nests, assemble in a rookery in the marsh in the northern section of the conservation area.

About 30 miles north, **Starr's Cave State Preserve❖** is on the northern edge of the quaint Mississippi river town of Burlington. The 200-acre sanctuary lies in the precipitous valley of Flint Creek, which has sliced through 325-million-year-old limestone revealing ancient deposits of fossil crinoids. The site, which contains 4.5 miles of meandering hiking trails, combines

118

ABOVE: *Marsh marigolds bloom among dried grasses at Cedar Hills, where a fringe of flames marks the progress of a controlled burn. Long suppressed, fire is now used to stimulate the growth of native grasslands.*

mature oak-hickory forest with breezy ridgetop prairies.

About 25 miles north of Burlington (via Routes 61 and X61) the **Louisa Division** of the **Mark Twain National Wildlife Refuge❖** offers a three-quarter-mile hiking trail that descends uplands to a bottomland slough. The 2,500-acre refuge, critical for migratory waterfowl, is a complex of wetlands scattered along 259 miles of the Mississippi River in Iowa, Missouri, and Illinois. Many of its marshes and backwaters are accessible only by boat. Peak time for ducks and geese is late October through mid-November.

To the northwest, 12 miles east of Cedar Rapids, the 840-acre **Palisades-Kepler State Park❖** nestles in a big bend of the Cedar River, where it has carved its way through an ancient marine reef deposited some 415 million years ago. With the precision of a scalpel-wielding surgeon, the river has opened an incision in the deep glacial drift and revealed bedrock. The ancient dolomite cliffs are unexpected and lovely, and the oak-hickory forest cool and dark. A nature trail along the river provides a great opportunity to learn trees by bark and leaf shape—among them, bigtooth and quaking aspen, black cherry, shagbark hickory, basswood, white oak, and eastern hop hornbeam.

Seventy-five miles northwest of Cedar Rapids—and far-flung from every other prairie patch in Iowa—is the Nature Conservancy's **Cedar Hills Sand Prairie Preserve❖**. About seven miles northwest of Cedar

119

Falls, the 90-acre site is beloved by Iowa prairie watchers for its rolling topography and summer-long display of wildflowers. (Take Route 57 west from Cedar Falls to Route T75; go 2.5 miles to Route C67; go west 2.5 miles and turn north on the gravel road 1.5 miles.) The prairie occupies a mound of loam and sand dunes rising up between two drainages, the Cedar River and Beaver Creek, and includes a full gamut of grassland plants from moisture-seeking sedges to drought-tolerant little bluestem.

The 21-acre **Williams Prairie❖,** about ten miles west of Iowa City and almost four miles northwest of Oxford, features a sedge meadow and wet prairie in the Iowa River bottoms. It is likely to be squishy (rubber boots are recommended) and was almost completely inundated in the 1993 flood. A lovely changing show of summer wildflowers includes gentian and blazing star.

A journey to the Iowa heartland would be incomplete without a visit to a cemetery prairie. Here, amid the ghosts of the pioneers, where the last few acres of grassland surround the faces of tombstones, it is altogether fitting to succumb to prairie reverie and mourn the passing of millions of acres of tallgrass.

Rochester Cemetery Prairie is about 35 miles east of Iowa City, just north of I-80 near the town for which it is named. The cemetery sprawls across sandy rolling terrain above the Cedar River, in a classic savanna habitat where fingers of prairie and forest interlace. Magnificent bur oaks shade the cemetery amid woolly thickets of prairie grasses and wildflowers.

On the third weekend in May, the **Iowa Prairie Network❖,** a state-wide organization of prairie enthusiasts, conducts a field trip here to see shooting stars, the diminutive prairie wildflowers that resemble little meteor showers. Many other wildflowers blooming throughout the summer include blue-eyed grass, pussytoes, yellow coneflower, lobelia, black-eyed Susan, Culver's root, baptisia, and leadplant.

Rochester Cemetery Prairie is one of the most poignant places on the Great Plains. Herbert Clark, whose thoughts appear on the kiosk at the cemetery, was not exaggerating when he wrote, "In no other place in Iowa are the resting places of the dead more beautifully decorated."

RIGHT: *Wildflowers found on Iowa's prairies include (clockwise from top left) sawtooth sunflower, a robust late-summer bloomer; pink shooting star, which resembles a burst of miniature rockets; prolific gray-headed coneflower, which blooms all summer; and prairie lark-spur, whose genus,* Delphinium, *refers to its dolphin-shaped blossoms.*

NEBRASKA

NEBRASKA:
DUNES, RIDGES, AND A
LATTICE OF RIVERS

In a history of Nebraska entitled *Love Song to the Plains*, Mari Sandoz characterizes the lay of her native land as "a golden hackberry leaf in the sun, a giant curling, tilted leaf." What she describes as a leaf, geologists call a gangplank. Nebraska, as both analogies indicate, is flattish (although not as prostrate as many people assume), and it tilts. In essence, the state is a great slag of material slipping off the eastern face of the Rocky Mountains.

In large measure water shaped the land. Running down the "gangplank," gathering in swales, accumulating in the vast underground High Plains aquifer, it has profoundly affected the natural history of Nebraska. Water brings life. "Millions of ducks, geese, cranes and gleaming white swans," writes Sandoz in *Love Song*, "made their annual flights over the plains so conveniently laddered by the east-flowing streams, while on the rolling prairie the great buffalo herds grazed into the cyclonic winds in their own migratory rounds, their millions moving dark as vast cloud shadows over the earth."

Positioned at mid-continent, Nebraska lay at the heart of the great migratory processions. In the last century, though, European settlers slaughtered the bison and greatly reduced the numbers of birds, not only by hunting, but even more ruinous, by reconfiguring rivers and draining wetlands. Bison have now been reintroduced to a number of wild or semi-wild places in western Nebraska, and one impressive intimation of the

PRECEDING PAGES: *Weary of prairiescapes, immigrants waxed poetic about Scotts Bluff, comparing it to Gibraltar, Alhambra, and the Tower of Babel.*
LEFT: *The largest tract of dunes in this hemisphere, Nebraska's Sandhills comprise the most extensive undisturbed grasslands in the United States.*

great migratory bird flights that Sandoz describes still occurs each spring along the Big Bend Reach of the Platte River, in central Nebraska, and in the nearby wetlands of the Rainwater Basin.

A topographic map of Nebraska shows its copious network of rivers. All have one purpose: to seek the Missouri River, which forms the 200-mile eastern boundary of Nebraska, and eventually the Gulf of Mexico. Their evocative names—the Dismal, Loup, Frenchman, Calamus, Niobrara—represent an abridged history of the various peoples who crisscrossed the plains over the last several centuries. For instance, the Loup, a three-branched tributary of the Platte in central Nebraska, is the name that French traders gave the Wolf People, a band of Pawnee who once lived along the river's banks. The Wolf People called it the Plenty Potatoes River because edible tubers grew in its floodplain.

The 1,600 miles of streams in the Loup River system almost all rise in the Sandhills, the vast dunescape that undulates across 265 miles of north-central Nebraska. One of the most impressive landforms on the Great Plains, the Sandhills are immense grass-stabilized drifts of sand lying astride a portion of the High Plains aquifer. Because the Sandhills brim with water, the Loup, fed primarily by this groundwater, is noted for its remarkably uniform rates of flow.

Forming the northern boundary of the Sandhills and synonymous with this remote part of northern Nebraska, the Niobrara River is virtually the last free-flowing waterway on the northern Great Plains. This distinction was almost lost in the mid-1970s until plans to build a reservoir were halted. In addition to harboring a living flora and fauna that reflect the complex movement of ice across the continent, the Niobrara exposes sedimentary layers containing some of the richest fossil deposits on the continent.

Of all the rivers in Nebraska, the one that summons the strongest sense of place is the Platte. Rising in the Colorado Rockies, the Platte starts as two rivers—the North Platte and South Platte—which converge at the town of North Platte in western Nebraska to form the river's main stem. The Platte then flows 310 miles across the state to join the mother river of the Great Plains, the Missouri, about 15 miles south of Omaha.

By nature, the Platte is a wide, shallow slurry of gravels and sands. Much of this sediment now gathers behind the 15 dams that garrote the river system. (Most of these reservoirs lie along the North Platte and its tributaries in Wyoming; the last in the chain is Lake McConaughy, impounded by Kingsley Dam in western Nebraska.) Today about 70 percent of the water that once surged down the Platte is parceled out to irrigate

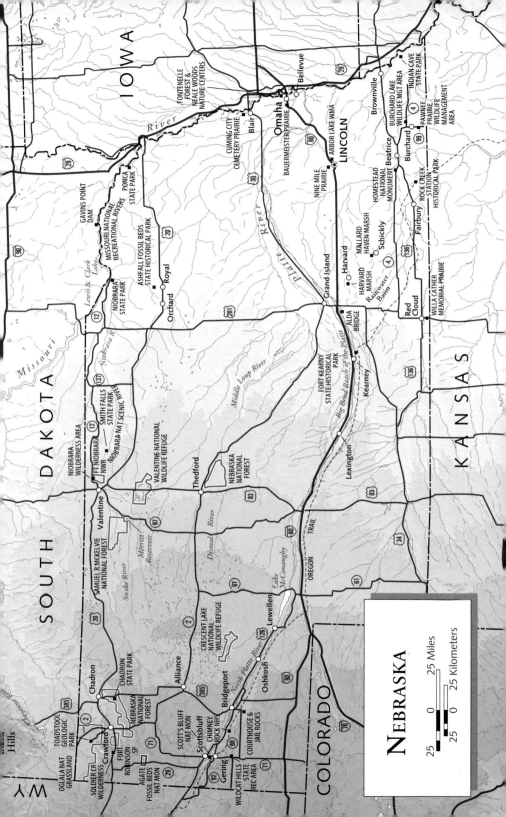

NEBRASKA

25 Miles

0

25 Kilometers

half a million acres of farmland. The river that William Henry Jackson painted in 1866 as a wide golden ribbon shimmering across the plain was not exactly beautiful, but it was awe-inspiring. The present river is tamer, tree-lined (floods and ice jams no longer strip vegetation from the sandbars and riverbanks), and as rivers go, rather unremarkable to behold.

The Platte's role in shaping the Great Plains and conveying human traffic across the continent more than compensates for its scenic shortcomings. It has inspired a body of art, prose, and poetry lavish in comparison to its ordinary appearance. Floating on its prosaic waters, for instance, brought out the cosmic best in Nebraska-born anthropologist Loren Eiseley, who wrote, "I was streaming over ancient sea beds thrust aloft where giant reptiles had once sported; I was wearing down the face of time and trundling cloud-wreathed ranges into oblivion."

To emphasize Nebraska's subtle but omnipotent tilt, this chapter moves down the geographical "gangplank" from west to east. Starting at about 5,000 feet in the ridge-and-tabletop country of western Nebraska, the itinerary meanders across the state, following streams and rivers until they discharge into the Missouri, a distance of some 450 miles and a drop of 4,600 feet.

128

NORTHERN PANHANDLE: THE PINE RIDGE

The Pine Ridge is Nebraska at its highest and most lonesome. Here a visitor can easily walk, ride a horse, or drive the better part of a day without encountering another person. Flatlanders, accustomed to the subtler terrains of the Great Plains, may at first be bewildered in this flagrantly scenic landscape of dramatic see-forever vistas, large fauna (pronghorn, mule and white-tailed deer, reintroduced elk, bison, and bighorn sheep), impressive flora (from stately ponderosa pines to rare stunted plants adapted to saline wetlands), weird geologic formations, and world-famous fossil beds.

Out in a beautiful nowhere of wedding-cake buttes near the Wyoming border, **Agate Fossil Beds National Monument**❖ encompasses Agate Springs Ranch, which was a hotbed of paleontological research and academic competition at the turn of the century. James and Kate Cook, owners of Agate Springs, took a keen interest in the fossil remains on their ranch and entertained many of the country's leading paleontologists, including rivals Edward D. Cope of Philadelphia and Othniel C. Marsh of Yale University.

About 45 miles northwest of the town of Scottsbluff on Route 29, the 2,762-acre reserve lies in the valley of the Niobrara River. Only 20 miles from its headwaters in Wyoming, the Niobrara barely warrants the status of river at this point. Twenty million years ago, however, it was a wide and powerful torrent, draining the uplifting Rockies to the west and watering a lush savanna where prehistoric herds of diminutive camels, horses,

---

OVERLEAF: *At Agate Fossil Beds, a storm brews and yellow irises glow in a wet meadow. In the distance the outlines of University and Carnegie Hills, sites of much paleontological discovery, pierce the horizon.*

rhinos, and deer- and piglike creatures roamed. Ensuing drought and changing vegetation caused massive die-offs of many species. Their fossilized remains, embedded in the cakelike layers of the surrounding buttes, provide abundant evidence of life during the Miocene epoch, 25 to 13 million years ago, a time aptly called the Age of Mammals.

A two-mile trail winds up and around Carnegie and University hills, prominent buttes—named for Pittsburgh's Carnegie Museum and the Uni-

versity of Nebraska—where much of the seminal collecting was done from 1904 into the 1920s. Interpretative displays along the way include an example of a devil's corkscrew, the burrow of a *Palaeocastor,* a common mammal of the Miocene that bears similarities to the modern-day beaver.

The trail meanders through a prairie-scape both lovely and edifying. During spring and summer, the staff at Agate Fossil Beds puts botanical labels on plants as they flower and grasses as they develop seed heads, providing a fine short course in grassland flora. Over-head, hawks such as red-tails, Swainson's, prairie falcon, and northern harriers patrol the vast, usually blue sky.

ABOVE: *The red-tailed hawk is the most conspicuous raptor on the plains; its cinnamon-colored tail is its hallmark.*

Some 20 miles up the road from Agate Fossil Beds is Nebraska's best precipice, the **Pine Ridge,** a 230-mile-long north-facing escarpment that arcs through eastern Wyoming, the northwest corner of Nebraska, and extreme south-central South Dakota. Its shimmering white cliffs, seen to best effect south of Route 20 between Crawford and Chadron, resemble a gargantuan ocean liner shearing through a sea of grass. The Pine Ridge was created when the Cheyenne River cut a valley around the south side of the Black Hills and erosion then carved away the land to the south. The Pine Ridge is high and cool, circumstances that favor ponderosa pine, Nebraska's only native *Pinus* species (pockets of ponderosa also grow in the Wildcat Hills and along hospitable stretches of the Niobrara River).

In this century, suppression of fire has produced denser stands of ponderosa in the Pine Ridge than occurred in presettlement times. Because more trees provide more fuel, fires can be Dantean events. In July 1989, four simultaneous lightning strikes in the Pine Ridge area ignited fires that burned across 50,000 acres of public and private land in a conflagration whose effects will be visible for years to come.

About 75,000 acres of the Pine Ridge are administered by federal and state agencies. Within this sprawling, rugged area, travelers can be as sociable or secluded as they choose. **Chadron State Park❖** (off Route 385 south of Chadron) and **Fort Robinson State Park❖** (north of Route 20 near Crawford) are often crowded with visitors in summer, but both make excellent base camps for forays into the backcountry.

Fort Robinson is the larger of the two (22,000 acres) and lies on more poignant terrain. The fort was established in 1874 to keep order among the Sioux and to coerce them into exchanging their nomadic bison-hunting existence for a more settled agrarian life—even though these arid plains, and the bison that roamed here, dictated a nomadic life. The nadir of this cultural confrontation occurred at Fort Robinson in 1877, when Sioux leader Crazy Horse was assassinated during a botched arrest.

ABOVE: *An owlish face and long tail mark the northern harrier, which flies near the ground like a teetering crop duster.*

Crisscrossing the park are some 30 miles of hiking, horseback, and mountain bike trails, including one across the Red Cloud buttes that offers commanding views. From a perch on the Pine Ridge escarpment, the mind's eye can readily populate the vast plain below with the former heirs to this magnificent landscape. And these days, not everything must be left to the imagination: A herd of about 400 bison has been reintroduced at Fort Robinson State Park. In summer some of the animals can be seen in a pasture about half a mile from the entrance to the fort. The remainder of the herd ranges in a restricted part of the park, where guided tours to see them are conducted in summer and fall.

Visitors to Fort Robinson may also spot reintroduced bighorn sheep. Once estimated to number 1.5 to 2 million, the bighorn population in North America had declined to fewer than 20,000 by 1960. In an effort to

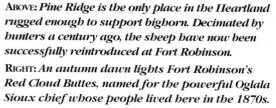

ABOVE: *Pine Ridge is the only place in the Heartland rugged enough to support bighorn. Decimated by hunters a century ago, the sheep have now been successfully reintroduced at Fort Robinson.*

RIGHT: *An autumn dawn lights Fort Robinson's Red Cloud Buttes, named for the powerful Oglala Sioux chief whose people lived here in the 1870s.*

return free-roaming bighorn to Nebraska, biologists established a captive herd of 12 animals at Fort Robinson in 1981. Twenty-one individuals were released into the wild in 1988, and by 1993, the remaining captive bighorns had also been freed. A year later, the wild population was breeding successfully and estimated to be 60 animals. The bighorns usually frequent the higher, more remote sections of the park.

The Nebraska National Forest and Fort Robinson provide trailheads into the 7,794-acre **Soldier Creek Wilderness❖** to the west, where three forks of Soldier Creek have etched deep, cool draws through high, dry pine savanna. Ponderosa pines—many blackened, skeletal remains from the 1989 fire—rise from expanses of western wheatgrass, side-oats and hairy grama, prairie sandreed, and other grasses found in semiarid land, while ash, willow, and cottonwood grow in the stream-laced valleys. (The charred pines add a slightly macabre touch to the scene, as well as a random risk. On windy days, visitors are advised to withdraw to stream valleys to avoid being bludgeoned by falling limbs and trunks.) From the pasqueflowers of spring to the asters of late summer and fall, however,

Soldier Creek is a wildflower heaven, which will remind well-traveled hikers of the foothills of the Rockies. Trooper Trail, one of two hiking paths through the wilderness area, boasts the most dramatic vistas. The middle fork of Soldier Creek supports a trout fishery.

Similar in aspect to Soldier Creek Wilderness—except that it escaped the 1989 fire—the 49,931-acre **Pine Ridge National Recreation Area❖** of **Nebraska National Forest** is a patchwork of ponderosa pine and grassy meadows, reached via Route 2 south of Crawford and Route 385 south from Chadron. A detailed map of backcountry roads and hiking trails is available at the Pine Ridge District Office at Chadron. Visitors can see the country on foot or mountain bike or astride a horse. Of the roughly 75 miles of hiking trails that wander through the Pine Ridge district, the 25-mile Pine Ridge Trail is particularly scenic.

Ranchers can obtain permits for cattle grazing in the national forest from mid-May to late September, and where livestock range, windmill-fed water tanks dot the terrain. Because they provide a permanent source of water in an arid landscape, the tanks attract wildlife as well, including

LEFT: *The rushing water of the Middle Fork of Soldier Creek has carved a cool ravine, providing a gauzy green contrast to the stark escarpments of the Pine Ridge.*
RIGHT: *Once common on tall-grass prairies, the threatened western prairie fringed orchid, an early summer bloomer, is now a rare and thrilling sight.*

such little gems as red crossbills, small finches with bills designed to pry open pinecones so the birds can eat the seeds.

On a clear day, from vantages along the Pine Ridge escarpment, the southern rim of South Dakota's Black Hills is visible on the horizon. The land in between is a rumpled bedspread of badlands and short-grass prairie. Some 94,000 acres of this stark, beautiful, and vaguely menacing country is the **Oglala National Grassland❖.** Equipped with a good map (provided by the Pine Ridge Ranger District Office at Chadron), a four-wheel-drive vehicle, drinking water, and assorted guidebooks (geology, botany, birds, Native American history), a resourceful and curious visitor can spend days exploring this vast, quiet moonscape. Two prairie-dog towns are accessible with four-wheel-drive. One of them, Montrose, is near the **Buffalo Bill Cody Monument.** Here in 1876 Cody and members of the Fifth Cavalry confronted and forced the return of 800 Cheyenne who had fled the nearby Red Cloud Agency.

In spring and early summer, hikes along Hat and Whitehead creeks provide the customary joys associated with birding in riparian areas surrounded by semiarid land. Sugarloaf Road (Forest Road 900), between Orella (a town that persists only on maps) and Route 2, is highly recommended by local bird authorities. Its grasslands and sagebrush are summer

OVERLEAF: *Sugarloaf Butte dominates the Oglala National Grassland, an exquisite emptiness of prairie, badlands, willow-lined draws, and ponderosa pine forest that lies between the Pine Ridge and the Black Hills.*

ABOVE: *A taste of the badlands in Nebraska, Toadstool Geologic Park's landscape of gnarled sandstone is both zany and a bit menacing.*

homes for Brewer's sparrows, sage thrashers, ferruginous hawks, and those most stately of Great Plains birds, long-billed curlews.

About 20 miles north of Crawford on the South Dakota border, **Toadstool Geologic Park** offers the perfect brief foray into the Oglala badlands. A one-mile trail winds through a grotesquerie of weirdly eroded sandstone figures and fossil footprints of ancient rhinoceroses and pigs from the Oligocene Epoch, 40–35 million years ago. Toadstool is the place for people who take pleasure in the goatlike exertions of rock hopping in the hot sun. In summer, the delicate cascading songs of the rock wren are among the few sounds breaking the badland silence.

SOUTHERN PANHANDLE: NORTH PLATTE VALLEY AND WILDCAT HILLS

Among imposing eroded landscapes, few surpass the spires and palisades of the North Platte Valley, a hundred miles south of the Pine Ridge. These signal rocks, visible on the horizon for miles, guided westward-bound settlers on the Oregon and Mormon trails in the mid-1800s. The sandstone and siltstone buttes named **Courthouse and Jail Rocks** were the first of these landmarks that the pioneers encountered. Crouching sphinxlike on the plain, they can still be seen from Route 88 about five miles south of Bridgeport. **Chimney Rock,** the centerpiece of **Chimney Rock National**

ABOVE: *Paul Kane (1810–71) traveled through the Platte Valley in 1847; his watercolor entitled* Pyramid Rock *actually depicts Chimney Rock.*

Historic Site❖, is commemorated by countless pioneer artists and diarists. This 450-foot steeple towering above the North Platte River valley lies about 4 miles south of Bayard at the intersection of Routes 26 and 92.

Scotts Bluff, a massive curtain of sandstone and siltstone, was an impediment rather than a beacon. Plains Indians called it Me-a-pa-te, "the hill that is hard to go around." Located 2.5 miles west of Gering, **Scotts Bluff National Monument❖** hunkers amid 3,000 acres of prairie dominated by little bluestem. The 1.6-mile Saddle Rock Trail zigzags through a million or so years of sandstone and volcanic ash deposits up to the pine- and juniper-clad summit, which affords stunning views of the North Platte Valley (visitors can also drive to the top). A one-mile hiking trail leads to **Mitchell Pass,** where 130 years ago bottlenecked wagon traffic plowed one of the more impressive troughs on the Oregon Trail. A 1.2-mile bike trail into Gering cuts across the prairie, which is strewn with wildflowers in May and June.

Just south of Scotts Bluff is a scattering of sandstone outcrops known collectively as the **Wildcat Hills.** Paralleling the North Platte River south of the town of Scottsbluff, the skeletal white hills resemble an immense rib cage protruding from the earth. At **Wildcat Hills State Recreation Area❖,** ten miles south of Gering on Route 71, more than three miles of trail in 935 acres skirt a scenic ridge through a garden of botanical delights. From May

LEFT: *A pregnant black-tailed prairie dog sits buddhalike by her burrow. She will bear a litter of four or five. These highly social rodents congregate in "towns" and devour all nearby vegetation, leaving no place for predators to hide.*
RIGHT: *An early morning walk along Saddle Rock Trail finds the sandstone formations of Scotts Bluff and Dome Rock beyond lit by the sunrise.*

to September, something is always in bloom. By late summer, the various grasses have donned distinctive seed heads, the yuccas have raised white-flowered stalks, the blazing stars have unfurled their deep purple spikes, and the mountain mahogany has borne seeds attached to peculiar fuzzy swizzle sticks.

NORTH-CENTRAL NEBRASKA: THE SANDHILLS

To the east, away from the jagged edges of the Pine Ridge and Wildcat Hills, the land changes dramatically to a succession of serene and voluptuous dunes called the Sandhills. About 19,000 square miles of Nebraska—an area three times the size of Massachusetts—are blanketed with sand as sugar-fine as any that adorns a pristine beach.

The dunes, many reaching heights of 300 feet, are covered with prairie grasses and forbs, which knit the underlying sands in place with the warp and weft of their roots. The Sandhills are like a Sahara enjoying the benediction of water. They are the largest dune formation in the Western Hemisphere and one of the last extensive unfragmented grasslands in this country, thanks largely to the husbandry of Sandhills ranchers, who have a vested interest in conserving the native grasses that feed their cattle.

The Sandhills are bejeweled with aquamarine lakes. A particularly impressive cluster of them lies along the region's western edge in an aptly named earthly paradise called Garden County. In its northwest corner, 28 miles by dirt road north of the village of Oshkosh, is **Crescent Lake National Wildlife Refuge❖,** which encompasses roughly 30 lakes—the number varies with the amount of precipitation—scattered across 46,849 acres of Sandhills grassland.

Remote by human measure, Crescent Lake is a metropolis for migratory waterfowl, one of the great gathering places for ducks on the Great Plains Flyway. The third week in April is usually the peak of spring migration; the

LEFT: *Western grebes nest in Sandhills wetlands and at Lake McConaughy. These sleek waterbirds are famed for elaborate mating displays, including a "dance" in which they dangle aquatic plants enticingly from their bills.* RIGHT: *An aerial perspective of the Crescent Lake refuge hints at the immensity of the wetlands hidden deep in the Sandhills. This view also suggests how inviting this area must appear to a migrating duck flying by.*

equivalent in fall is mid-October. At these times, the lakes are spangled with pintail, green-winged and blue-winged teal, gadwalls, redheads, canvasbacks, and ruddy ducks, to name a few of the most common birds. Some linger to nest in the marshes, and others press northward to the Dakotas and Canada. By April, the nesting of Canada geese is well under way, and off in the dunes sharp-tailed grouse males congregate on their booming grounds, called leks (observation blinds are available by reservation). Eagles (bald and golden) and hawks hunt from above, coyotes patrol the watery fringes, and deer and pronghorn roam the grasslands.

On the Great Plains, spring is not a clear-cut season. From March through May, the weather jerks between extremes that can vary from the low 90 degrees Fahrenheit to the teens. Because snow, thunderstorms, high winds, and tornadoes are standard events, visitors to remote places like Crescent Lake should always take weather reports seriously.

About 70 miles southeast of Crescent Lake on the southern rim of the Sandhills, water assumes a totally different appearance. On clear days **Lake McConaughy❖**, an impoundment on the North Platte River, resembles a mini-Mediterranean. In terrain where natural lakes are demure gemstones scattered amid the dunes, McConaughy—22 miles long with 105 miles of shoreline—is exposed and oceanic. Its tempo—ordained by anglers, waterskiers, jet-skiers, and sunbathers predominantly of college age—may also be a bit raucous for some nature seekers. Lake McConaughy has its rewards, however, chiefly of the avian persuasion. Because a number of habitats intersect here, the reservoir and surrounding terrain constitute one of the richest birding spots on the Great Plains. In addition, frequent drawdowns at Lake McConaughy, which stores water for irrigation, create instant and extensive mudflats for migrating shore and water birds.

The lake also supports extensive marshes on its western end (Route 26 crosses one near Lewellen), riparian cottonwood and willow woodlands, man-made shelterbelts (barriers of trees and shrubs that protect against wind), grasslands, and of course a great deal of open water, where rafts of common loons, various diving ducks, common mergansers, and western grebes bob in proper season. The lake is one of the few places in Nebraska where Clark's grebes—which look so similar to western grebes that they were not described as a new species until 1985—are regularly, if rarely, seen.

From mid-November to mid-April, bald eagles are common at the reservoir, where these consummate scavengers feed on dead fish and weakened waterfowl. They are especially abundant in March, when ice is breaking up and winter-killed carp and other fish litter the lake's beaches.

To move deeper into the Sandhills, head north from Lake McConaughy on Route 61, which in about 70 miles intersects Route 2, considered by many veteran prairie ramblers the highway through heaven. Visitors who can travel only one road in the Great Plains should choose Route 2 between Alliance and Grand Island. At least a portion of the 274-mile trip is best driven at dawn or dusk. Low light becomes the prairie.

ABOVE: *Fertile by necessity, cottontails (left) produce 15 to 20 young per season. The coyote (right), a wily carnivore, helps keep this burgeoning rabbit population in check; cottontails rarely live more than a year.*

About halfway between Alliance and Grand Island, wedged between the Dismal and Middle Loup rivers, is one of those madcap experiments for which *Homo sapiens* is so renowned: a man-made forest. The **Bessey Ranger District❖** of the **Nebraska National Forest** is the largest publicly supported tree planting operation in the country and the only human-engineered stand of timber in the federal forest system. Against a vast backdrop of sandy hills, this beautiful green island of pines looks like the Emerald City of Oz.

In 1891 the first federal tree planting commenced in the Sandhills; in 1902, President Theodore Roosevelt, an admirer of trees and human ingenuity, established two forest reserves, one near the Dismal and Loup rivers (the Bessey Unit) and one between the Snake and Niobrara rivers near Valentine (the Samuel R. McKelvie National Forest). By far the bigger of the two at 22,000 acres, the forest at the Bessey Unit is primarily ponderosa pine, eastern redcedar, and jack pine; the remaining 68,000 acres at Bessey are grassland. In spring and fall the forest hops with myriad small songbirds that migrate along rivers like the Middle Loup and Dismal. Birders call such places migrant traps—partly because isolated pockets of woodlands lure both eastern and western species that have strayed from their normal migratory paths.

A 400-mile maze of roads loops through the forest, around its perimeter, and across the sandy hills. One forest road leads to Scott Lookout, the only

ABOVE: *Migrating through Nebraska, loons (left) keep to large bodies of water such as Lake McConaughy. Because of its potent spray, the striped skunk (right) has only one real predator, the great horned owl.*

operating fire tower in Nebraska, which is open to the public during summer and provides a spectacular perch for viewing the surrounding Sandhills landscape. A number of these roads require a four-wheel-drive vehicle, and no trip should be attempted without a detailed map. Humans share these spaces with cattle, which graze the grasslands from June to November.

Observation blinds for viewing the intricate mating dances of the sharp-tailed grouse and greater prairie chicken have been constructed in the sandy hills and are available by reservation from April to mid-May. Vying for the attention of females lurking nearby in the grass, the males strut and spar on the lek, in the process making odd noises and revealing gaudy body parts usually concealed under their mottled brown plumage. The greater prairie chicken, for example, inflates brilliant orange cheek pouches, puffs up bright yellow eyebrows, flips pointed feathers up over its ears, and cocks its fan-shaped tail. An eerie, unforgettable morning in the Sandhills begins about 4 A.M. with a trek—first by vehicle, then on foot—across the pitch-dark hills to a ghostly blind. Here, the physical discomfort of hunkering in a small box for an hour and a half is a small price to pay for watching the ritual combat of pumped-up grouse.

NORTHERN NEBRASKA: THE NIOBRARA VALLEY
Up Route 83, 50 miles north of the Bessey Unit, amid another cluster of Sandhills lakes, **Valentine National Wildlife Refuge❖** encompasses

ABOVE: *White pelicans rely on Nebraska's lakes and rivers during migrations. Stocky birds, they ride high in the water, wings positioned up behind.*
RIGHT: *Thousands of waterbirds migrate through the Valentine refuge, where grasses blanket the land and bulrushes and cattails fringe the lakes.*

71,516 acres of billowing prairie. Between the crests of the dunes, the broad valleys and swales are natural basins for lakes and marshes. The native grasses, especially in the wet meadows, are plush green in summer, and by August, a galaxy of sunflowers, predominantly *Helianthus rigidus,* are in buttery bloom across the hills.

The large and permanent lakes at the Valentine refuge attract big birds such as white pelicans and diving ducks such as scaup and common goldeneye. Smaller, ephemeral lakes governed by the whims of rain and snow generally appeal to the puddle ducks—blue-winged and green-winged teal, northern shovelers, and mallard. The peak migration times are May and October. Fall migration is often the more dramatic because the birds, fleeing Arctic cold fronts, push southward in large swells. Coordinating visits to Valentine (and to any other Great Plains wetlands) with approaching Arctic air masses can be very rewarding. By comparison, the spring pace is more desultory: Ducks and other waterbirds seem to dawdle northward as they feed and rest in preparation for the strenuous nesting season ahead.

In years of ample rain, so much aquatic habitat lies along Route 83, both in and outside the refuge, that the 65-mile trip from Thedford to Valentine takes most of the day for visitors stopping to bird every pond, puddle, marsh, and mudflat.

The 116,000-acre **Samuel R. McKelvie National Forest❖**, 25 miles southwest of Valentine, is a forest in name only because a mere 2,500 acres of trees—mostly ponderosa pine, eastern redcedar, and jack pine—are engulfed in an immensity of grass. Despite the much-needed shade they provide, the trees at Steer Creek Campground impart a peculiar artificial aura to an otherwise wild and woolly landscape.

The isolated sand-track roads that crisscross McKelvie are used primarily by cattle ranchers with grazing permits who must periodically tend their windmills. Although visitors can drive these roads, the sand is often too much even for four-wheel-drive vehicles, and hiking out is the only way to get help. A more reliable and equally spectacular route through the grassland is Route 16F, which enters the national forest from the north, 10.5 miles south of Route 20, and then doglegs east, exiting at the northern edge of Merritt Reservoir, an impoundment on the Snake River. Something of botanical interest can be found along this road from May, when the wildflowers start blooming, through September, when the little bluestem turns mauve.

The Niobrara River, its headwaters barely within Wyoming, flows 400 miles across extreme northern Nebraska before joining the Missouri River on the eastern shoulder of the state. It is one of the last free-flowing rivers on the Great Plains, a distinction that was almost forfeited in the early

1980s, when the Niobrara came very close to being impounded to store water for irrigation. In 1991, however, some 76 miles of the river—from east of Valentine to the Route 137 bridge—were designated the **Niobrara National Scenic River❖**.

The Niobrara's charms are obvious. Shallow and gentle, it is fed by springs that keep it cool on even the hottest summer days. Its peculiar and abundant contribution to biological diversity on this part of the continent helped to save it from imminent damming. A slender green wand waving across the Great Plains, the Niobrara Valley inserts an unusually rich assortment of habitats into an immense expanse of grassland that has its own subtle and complex variables. This distinctive compression and converging of ecosystems can be witnessed at a number of public sites along the river.

ABOVE: *Late summer bloomers, stiff goldenrod and its allies in the genus* **Solidago** *are the state flower.*

RIGHT: *In the Niobrara River canyon, East meets West and prairie plants mingle with woodland species.*

Ice Age pockets of boreal vegetation, of which paper birch is the most conspicuous representative, are tucked along cool, shady steep-banked streams that lace the north-facing slopes of the river. Here also bur oak, basswood, and other eastern deciduous trees poke a last little botanical finger into the West. The drier, sunnier slopes on both sides of the river mark the farthest point from the Rocky Mountains that ponderosa pine grows. And embracing it all is a glorious breadth of prairie.

Five miles northeast of Valentine, **Fort Niobrara National Wildlife Refuge❖** provides canoe access at Cornell Bridge, at the entrance to the refuge. This 19,000-acre preserve is most conspicuously a living-history landscape of large Great Plains mammals. The 1.5-mile wildlife drive, which loops through 400 acres of Sandhills grassland, brings visitors as close as feasible for both viewer and viewed to free-ranging herds of bison and elk. Other regulars in this impressively authentic tableau are white-tailed deer and Texas longhorns (a potent, albeit brief constituent of the turn-of-the-century Great Plains landscape), as well as wild turkeys, prairie dogs, burrowing owls, and in winter golden and bald eagles.

A newborn bison calf (above) reclines by its mother; its life expectancy is about 25 years. Easy to maintain and tolerant of cold, bison are experiencing a renaissance on the Great Plains. A managed herd (right) grazes on fall grasses at the Fort Niobrara National Wildlife Refuge.

The refuge was established in 1912 to protect a few bison and elk bequeathed to the federal government by Nebraskan J. W. Gilbert. The site chosen was the former military installation of the same name, which had been rendered unnecessary by a truce between the Sioux and settlers of the area. In 1936 the Texas longhorns were added. One mile east of the refuge's visitor center, the one-mile Fort Falls Nature Trail descends along a tributary typical of the Niobrara River. The trail provides a quick and intimate survey of the plant life—including bur oak, paper birch, basswood, ironwood, and native columbine—that distinguishes these cool crannies.

The Niobrara River cuts an arc through the northern tier of the refuge. The land north of the river comprises the 4,635-acre **Niobrara Wilderness Area❖.** Day hiking is permitted in this hilly section, which is also the wintering range for the bison herd.

Perhaps the most popular destination for canoeists on the Niobrara is the 244-acre **Smith Falls State Park❖,** 12 river miles from the Cornell Bridge put-in at Fort Niobrara refuge. The park straddles the river, and its land entrance is on the north side of the Niobrara, about 15 miles east of Valentine on Route 12 and 3.5 miles south via a gravel road. The park's

namesake, the highest waterfall in Nebraska, is a 70-foot plunge in a spring-branch canyon on the south side of the river. A 300-foot boardwalk leads up the narrow canyon to a deck overlooking the falls. The park provides canoes for visitors entering from the north who wish to paddle across the river and hike up to see the cascade, and a footbridge across the river is expected to be completed by late 1996.

The **Niobrara Valley Preserve❖,** owned and operated by the Nature Conservancy, is a 55,000-acre expanse of Sandhills prairie bounded on the north by a 30-mile ribbon of the Niobrara River. In conjunction with a number of other Conservancy preserves across the Great Plains, Niobrara Valley strives to determine and maintain the dynamic elements that sustain biodiversity within grassland systems. Although bison and fire are the most obvious shapers of these landscapes, smaller, largely subterranean players, such as badgers and pocket gophers, contribute as well to the day-to-day reshuffling of soil, which makes prairies the wild, ever-changing gardens that nature designed them to be. The Niobrara Valley's 300 bison, which range over about 7,500 acres of the preserve, can be seen on tours during the preserve's annual open house in June.

Two self-guided nature trails on the preserve reveal the remarkable compression of ecosystems along this stretch of the Niobrara. In less than two miles, the south trail moves through a shady basswood–bur oak forest into even cooler spring-branch ravines lined with paper birch and then up to bluff tops covered with ponderosa pine and out onto full-bore big-sky prairie. The three-mile north trail traverses the flatter tableland prairies and drier, more rugged canyons that characterize the north side of the river.

THE BIG BEND REACH OF THE PLATTE RIVER

The continent offers no more overwhelming affirmation of spring than the annual gathering of sandhill cranes and waterfowl along the Big Bend Reach of the Platte. In March, birds are everywhere. The air thrums with wing beats, and the cacophony of their calls—the tremolos of cranes, honks of Canadas, chortles of white-fronts, and raspings of mallard—is one of nature's most impressive concertos.

On a river much diminished by damming and diversion, this 80 mile stretch of the Platte, from the cities of Lexington to Grand Island, retains enough of its essential native charms to attract nearly half a million sandhill cranes (80 percent of the world's population) from late February to early April. Accompanying the cranes are millions of geese—snow, Canada, and white-fronted—as well as mallard, common mergansers, pintail, and scatterings of other puddle and diving ducks. Depending on weather, these waterfowl arrive early and head north by mid-March, while the cranes linger for a few more weeks.

The name Platte—French for flat—describes a long-gone landscape. In 1910, the first major dam was completed on the North Platte River in Wyoming. Since then 14 others have been built to irrigate crops, produce electricity, and create jobs, and some 70 percent of the Platte's annual volume no longer flows down the river. Once described as "a mile wide and an inch deep," the Platte has dwindled to a series of narrow tree-lined channels that move 310 miles across Nebraska through a valley largely converted to agriculture.

The sandhills stop at the Platte for about a month to fatten up for the nesting season ahead in Canada and Siberia. At night, the cranes roost in water on shallowly submerged, unvegetated sandbars, which provide the safest havens from predators, primarily coyotes. The Big Bend Reach still contains enough sandbars to suit the birds. In adjacent prairies and wet meadows, the cranes probe for grubs, snails, and earthworms, which provide essential nutrients, and in the fallow fields they feed on tons of waste

ABOVE: *Sandhill cranes are nervous and energetic during spring stop-overs on the Platte. Their nimble dances may strengthen pair bonds; hunters in surrounding states may also explain their skittish behavior.*

corn, an abundant source of carbohydrates. One way to witness the spectacle of the sandhill cranes is to drive the network of farm roads paralleling I-80 south of the river, preferably at dawn or dusk, when the cranes are rising from the river or returning to roost for the night. **Fort Kearny State Historical Park❖,** six miles southeast of the city of Kearney, maintains a hiking and bike trail across the river that is a popular crane-viewing spot. The **Alda Bridge,** three miles south of I-80 at Exit 305, affords spectacular views of the cranes, although bumper-to-bumper traffic on weekends can be a distraction. An informative guidebook is Gary R. Lingle's *Birding Crane River: Nebraska's Platte.*

Every spring, three private organizations—the National Audubon Society, the Nature Conservancy, and Crane Meadows Nature Center—provide crane-viewing opportunities in blinds along the Platte River; all require advance reservations, and most charge a fee. Although cold and somewhat

OVERLEAF: *In March, sandhills congregate by the tens of thousands on the Big Bend Reach of the Platte. Lack of other roosting sites and a surfeit of corn in nearby fields help explain the remarkable gathering.*

ABOVE: *The ring-necked duck (left) is best identified by the bold white ring on the tip of its bill. During the breeding season, the bill of the male ruddy duck (right) turns a distinctive and amazing shade of blue.*

claustrophobic, blinds offer incredible proximity to the cranes.

The sandhill crane's federally endangered North American cousin, the whooping crane, appears more frequently on the Platte than anywhere else along its Great Plains migration route and has consequently provided much of the legal impetus for protecting and restoring the last wild vestiges of the Platte River. The first three weeks of April and late October are peak times for whoopers in Nebraska, but because the entire wild population numbers just less than 160 individuals, seeing one of these ghosts of the plains requires more luck than skill.

THE RAINWATER BASIN AND WILLA CATHER COUNTRY

South of the Platte River lies the Rainwater Basin, a 4,200-square-mile arc of wind-blown silt deposits called loess. The almost imperceptibly undulating landscape contains thousands of impervious shallow depressions, or swales, which gather and hold rain and melting snow like cupped hands. Only 10 percent of the region's original wetlands remain, making Rainwater Basin a poignant name for terrain that is now horizon-to-horizon fields of corn and soybeans. In spring—when sufficient moisture fills the basins or water is pumped into them by state and federal agencies—pandemonium reigns as an estimated ten million geese and ducks funnel into these wetlands and junket among them and the nearby Platte River.

Most numerous are snow geese (including the blue phase of that species), white-fronted geese, Canada geese, mallard, northern pintail, wigeon, northern shovelers, ruddies, and blue-winged and green-winged teal. Lesser numbers of other waterfowl include Ross' geese (relatives of snow geese), gadwalls, ring-necked ducks, redheads, canvasbacks, and occasional cinnamon teal popping up in the horde. The waterfowl gather in the Rainwater Basin from late February to late March, but the largest, most spectacular concentrations usually occur over about ten days in mid-March.

Efforts are under way to protect and restore wetlands in the Rainwater

ABOVE: *A pair of redhead ducks displays the bold and subtle character-istics of the species. He sports a black chest, slate blue bill, smoky flanks, and mahogany red head; she is a study in browns and grays.*

Basin. For instance, the U.S. Fish and Wildlife Service manages 22,436 acres at 57 sites, which vary in size from 40 to 2,000 acres. Two of the largest wetlands, where the most predictable multitudes of birds can be seen, are the 1,484-acre **Harvard Marsh❖,** three miles west of the town of Harvard, and the 927-acre **Mallard Haven Marsh❖,** two miles north of the town of Schickly. To see 200,000 or more ducks and geese on a given day in these wetlands is not unusual.

Visiting the Rainwater Basin, a do-it-yourself proposition, consists of cruising from marsh to marsh along the tidy grid of section-line roads while all available eyes search the horizon for skeins of geese. An essential tool is the *Visitor's Guide to Waterfowl Production Areas of the Rainwater Basin,* which contains maps of all the major marshes and is available through the U.S. Fish and Wildlife Service's **Rainwater Basin Wetland District❖** in Kearney. Lingle's *Birding Crane River* also contains much information on the Rainwater Basin.

A drive along Route 136, which parallels the southern border of Nebraska, is a latter-day reprise of *My Antonía, The Song of the Lark, O Pioneers!,* and other prairie stories of the acclaimed American author Willa Cather. In 1885, when she was nine, her family moved here from Virginia, and she spent much of her childhood in Red Cloud, a small railroad town surrounded by a sea of prairie. Today farming has appropriated much of the area, but the essential prairie details—the pervasive silence, the uncomplicated encounter of earth and sky—remain intact. The terrain still seems at times to be the landscape of "uninterrupted mournfulness" that Cather described so evocatively in *O Pioneers!.*

Here and there along the highway, scattered parcels of the prairie that so enthralled Cather survive. Botanically speaking, these spots may not rank with the best prairies in Nebraska, but they create a time warp, allowing passersby to slip back a century and more to an era when this empty space was on the cusp of major cultural change. The 640-acre

159

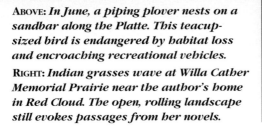

ABOVE: *In June, a piping plover nests on a sandbar along the Platte. This teacup-sized bird is endangered by habitat loss and encroaching recreational vehicles.*

RIGHT: *Indian grasses wave at Willa Cather Memorial Prairie near the author's home in Red Cloud. The open, rolling landscape still evokes passages from her novels.*

Willa Cather Memorial Prairie❖, owned by the Nature Conservancy, is five miles south of Red Cloud on Route 281.

The prairie restoration at **Rock Creek Station Historical Park❖** adds a lovely authenticity to the scene. Seven miles east of the present-day town of Fairbury, Rock Creek was a way station on the Oregon Trail where trappers, traders, California gold seekers, and westward-bound settlers often paused to rest. In 1860 it became a swing station (where riders quickly changed mounts) on the short-lived Pony Express, which operated between Saint Joseph, Missouri, and Sacramento. In 1861 James Butler "Wild Bill" Hickok was involved in a gunfight here in which he killed one man and wounded two others who later died. The myth has long obscured the actual event.

The **Homestead National Monument❖,** 4.5 miles west of Beatrice, encompasses 160 acres thought to be among the first claims filed under the Homestead Act of 1862. In one of the first such programs in the country, restoration of the 100-acre prairie on the site began in 1939.

Burchard Lake Wildlife Management Area❖, about four miles northeast of the town of Burchard, is a tuft of native prairie surrounding an impoundment installed in the mid-1950s to provide local recreation

and halt stream-bank erosion. Although today it is mainly a fishing and picnic spot, greater prairie chickens, once astoundingly abundant on the plains, still live here. Perched on the knobs of hills by the prairie chickens' booming grounds, blinds afford intimate views of the birds in action. Peak strutting season is mid-March to mid-May. Familiarity with the site is recommended, because visitors must hike in to the blinds in pitch dark before sunrise.

Pawnee Prairie Wildlife Management Area❖, about seven miles south of Burchard on Route 99, is a 1,120-acre tallgrass prairie sustaining an impressive assortment of wildflowers, from leadplant to blazing star.

THE LINCOLN AREA: SALT MARSHES AND FRINGES OF TALLGRASS PRAIRIE

Built in a shallow basin that oozes salt, Nebraska's capital city, Lincoln, occupies a low lens-shaped valley etched by Salt Creek and its sluggish tributaries. This network of streams once fed sprawling saline wetlands that accommodated the conspicuous (waterfowl and shorebirds) and the unobtrusive (diminutive salt-tolerant plants and seldom-seen inverte-

161

brates). The salts, which precipitate from the water and leave a characteristic snowlike dusting on the ground, apparently derive from Cretaceous
shales deposited some 100 million years ago when Nebraska was part of
a great inland ocean.

The natural deposits attracted Native Americans, then settlers, and
eventually, in the 1860s, entrepreneurs. Many of the first residents of the
city came to make money on salt. As the city grew, the salt marshes
shrank. Today barely 1,200 of an estimated 16,000 original acres are still
intact, and even these are in various stages of decline as a result of road
construction, overgrazing, siltation, erosion, and dilution with freshwater.

The first step in protecting the vestiges is to restore the water patterns
and hence the habitats needed by plants and animals adapted to prodigious levels of salt. **Arbor Lake Wildlife Management Area❖,** on the
northeastern fringe of Lincoln, is an example of the benefits that result
from stabilizing and manipulating water levels. This 80-acre expanse of
marsh and salt-encrusted mudflat harbors all the classic plants of this harsh
environment—such as saltwort, inland saltgrass, and sea blite—and in
proper season, usually late April to early May, the place dances with
phalaropes, yellowlegs, avocets, black terns, and other migrating birds.

Nine Mile Prairie❖ unfolds across 230 acres of rolling hills on the
northwest outskirts of Lincoln. Because this preserve is right on the climat-
ic brink, enough rain falls here to produce the five- and six-foot stands of
big bluestem and other grass species that constitute a tallgrass prairie.
Nine Mile refers to the distance from botanist J. E. Weaver's office on the
University of Lincoln campus to the prairie. A leader in grassland ecology,
Weaver conducted numerous botanical studies at Nine Mile from the
1930s into the mid-1950s. This splendid prairie is rich in grasses and wildflowers, which bloom from April through the first frosts of late September.

THE EASTERN SHOULDER:
FOSSIL BEDS AND THE MISSOURI RIVER

Ten million years ago, a volcano in the present-day corner of southwestern Idaho blew its top. Tons of ash carried on prevailing westerly winds
dropped across a landscape of subtropical savannas, creating a dusty

---

RIGHT: *A lovely but noxious invader, foxtail barley brandishes its frothy
plumes at Arbor Lake, the last of Lincoln's once abundant salt marshes.*

OVERLEAF: *In autumn big bluestem grasses turn a tawny gold at Nine Mile
Prairie, a remnant swath of tallgrass prairie on the outskirts of Lincoln.*

blanket that paleontologists estimate at 300 miles long and 150 miles wide. Although the forces of erosion obliterated the blanket over time, in 1971 a tatter of the ash that had escaped wholesale erosion was discovered in northeastern Nebraska by Nebraska paleontologist Michael Voorhies. Embedded within six feet of the glittering, glassy dust were hundreds of perfectly preserved skeletons of Miocene mammals, reptiles, and birds.

Ashfall Fossil Beds State Historical Park❖, six miles north of Route 20 between Royal and Orchard, preserves a watering hole where hungry and weakened animals, their lungs filled with suffocating dust, gathered to die. More than 300 complete skeletons of 17 species have been discovered at Ashfall, including an ancient relative of the crowned crane and five distinct kinds of horses. Constructed over a portion of the site, a building called the Rhino Barn allows visitors to peer into an arena where barrel-bodied rhinos, a llama-like camel, and other fossilized skeletons have been painstakingly exhumed from their ashen grave.

Ashfall Fossil Beds is in the lovely valley of Verdigre Creek, a tributary of the Niobrara River. Today's landscape—grassland scattered with vetch, milkweed, mullein, and other prairie wildflowers—is a more arid but strikingly similar version of the Miocene savannas that predominated at the time of the catastrophic eruption.

About 30 miles north of Ashfall Fossil Beds, the Missouri River descending from South Dakota forms the hunched shoulder of northeastern Nebraska. Where the babbling, spring-fed Niobrara River converges with the cloudy silt-laden waters of the Missouri, **Niobrara State Park❖** offers impressive views of the confluence from its perch on the bluffs above. This grand vista is particularly affecting because it encompasses one of the last relatively untamed stretches of the Missouri. Weaving like a lazy serpent through its spacious valley, the shallow dun-colored river is poignantly

similar to the Missouri that Karl Bodmer painted and sketched on his trek up the river with Prince Maximilian of Wied-Neuwied in 1833. The Missouri is now a vanquished river: Nearly 70 percent of its 2,300 miles are impounded or channelized. Its floodplain, a rich matrix of bottomland forests, grasslands, and wetlands, has been converted to farmland, cities, or industrial sites. Besides unaltered portions of the Missouri near its headwaters in Montana, two last seminatural stretches of the river occur along the South Dakota border and together form 98 miles of the **Missouri National Recreational Rivers❖.** One 39-mile section runs from Fort Randall Dam in South Dakota to the western end of Lewis and Clark Lake (this segment is visible from the bluffs in Niobrara State Park). The other is a 59-mile portion flowing from Gavins Point Dam, which impounds Lewis and Clark Lake, to **Ponca State Park❖.** Access points for canoeists are found along both stretches.

Downriver a hundred miles in the Omaha metropolitan area, **Fontenelle Forest and Neale Woods Nature Centers❖** provide intimations of the Missouri River valley in the early nineteenth century. The larger of the two, Fontenelle Forest covers 1,311 acres of steep loess bluffs and superb marshy bottomlands. More than 17 miles of trails wind through the preserve, including a one-mile boardwalk that loops through a stately upland forest of bur oak, shagbark hickory, and basswood. In spring, warbler migration can be quite an event at Fontenelle Forest, as black-and-white, blackpoll, Blackburnian, and Canada warblers (to name a few) flit through the trees. Many warbler species are at the western limit of their range in the Missouri Valley, the largest finger of eastern deciduous forest poking through the plains. The peak of warbler migration is usually the first week of May. Fontenelle, surrounded on its western flank by the city of Bellevue, suffers like many nature centers in urban settings from an oversupply of white-tailed deer, which severely overgraze the forest understory. A regulated hunt, instituted in 1996, should begin to alleviate the problem.

The 554-acre **Neale Woods,** on the northern outskirts of Omaha, is a combination of woodlands, Missouri River floodplain, and restored prairie atop loess hills, which afford clear views of the immense Missouri Valley, seven miles wide at this point. In the fall, Neale Woods is a fine place to watch turkey vultures and various hawks—red-tails, broad-wings, rough-legs, sharp-shins, and others—mosey south along the broad river valley.

The small parcels of tallgrass prairie that managed to survive the plow have stood little chance of withstanding the onslaught of Omaha's westward-marching suburbs. Two miraculous patches are the 40-acre **Bauer-**

meister Prairie❖, near 156th and F streets adjacent to Zorinsky Lake, and the 24.5-acre **Stolley Prairie❖,** east of 168th Street between Blondo and West Dodge roads.

A poignant place with a beautiful view, the 11-acre **Cuming City Cemetery Prairie❖,** about 30 miles north of Omaha on the northern edge of Blair, stands atop a lovely loess hill overlooking the Missouri Valley. Virtually the only places on the plains exempt from the plow, cemeteries such as this one are tiny islands of prairie biota engulfed in oceans of monoculture. Weathered old gravestones, most bearing nineteenth-century dates, peek through a bedlam of grass and wildflowers. In some years, the big bluestem towers over the heads of all but the tallest visitors.

Sprawling across 3,000 acres of roller-coaster loess hills in southeastern Nebraska 14 miles south of the quaint Missouri River town of Brownville, **Indian Cave State Park❖** is the largest expanse of this dramatic loess landform accessible to the public in the state. Within easy reach of Omaha (90 miles) and Kansas City (110 miles), the park can be jammed on weekends, and its trails suffer the incessant pounding of hikers, horseback riders, and mountain bikers.

However, the terrain is impressive—an uncommon botanical mingling of forest and prairie—and evocative of that most famous American event, Lewis and Clark's 1804–6 expedition up the Missouri River. A copy of Bernard DeVoto's *Journals of Lewis and Clark* is a valuable companion on a visit to Indian Cave. Outward bound, the Corps of Discovery passed along this stretch of the Missouri in July, a time, William Clark noted, distinguished by its sultry days, furious thunderstorms, ticks, and mosquitoes. Although much has changed along the Missouri since 1804—most notably the river, which has been constricted by dams and levees and divorced from its floodplain—Clark's complaints still pertain at the height of summer.

About 20 miles of trails crisscross the bluffs in the park. Some are steep and strenuous, and the loess soil provides very poor purchase. The 1.5-mile Rock Bluff Run Trail demonstrates how the woodland, on the shady, moister northern exposures, interfaces with the prairie, which clings to the south-tending bluffs. Late summer is a splendid time for prairie wildflowers and for a profusion of butterflies, including monarchs, red-spotted purples, eastern tiger swallowtails, and hackberry emperors. Wheeling on thermals along the bluffs, turkey vultures and hawks are starting to migrate southward by late August and early September. The forest of bur, chinquapin, and red oaks, basswood, and papaw reaches peak fall color in mid-October.

KANSAS

CHAPTER FIVE

KANSAS:
WINDY PLAINS, HAZY HILLS, AND SPACIOUS SKIES

L ike Nebraska, Kansas straddles the 100th meridian, the longitudinal demarcation that biogeographers and historians use to divide East from West. The line runs through the western third of the state, a landscape of vast skies, strange chalk-rock formations, wheatfields-née-grasslands, and few people (Dodge City is the only sizable town on the meridian). More a smear than a distinct margin, the 100th marks the transition between eastern and western flora and fauna, making the natural landscapes of Kansas particularly interesting.

Here the great hardwood forests of the East ease into the grasslands of the West in a gradual but momentous shift that produces impressive divergences across the 400-mile breadth of the state. The desertlike topography of the Red Hills in south-central Kansas, for example, is a sharp contrast to the humid bottomland forest along the Missouri River in the northeast.

At least during the last 400 million years, the state's geologic history has been a fairly quiet progression of deposition and erosion. Oceans have come and gone, and at one time or another Kansas has been "a shallow sea, a dismal swamp, or a vast salt plain," notes geologist Rex Buchanan.

Kansas landscapes reveal the subtle insinuations perpetrated by weather, wind, and water seeking a course to the sea. Not coincidentally, this third-windiest inland area in the country is named for the Kansa Indians, whose name means "People of the South Wind." From the great pile of

---

PRECEDING PAGES: *Bison browse the High Plains of Kansas. Once Arapaho and Cheyenne hunted here; now ranches and wheat farms predominate.*
LEFT: *Presiding over the unpeopled valley of the Smoky Hill River, the Chalk Pyramids are remnants of 100-million-year-old ocean sediments.*

sands and gravels composing the Ogallala formation of the High Plains in western Kansas to the majestic Flint Hills in the eastern quarter of the state to the stair-stepping Osage Cuestas in the southeastern corner, Kansas manifests the powers of erosion.

Beyond the 100th meridian, western Kansas is dominated by the High Plains, vast steppes of grass that once stretched from Saskatchewan to northern Texas. Craig Miner, writing about the settling of the Kansas High Plains in *West of Wichita,* describes the region as one of "marginality, extremes, and variability"—an area that almost defies domestication. The High Plains remain a sparsely populated region, but they have, despite the odds, been tamed. Most native grasslands have been converted to row crops, and rivers have been dammed to create mammoth reservoirs.

The most notable natural feature in western Kansas is the Ogallala formation, which stretches beneath the High Plains. Because it lies unseen and underfoot, to appreciate it fully requires both a vivid imagination and a copy of John Opie's *Ogallala: Water for a Dry Land.* The Rocky Mountains reconstituted, the High Plains are as horizontal as their source is vertical. The plains are immense fans of sand and gravel carried off the Rockies by water. This porous material worked like a gargantuan sponge, soaking up vast quantities of water 25,000 to 10,000 years ago. "The scale of water held in the Ogallala formation," writes Opie, "is almost beyond reckoning. . . . Unlike most of the world's water supplies, Ogallala groundwater is largely nonrenewable because its sources were cut off thousands of years ago. It is essentially fossil water."

By the 1960s, farmers had tapped this water, transforming the parched land atop this vast underground ocean into lush, orderly fields of wheat, corn, and sorghum. Between 1960 and 1990, about one-sixth of the water stored in the Ogallala aquifer was drawn out, primarily by farmers in southwestern Kansas and the panhandles of Oklahoma and Texas. This depletion of the Ogallala is profoundly affecting the natural landscapes of Kansas, most noticeably the High Plains, where rivers, streams, springs, and wetlands fed by the aquifer are being sucked dry. The biggest river in Kansas, and the only one that drains off the Rockies, is the Arkansas, which crosses the southern tier of the state, making a grand sweep south near the town of Great Bend and flowing into Oklahoma by way of Hutchinson and Wichita. Upstream impoundments and irrigation have taken their toll: The Arkansas is now bone-dry between Lakin and Dodge City and barely a trickle from Dodge to Great Bend.

Although glaciers never reached this far into southern Kansas, water and

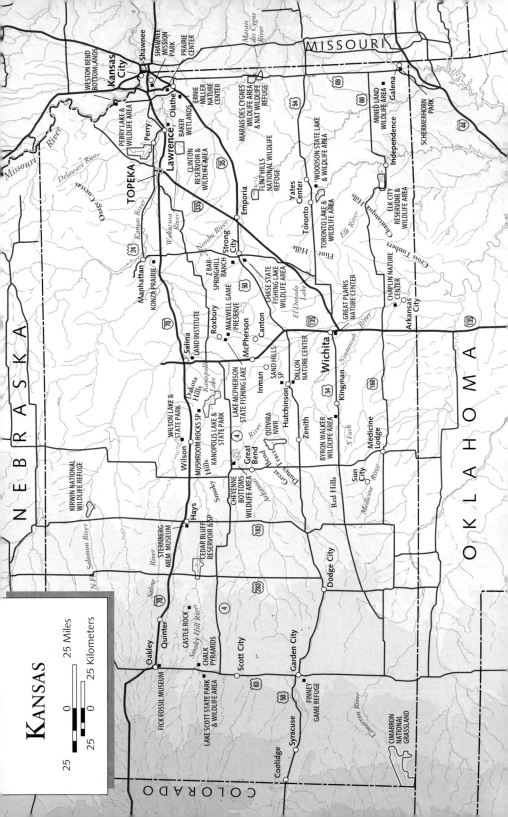

wind transported glacial sediments far and wide. In the huge pocket of displaced sand south of Great Bend, sites such as Great Bend Prairie illustrate the wind at work. There dunes and plains were stabilized over time by big bluestem, little bluestem, sand bluestem, prairie sandreed, and switchgrass.

Also near the great bend of the Arkansas, two of the largest wetland complexes remaining on the Great Plains form a critical rung on the avian migratory ladder up the Plains. From mid-March through April, about half the continent's shorebirds visit the marshes and mudflats of Cheyenne Bottoms and the nearby Quivira refuge, along with a boggling succession of sandhill cranes, geese, and ducks. Maintained by systems of canals and water-control structures, both wetlands—particularly Cheyenne Bottoms—are threatened by continuing agricultural demands on the water that feeds the marshes.

Lying between the 97th and 100th meridians, the broad middle of Kansas is an area of incrementally declining rainfall. In this renowned transition zone of the Great Plains, the lush tallgrass prairie of the eastern plains segues into the progressively more arid mixed-grass prairie and short-grass prairie that predominate west of the 100th meridian. The mixed-grass prairie was once home to huge herds of bison, whose roaming patterns shaped this vast grassland.

Although the fabric of the state's tallgrass and mixed-grass prairies is full of tears, numerous whole pieces survive. In the five-state area covered in this volume, only the Nebraska Sandhills harbor a larger expanse of uninterrupted grassland than areas of Kansas. Forever dispelling the notion that prairies are flat, featureless places, these prairie remnants unfurl across lovely congregations of hills—the Smoky Hills, a series of chalky cliffs and buttes in north-central Kansas; the Red Hills, a phalanx of buttes and mesas along the state's southern border; and the Flint Hills, a narrow north-south band running from Manhattan to Arkansas City.

Extending almost to Topeka, fingers of forest stretch into the eastern fifth of Kansas; along watercourses, long slender digits reach even farther west onto the prairie. Woodland songbirds often follow the shade-giving greenery into these sunburned places, and it is strange indeed to stand on a baking summer slope at Konza Prairie and hear a wood thrush singing from a sliver of streamside trees.

In its northeastern corner, Kansas boasts one of the last large remaining floodplain forests on the Missouri River at Weston Bend, an eastward bulge of the river that lies on the grounds of Fort Leavenworth. Some trees in this woodland of cottonwood, walnut, pecan, sycamore, and hackberry were standing in 1804 when Lewis and Clark passed through; large stands of horsetail, a primitive-looking fern relative, grow in the silty, murky soil. The forest offers excellent birding in any season. Finally, Weston Bend exemplifies the power of bottomland forests to mediate floods. During the high waters of 1993, the over-engineered Missouri River performed like a sluice, flushing flood waters at increased velocity and depth. At Weston Bend's floodplain, however, the waters slowed, spread out, and lapped into the bottomland, causing no economic, social, or ecological catastrophe.

After beginning near the Colorado border in the western High Plains, this chapter wends its way east along the Arkansas River visiting dune tracts, wetlands, and native grasslands. Across the remnant prairies in the hilly transitional zone where West becomes East, the tour explores mesas, valleys, and rangeland in southeastern Kansas and then concludes north of Kansas City in the lush bottomlands along the Missouri River.

SOUTHWEST CORNER: THE CIMARRON NATIONAL GRASSLAND

Depending on the season, recent rainfall, and even the traveler's state of mind, the High Plains of Kansas resemble either the Garden of Eden or Sheol, the biblical abode of the dead. Three elements, however, are constant: endless horizons, spectacular sunrises and sunsets, and cool night skies so full of stars that even the constellations are eclipsed.

Most of the state's High Plains lie west of the 100th meridian, where annual rainfall averages between 15 and 20 inches. Because clumps of grass grow no more than two feet high, this semiarid landscape is aptly called short-grass prairie. Dominating the terrain are buffalo grass and blue grama, both diminutive species whose delicate inflorescences require observers to get down on all fours for a proper appreciation. Because the blue grama flower resembles a false eyelash, the grass is sometimes called eyelash grama. Both male and female buffalo-grass plants possess tiny, distinctive flowers. Sand-sage prairie—home of sand sagebrush, a three-foot-tall gray-green shrub—occupies the sandier, more arid hills along the rivers. Both short-grass and sand-sage prairies contain expanses of exposed ground, giving these grasslands a mangy appearance. The descrip-

OVERLEAF: *Point of Rocks in the Cimarron National Grassland provides a sweeping vista of the Cimarron River valley and the endless short-grass prairie. This landscape was a Dust Bowl wasteland in the 1930s.*

tion, however, is almost moot: Little short-grass or sand-sage remains in this province of waving wheat. Indeed, after the summer harvest, most of western Kansas looks not mangy but utterly bald.

One of the finest attributes of short-grass and sand-sage prairies is their sharp, resiny air. Especially at dawn and dusk, when the atmosphere is cool and moist, the grasslands of western Kansas are redolent with aromatic *Artemisia* sages, whose fragrances are similar to those wafting from a newly opened bottle of retsina.

ABOVE: *In 1981, elk were reintroduced at Cimarron. The herd prospered but was cut in half to prevent damage to irrigated cornfields nearby.*

An important waterway of the southern High Plains, the Cimarron River arises in northeastern New Mexico, winds east through the Ogallala sands of the Oklahoma panhandle, sweeps through southwestern Kansas, and then returns to Oklahoma, finally entering the Arkansas River at Keystone Lake, west of Tulsa. Called dune tracts, the sand dunes flanking the Cimarron were created when tremendous winds tumbling from retreating Pleistocene glaciers blew silt, or loess, across the Great Plains and swept sand into hills along rivers.

Pools along the Cimarron River—and springs seeping from its banks—have attracted wildlife for eons. Drawn by this natural bounty, Native Americans have followed the wildlife trails along the river's 600-mile course for thousands of years. The earliest Cimarron hunters were probably Folsom—perhaps even Clovis and Sandia—peoples, who lived more than 10,000 years ago. Native Americans continued to use this region well into the 1880s; the last Plains tribes to hunt here were the Kiowa and the Comanches.

The Cimarron River in its brief foray into Kansas bisects the **Cimarron National Grassland❖,** which occupies 108,175 acres in the state's far southwestern corner. For its history and beauty—and for the lessons it teaches about mid-twentieth-century attempts to restore natural ecosystems within intense agricultural settings—this landscape is priceless.

Two miles north of Elkhart on Route 27 is the start of a 50-mile self-guided driving tour through the grassland. (A map is available from the

U.S. Forest Service.) One impressive stop on the tour is **Point of Rocks,** a Jurassic Age limestone bluff that juts over the Cimarron Valley like the prow of an ocean liner. It is one of the few high spots along the river and the view is spectacular.

Nearby **Middle Springs** provides an essential oasis in a parched landscape—a place to replenish water supplies. Coronado visited this area in 1541 on his search for the City of Quivira. In 1821 William Becknell established the Santa Fe Trail, which stretched from the Arkansas River to Santa Fe, New Mexico. The portion crossing the hostile, waterless Cimarron Desert to Middle Springs became known as the Cimarron Branch of the trail. Many died on this branch of the trail, including mountain man Jedediah Smith, who was killed by Native Americans in 1831 while seeking water.

Homesteaders were slow in coming. Established by the Beaty brothers of Colorado in 1879, the Point of Rocks Ranch was the area's first permanent enterprise, running up to 30,000 head of cattle. A 1914 flood destroyed the ranch and drowned two children. Farmers used the land to pasture livestock and grow wheat; during the 1920s a string of wet years and the introduction of the tractor turned the short-grass and sand-sage prairie into golden waves of grain. Combined with powerful prevailing winds and the drought of the 1930s, how-

ABOVE: *The graceful, fleet-footed pronghorn is the fastest large mammal on the Great Plains; it can race up to 60 mph to escape predators.*

ever, plowing released the loess and turned the short-lived cornucopia into a wasteland. In the Dust Bowl era, this corner of Kansas was the hardest hit. When Congress passed legislation to buy out bankrupt farmers, the concept of a national grassland was born. In 1938 the U.S. Soil Conservation Service began to restore native prairie plants to the region, and in 1954 the U.S. Forest Service assumed management.

Today botanists have identified more than 230 species of plants growing in this "desolate" land. Although these grasses and flowering species bloom from April to October, the prairie is truly green only in early spring and, if rainfall is adequate, in the fall. As summer wears on and water grows scarce, the grasses become dormant, assuming the wonderfully muted

ABOVE: *Native Kansan John Steuart Curry (1897–1946) knew the violent weather of the High Plains. In this detail of* Spring Shower, Western Kansas Landscape *(1931), the sky is as dramatic as the setting is placid.*

dusty-gray aspect that is characteristic of short-grass and sand-sage prairie.

In the dune tracts south of the Cimarron River, sand bluestem, sand sagebrush, big sandreed, sweet sand verbena, sand milkweed, and prairie spiderwort dominate the sand-sage prairie. The northern short-grass prairie sustains blue grama, buffalo grass, plains larkspur, Indian blanket, scarlet gaura, blazing star, and prairie coneflower.

Pronghorn and elk, reintroduced in 1979 and 1981 respectively, roam the vast plains of the national grassland. Colonies of prairie dogs—as well as burrowing owls, mountain plover, and swift foxes—occupy the heavily grazed areas; badgers, scaled quail, and lesser prairie chickens inhabit the sand hills; and rock wrens nest in the canyons. Floating the thermals above are Swainson's hawks, turkey vultures, and golden eagles.

WESTERN KANSAS: DUNES, BISON, AND BADLANDS

One of the Mississippi's major western tributaries, the **Arkansas River** begins near Colorado's Tennessee Pass on the east side of the Continental Divide. The river passes through the High Plains of eastern Colorado and western Kansas (where it is a major source of irrigation), swings northward in central Kansas, then dives south into Oklahoma and southeastern Arkansas, where it finally meets the Mississippi after traveling 1,450 miles.

Route 50 follows the Arkansas River Valley for about 120 miles from the town of Coolidge, on the Colorado border, east to Dodge City. The

ABOVE: *A welcome oasis on the arid High Plains, Lake Scott attracts humans and wildlife with its cool springs and shade-giving trees. This hidden valley on Ladder Creek became the first state park in Kansas.*

Syracuse Dune Tract is a series of sandy hills fringing the south side of the Arkansas. For a closer look at these desertlike dunes take the 19-mile unnamed dirt road between Syracuse and Coolidge. (From the intersection of Routes 50 and 27 in Syracuse, go south on Route 27 for 1.4 miles and take the road west.) The drive provides a fascinating primer on dune topography, including examples of stabilized sand dunes and shifting blowouts. Stands of cottonwoods along the river support the large stick nests of black-billed magpies, and scaled quail, lesser prairie chickens, wild turkeys, and mule and white-tailed deer often appear. Porcupines perch in the trees, and at night kangaroo rats bound along the road.

In 1905 the now-defunct Kansas National Forest was established on 30,000 acres of sand-sage prairie south of the Arkansas River, just west of Garden City; by 1908 an additional 270,000 acres stretched west to the Colorado border. More than 800,000 trees of various species were planted here in an effort to find varieties suited to the Great Plains. When the experiment failed, irrigation transformed most of the sand-sage prairie into cropland.

A 3,670-acre portion of this forest survives as the **Finney Game Refuge❖**, one mile south of Garden City on Route 83. The preserve is home to the oldest publicly owned herd of bison in Kansas; the first animals were brought from Oklahoma's Wichita Mountains National Wildlife Refuge in 1924. Today the managed herd at Finney numbers about a hundred buf-

183

ABOVE: *Swainson's hawks nest on North American grasslands, but pesticides imperil them on South American wintering grounds.*

RIGHT: *The rising sun casts a warm glow over Castle Rock, a chalky sentinel in the lonesome landscape of western Kansas.*

falo. Although access to the bison is limited, other sand-sage prairie animals to watch for are scaled quail, Cassin's sparrows, western meadowlarks, black-tailed jackrabbits, spotted ground squirrels, black-tailed prairie dogs, and mule deer.

About ten miles north of Scott City and three miles west of Route 83, the 1,120-acre **Lake Scott State Park and Wildlife Area**❖ is a green oasis in an arid land. Located in a canyon etched by Ladder Creek, this valley has been a garden spot of the plains for millennia. Wildlife and humans alike have refreshed themselves with the waters gushing from Big Springs and Barrel Springs. In the 1600s Taos Indians came here from northern New Mexico to escape the Spanish. They built a pueblo—now called El Cuartelejo, or "old barracks"—dug irrigation ditches, planted crops, and shared this site with their Apache friends for 20 years. The remains of **El Cuartelejo,** which have been restored, are modest but evocative. In 1888 Herbert Steele moved into the canyon and used some of the remaining irrigation ditches to establish a successful truck garden enterprise. In 1928 he and his wife, Eliza, donated their land to become the first state park in Kansas.

184

As might be expected in an oasis, birding is great. Among the resident species are the rock wren, lazuli bunting, black-headed grosbeak, yellow-breasted chat, and Say's phoebe, and the endangered Scott riffle beetle lives in Big Springs. Near the park, the last battle of the Indian wars in Kansas occurred along Beaver Creek. On September 27, 1878, a band of Northern Cheyenne escaping a reservation in Oklahoma repelled the U.S. Cavalry here and then, led by Chief Dull Knife and Little Wolf, fled north to Nebraska, killing settlers in northwestern Kansas on the way.

A few miles north of Lake Scott State Park to the east of Route 83 are the **Badlands of Kansas,** an area of chalky bluffs, flats, and pinnacles famous for fossils. Eighty million years ago this landscape lay under an ocean brimming with foraminifera (microscopic calcium-shelled protozoans), giant oysters, sharks, bony fish, swimming reptiles, and—overhead—flying reptiles. As they died, the tests (little shells) of trillions of foraminifera fell like snow to the sea bottom, forming a thick limy ooze that enveloped the corpses of larger animals. In time the ooze was covered by other sediments and pressed into chalk.

Over thousands of years, the Smoky Hill River sculpted the **Chalk Pyramids** (also known as Monument Rocks), majestic pedestals that look remarkably like Stonehenge, which rise just north of the Smoky Hill River, about eight miles east of Route 83 on dirt and gravel roads. Another chalk formation, **Castle Rock,** lies about 30 miles northeast on the old Butterfield Overland Dispatch trail (follow Castle Rock Road about 20 miles south from the Quinter exit of I-70; be warned that back roads out here are treacherous when muddy). In this vast, empty part of Kansas, the sky can be so blue it almost seems purple. The chalk-flat prairie is dominated by little bluestem, side-oats grama, and salt grass; the open spaces and big sky suit raptors—ferruginous hawks, American kestrels, red-tailed hawks, golden eagles, northern harriers, and prairie falcons. Although both the Chalk Pyramids and Castle Rock are on private land, visitors are welcome as long as they do not damage the formations.

Two museums just off I-70 in western Kansas are noted for their fossil collections: the **Fick Fossil and History Museum❖** in Oakley and the **Sternberg Museum of Natural History❖** (under renovation) in Hays. The Sternberg is well-known for its displays of Miocene fossils: rhinoceroses, camels, horses, and saber-toothed cats taken from Rhinoceros Hill in extreme western Kansas and other private quarries in the state.

NORTH-CENTRAL KANSAS:
THE CHALKY FINGERS OF THE SMOKY HILLS

Tucked between the High Plains to the west and the Flint Hills to the east, the **Smoky Hills** are a rolling landscape of knolls, buttes, and hazy valleys. At high noon, this part of Kansas seems pallid and interminable, but during the low light of morning or evening, it is exquisite. Vast herds of bison and pronghorn roamed this mixed-grass prairie, hunting grounds of the Cheyenne and Pawnee.

Today the defining element of the Smoky Hills is the artificial reservoir, and the map of Kansas twinkles with these azure orbs. Reservoirs interrupt one of the most fundamental natural processes—the way water shapes continents. Nothing is quite so unnatural as a big bath of water where a river once flowed. Ironically, much that remains natural in Kansas appears around its reservoirs, which are magnets for nesting, migratory, and wintering birds. Zimmerman and Patti's *Guide to Bird Finding in Kansas and Western Missouri* ranks many of these impounded lakes among the prime birding spots in the state.

The Smoky Hills comprise three distinct upland regions composed of

ABOVE: *At Cedar Bluff Reservoir, a chalk bulwark meets the blue water of the Smoky Hill River. Open water, trees, and mixed-grass prairie make this a haven for birds, from black-billed magpies to Bell's vireos.*

sediments deposited 165 to 65 million years ago during the Cretaceous period. The westernmost hill range is the **Niobrara Chalk Hills,** most vividly displayed at Castle Rock and the other sculpted monuments of the Kansas Badlands. The middle range of hills is known as the **Post Rock country** because settlers found its abundant Greenhorn limestone ideal for making fence posts (limestone bridges, buildings, and fence posts are still a distinctive part of the landscape). The easternmost range, the **Dakota Hills,** is characterized by dramatic sandstone buttes and outcrops.

Hidden in the lonesome vastness of the Niobrara Chalk Hills, **Cedar Bluff Reservoir and State Park❖** encompasses a 15,242-acre expanse of

ABOVE: *A stand of cottonwoods flanks Wilson Lake on the Saline River, one of many artificial reservoirs in Kansas. These impoundments are magnets for wildlife, especially migratory ducks, geese, and shorebirds.*

mixed-grass prairie amid a preponderance of wheat. The reservoir on the Smoky Hill River is east of Route 283 about 15 miles south of the town of WaKeeney and I-70. Built in 1951 by the Bureau of Reclamation for flood control and irrigation, Cedar Bluff is a prime birding area in any season. Spring and fall migrations bring ducks, geese, and shorebirds. Winter is especially good for finches, sparrows, longspurs, black-billed magpies, long-eared owls, and prairie falcons. The chalk bluffs on the south side of the reservoir make fine perches for viewing wildlife and the landscape. The chalk and gravel areas are noted for fossils, and numerous petroglyphs have been found in the vicinity.

Also in Niobrara Chalk country, the **Kirwin National Wildlife Refuge❖** is 60 miles north of Hays on Route 183. The first national wildlife refuge in Kansas, this 10,778-acre preserve encompasses a reservoir at the confluence of Bow Creek and the North Fork of the Solomon River that was constructed in 1954 to provide habitat for migratory waterfowl. Partly because it lies in the transition zone between western and eastern avifauna, Kirwin is a birder's paradise and a major feeding stop for migrating waterfowl. In spring the cacophony of ducks and geese is a seasonal wake-up call that sends

188

ABOVE RIGHT: *The Texas horned lizard prospers on sun-baked plains from Kansas to Texas. While it dislikes cold temperatures, the reptile's real nemeses are the pet trade and pesticides, which poison the ants it eats.*

shivers down the spine. In addition, horned and eared grebes, American white pelicans, and Franklin's gulls can be spotted on the lake. At Dog Town, on the south side of the reservoir, conspicuous underground homes announce the presence of black-tailed prairie dogs, thirteen-lined ground squirrels, plains pocket gophers, and Ord's kangaroo rats.

In the heart of Post Rock country but containing features of the Dakota Hills, **Wilson Lake❖** and **Wilson State Park❖** lie on the Saline River about ten miles north of I-70 and the town of Wilson. The clear blue waters of Wilson Lake sparkle like diamonds amid the ruddy bluffs of Greenhorn limestone and Dakota sandstone, making this spot one of the loveliest in Kansas. Close to a hundred miles of woody and brushy shoreline attract abundant wildlife, including beavers, red bats, great horned owls, and migrating warblers. In migration season, ducks, geese, grebes, double-crested cormorants, sandhill cranes, and various shorebirds visit the lake and lakeshore. The upland prairie is home to upland sandpipers, greater prairie chickens, western kingbirds, dickcissels, grasshopper sparrows, loggerhead shrikes, coyotes, and mule deer. Western chorus frogs can be heard in the spring, and ornate box turtles, Texas horned lizards,

and six-lined race runners appear daily in summer.

The three-quarter-mile Bur Oak Nature Trail below the dam is an excellent introduction to the natural history and geology of the area. On the north side of the reservoir, the three-mile Rock Town Natural Area Trail traverses massive Dakota sandstone formations and offers glorious views of the lake and mixed-grass prairie.

The Dakota Hills are at their most rugged and picturesque in the vicinity of **Kanopolis Lake and State Park❖,** a 5,100-acre expanse of open water, mixed-grass prairie, and riparian woodland flanking the Smoky Hill River 30 miles southwest of Salina. From spring to fall, wildflowers spread their coat of many colors across the grasslands here. One of the most prolific wildflower sites in the mixed-grass prairie, **Horsethief Canyon** in Kanopolis park boasts 400 species of wildflowers, including prairie larkspur, prickly poppy, purple poppy mallow, butterfly milkweed, and purple coneflower. At **Mushroom Rocks State Park❖,** just north of Kanopolis Lake, and **Rock City❖,** near Minneapolis, about 20 miles north of Salina on I-35, visitors can admire the region's Dakota sandstone, which has eroded into a variety of bizarre formations.

Situated on 275 acres of rolling hills on the southeast outskirts of Salina, the **Land Institute❖,** in operation since 1976, is dedicated to developing agricultural practices that replicate, rather than consume, natural ecosystems. To find methods of farming that replenish soil, its researchers and interns are seeking viable perennial polycultures—grain crops that do not have to be seeded and harvested annually as do grains in conventional row-crop agriculture. Native prairie is the granddaddy of perennial polycul-

ABOVE: *Kansas is quite rightfully called the Sunflower State. A dozen varieties of the robust and radiant wildflower (including the prairie sunflower pictured here) grow throughout the state.*

LEFT: *At Mushroom Rocks State Park, purple poppy mallows bloom among formations reminiscent of* **Alice in Wonderland** *Erosion whimsically sculpted the area's giant spheres and balanced rocks by whittling away the soft Dakota sandstone.*

191

LEFT: *Bison now thrive at the Maxwell refuge. In 1873 one observer described the climax of the bison slaughter in western Kansas: "The vast plain which only a short 12 months before teemed with animal life, was a dead, solitary, putrid desert."*

RIGHT: *A black locust changes color at Cheyenne Bottoms, a patchwork of wetlands and native prairie that supports one of the largest assemblages of migratory shorebirds in the Western Hemisphere.*

tures. On the site, a 90-acre native tallgrass prairie, open to the public, shows how, in the words of Land Institute ecologist Jon Piper, "interdependent plants, animals, and microbes garner, retain, and efficiently recycle critical nutrients."

About 15 miles northeast of McPherson between the towns of Roxbury and Canton, the **Maxwell Wildlife Refuge**❖ is named for McPherson businessman Henry Maxwell, who donated the land to the state in the 1940s. At the 2,254-acre wildlife refuge, which is home to nearly 200 bison and 50 elk, tours on covered trams bring visitors close to these daunting plains animals. The surrounding Smoky Hills are accented from spring to fall with exquisite wildflowers. The 1.5-mile Gypsum Creek Nature Trail is on the southwestern edge of **McPherson State Fishing Lake**❖.

SOUTH-CENTRAL KANSAS: WETLANDS, DUNE TRACTS, AND THE RED HILLS

The **McPherson-Wellington Lowlands** form a triangle of wetlands in south-central Kansas that runs from about Salina to the Oklahoma border. Once part of an ancient Permian sea, the lowlands combine thick layers of shale with beds of salt and gypsum. Shallow depressions, which formed as the salt and gypsum dissolved far below the surface, produced 126 square miles of wetlands in 52 separate marshes. This magnificent constellation of wetlands was once rivaled only by Cheyenne Bottoms, just north of Great

192

Bend, as a stopover for migrating waterbirds in Kansas. Beginning at the turn of the century, when much of the area was drained for farming, the McPherson Valley wetlands were reduced to a handful of marshes and lakes. Efforts are under way to restore portions of this system. **Lake Inman,** about three miles northeast of Inman, is a half-mile-wide sink and the largest natural lake in Kansas, and **Clear Pond** is seven miles northwest of McPherson. The two sites are currently the most accessible wetland areas for viewing a variety of nesting and migratory waterbirds.

About 10,000 years ago, during the Pleistocene epoch, windblown sands whipping out of the Arkansas River valley created the **Hutchinson Dune Tract,** just north of the city of Hutchinson. Over time the roots of grasses and shrubs have kept the dunes from shifting like the sands of the Sahara. A fine group of stabilized dunes lies within the 1,123-acre **Sand Hills State Park❖,** on the north edge of the city just east off Route 61. Numerous trails wander through a gently undulating landscape of high dunes and ridges, sand prairie, marshes, and woodlands. The major grasses of the sand prairie—sand bluestem, little bluestem, switchgrass, and sand dropseed—leave ample space for wildflowers, shrubs, and areas of exposed sand. Exploring these dunescapes is like walking on a vast beach. **Dillon Nature Center❖,** about two miles south of Sand Hills State Park, provides an excellent introduction to the natural history of the area and is a good place to spot sparrows and warblers during songbird migration.

Mid-March to mid-May is the best time to visit **Cheyenne Bottoms Wildlife Area❖,** one of the finest waterfowl and shorebird wetlands in the world. Just north of the Arkansas River and about six miles north of the town of Great Bend, the 19,857-acre marshland occupies an elliptical basin covering about 60 square miles and ringed on the north, south, and west by low terraced bluffs. Although the terrain is unremarkable, the life it supports is astonishing. In March geese, ducks, and sandhill cranes pushing north begin the procession. The cranes are bound for the Platte River in Nebraska, where they will spend almost a month before moving on to their nesting grounds farther north. The shorebird migration peaks from mid-April to mid-May. The numbers of birds that pack into the marsh are astounding. In a day's observation Kansas ornithologist John Zimmerman has recorded 101,500 white-rumped sandpipers, 62,580 Bard's sandpipers, 210,000 long-billed dowitchers, and 130,000 Wilson's phalaropes. The birds, especially the ducks and shorebirds, come to feed on the rich soup of invertebrate life that thrives in the marshes; bloodworms, the larval state of midges, are the predominant prey. Zimmerman describes the feast in *Cheyenne Bottoms, Wetland in Jeopardy.*

The state's other incredible wetland is **Quivira National Wildlife Refuge❖,** about 20 miles southeast of Great Bend via Route 281 and 4th Street Road. Even more desolate and remote than Cheyenne Bottoms, Quivira's 21,820-acre complex of marshes, mudflats, and sand prairie is the heart of the **Great Bend Dune Tract** of the Arkansas River, one of the largest accumulations of sand in the United States. In spring, Quivira, like Cheyenne Bottoms, is a major staging area for ducks, geese, sandhill cranes, white pelicans, and shorebirds heading to nesting grounds in the north. American kestrels, Mississippi kites, Swainson's hawks, and northern harriers visit in summer, and bald and golden eagles are common in winter. Quivira is also a stronghold for the much-maligned massasauga rattlesnake.

In south-central Kansas, almost reaching Hutchinson and Wichita, an arm of the southern High Plains extends beyond the 100th meridian, squeezing between the Red Hills and Great Bend Dune Tract of the Arkansas River. In this part of the High Plains, porous Ogallala sands and gravels function as a sieve that allows water from the Arkansas River

RIGHT: *Twining purple tendrils of native American vetch blanket a meadow at Byron Walker Wildlife Area on the South Fork of the Ninnescah River. Vetches are legumes, known for their soil-building properties.*

194

ABOVE: *Wavyleaf thistles colonize crevices in the Gypsum Hills. Because the soil here has high concentrations of calcium and magnesium sulfates, local waters offered native Plains peoples relief similar to Epsom salts.*

aquifer to flow under the Great Bend Dune Tract and replenish High Plains streams like the Ninnescah River.

Stabilized dunes along an eight-mile stretch of the South Fork of the Ninnescah River boast one of the foremost wildlife attractions in Kansas. Straddling Route 54 about seven miles west of Kingman, the 4,529-acre **Byron Walker Wildlife Area**❖ (named for a Kansas Department of Wildlife and Parks manager who spent a lifetime developing the site) features a mixture of native and fabricated landscapes that work in tandem to boost wildlife diversity. The riparian woodlands border extensive native sand prairie, with its typical undulations of dune ridges and swales. A small reservoir, **Kingman State Fishing Lake,** attracts migratory water-fowl, and a developed marsh at the western end of the lake provides habitat for nesting birds and migratory shorebirds, herons, and egrets. Extensive plantings of shrubs benefit such nesting birds as Bell's vireos and various migratory and wintering sparrows. From the pull-off on Route 54, east of refuge headquarters, a small herd of bison is visible.

Just south of the long arm of the southern High Plains stretches a pecu-

196

liar dreamlike topography of buttes and bluffs. Composed of layers of brick red shales, siltstones, and sandstones topped with pewter-colored caps of gypsum and dolomite, the **Red Hills** (also called the Gypsum Hills) look like desert but receive enough rainfall to support an unusual mixture of big bluestem, little bluestem, blue grama, hairy grama, and eastern redcedar. This cedar-prairie community is renowned for its seasonal display of wildflowers. In spring, citron paintbrush splatters the slopes of the Red Hills with bursts of yellow; in fall, scarlet cardinal flower brightens the moist sandy stream valleys. The Plains Indians called these red mesas the Medicine Hills, and the springs and streams indeed contain calcium and magnesium solutions similar to Epsom salts.

Although no land in the Red Hills is open to the public, visitors can enjoy the region's beautiful panoramas from the back roads that crisscross the area within a rectangle formed by Route 283 on the west, Route 160 on the north, Route 281 on the east, and the Oklahoma border on the south. The **Gyp Hills Trail,** a 20-mile marked route, runs from the city of Medicine Lodge northwest along the Medicine River to Sun City; the chamber of commerce in Medicine Lodge can provide maps and information on the Red Hills area.

In Wichita, the largest city in Kansas, the **Great Plains Nature Center❖** provides a fine introduction to the major ecosystems of the Heartland, with an emphasis on grasslands. Located in 240-acre **Chisholm Creek Park,** the center maintains a system of trails that wander through woodlands, prairie, and wetlands. The Wichita Audubon Society owns **Chaplin Nature Center❖,** a 230-acre wildlife sanctuary along the Arkansas River about three miles west and two miles north of Arkansas City. Prairies, streams, mature bottomland woodlands, and five miles of trails make the center a fine place to watch birds in all seasons.

EAST-CENTRAL KANSAS: THE FLINT HILLS

Because it averages 30 to 40 inches of rain per year, eastern Kansas, from the western border of the Flint Hills to the Missouri River, is moist enough to support a forest. However, dating back roughly 10,000 years to the end of the Pleistocene epoch, this region has been dominated by tallgrass prairie. Periodic droughts, heavy grazing by bison and elk, and fire kept trees and shrubs at bay. Lightning caused many natural conflagrations, and Native Americans set fires—to reduce vegetation and hence the threat of fire near their homes, to intimidate enemies, and to maintain forage for their most

197

needed commodity, the bison. Today the bison and elk herds are gone, and the grasslands have been converted to cropland or protected from fire. As a result, trees and shrubs have invaded much of the tallgrass, in some places even advancing to the hilltops. The tallgrass prairies of North America once stretched across much of the Midwest, occupying 400,000 square miles; at the end of the twentieth century less than 1 percent remains.

The country's largest remnant tallgrass prairie lies in the big, brawny **Flint Hills** of east-central Kansas. Some 40 miles wide and extending 200 miles from near the border of Nebraska into Oklahoma, the Flint Hills present an exquisite landscape of limestone-capped mesas and deep winding valleys carved by crystal-clear streams. Nodules of chert (also called flint) in the limestone and soil have slowed erosion, hindered the plow, and maintained the integrity of the Flint Hills. Sustained by managed fires, the big bluestem, little bluestem, Indian grass, and switchgrass provide nutrients for the thousands of cattle that roam this ranchland today.

To experience the magnitude of the Flint Hills and its tallgrass prairie, follow Route 177 north about 100 miles from El Dorado Lake to Manhattan. Along the way, back roads between Cassoday, Matfield Green, and Bazaar afford magnificent views. Except for the cattle, the land appears much as it did when the Osage hunted here. From spring thaw to autumn frost, wildflowers of all sorts brighten the grasslands, and by late summer the plush

LEFT: *In* Prairie Meadows Burning, *George Catlin (1796–1872) bears witness to the fact that fire on the plains was a formidable event. Not even the fleet bison could outmaneuver the raging flames.* RIGHT: *The dickcissel is the most vocal bird in the Kansas grasslands. In the United States, this finch lacks nesting habitat, and in South American rice fields, where it winters, it is considered a pest.*

green grasses of spring have turned a thousand subtle hues of yellow, orange, brown, purple, and crimson.

To walk on the tallgrass prairie proceed to the 383-acre **Chase State Fishing Lake Wildlife Area❖,** three miles west of Route 177 at Cottonwood Falls. Formed by the damming of Prather Creek, the small lake is surrounded by a lovely swatch of tallgrass. This preserve is the place to see—and hear—the septet of classic prairie birds: upland sandpiper, grasshopper sparrow, eastern meadowlark, dickcissel, common nighthawk, common poorwill, and greater prairie chicken. Writer William Least Heat-Moon sets his *PrairyErth* in Chase County, in the heart of the Flint Hills. The county seat, Cottonwood Falls, boasts a handsome French Renaissance courthouse built in 1873. A mile to the north is the rodeo town of Strong City, and two miles north of it on Route 177, the 10,894-acre **Z Bar/Springhill Ranch❖,** which dates from the early 1880s, is the site of a proposed **Tallgrass Prairie National Preserve.**

About six miles southwest of Manhattan, Kansas State University maintains one of the gems of the Heartland, **Konza Prairie❖,** an 8,616-acre tallgrass prairie research site for the study of natural prairie ecosystems. A 2.8-mile self-guided nature trail and two longer trails, the 4.7-mile Kings Creek Loop and 6.1-mile Godwin Hill Loop, are perhaps the best walkabouts in Kansas. The trails scale limestone-capped mesas affording spectacular views of the Flint Hills, then descend prairie slopes into the forest along clear-running Kings Creek.

SOUTHEAST KANSAS: OSAGE CUESTAS TO CHEROKEE LOWLANDS

East of the Flint Hills and south of the Kansas River, the **Osage Cuestas,** alternating beds of limestones and shales, were deposited 300 to 250 million years ago during the Permian and Pennsylvanian periods, when the

199

area was a shallow sea. Differential weathering of the shales and limestones has produced a series of crested hills with a steep face on one side and a gentle slope on the other. Known as cuestas, they are described by Kansas geologist Rex Buchanan as "tilted steps of a giant staircase."

Despite its name, the 18,500-acre **Flint Hills National Wildlife Refuge❖** is in the western portion of the Osage Cuestas on the upper reaches of **John Redmond Reservoir.** About 20 miles southeast of Emporia, the refuge is on Route 130 8 miles south of I-35. This Neosho River bottomland provides a variety of habitats, including flooded sloughs, marshland, tallgrass prairie, hardwood timber, and cropland. Migrating ducks, including redheads and canvasbacks, pass through in fall and spring, and in mild years, more than 55 bald eagles and thousands of snow geese winter here.

Penetrating the southwest reach of the Osage Cuestas, a fascinating sliver of sandstone known as the **Chautauqua Hills** is a remnant of the sandy deltas that formed where streams flowed into Pennsylvanian seas some 300 million years ago. Centered in this rugged terrain, the **Cross Timbers**—a savanna of oaks and grassland that stretches south into Oklahoma and northern Texas—traditionally separates the eastern blackland prairie from the western plains. Featured here are such tree species as blackjack, chinquapin, and post oaks, and bitternut hickory. Blooming redbuds and booming greater prairie chickens make spring a delightful time to visit the Chautauqua Hills.

Classic examples of the Cross Timbers and Chautauqua Hills can be seen at the 5,840-acre **Toronto Lake and Wildlife Area❖,** on the Verdigris River, and at the nearby 2,850-acre **Woodson State Fishing Lake and Wildlife Area❖** (both are just west of the town of Yates Center, which is on Route 54). The Kansas Department of Wildlife and Parks office at Toronto can help visitors schedule time in prairie chicken observation blinds.

Back on the Osage Cuestas, the 13,000-acre **Elk City Reservoir and Wildlife Area❖,** four miles northwest of Independence, is especially breathtaking in autumn, when the oaks and hickories covering the hills reach peak color. The reservoir, created by damming the Elk River, attracts large

---

LEFT: *Orange blossoms of butterfly milkweed brighten a slope at Konza Prairie, one of the first large tallgrass preserves in North America.*
OVERLEAF: *Twilight tints an outcrop of the Flint Hills, where bits of chert in the limestone and soil make the tallgrass prairie too rocky to plow.*

ABOVE: *In the Osage Cuestas, the first rays of dawn glance off splendid rock formations; a wind-shaped American elm is silhouetted against the*

numbers of waterfowl in both spring and fall. Snow, greater white-fronted, and Canada geese—and attendant bald eagles, which prey on weakened waterfowl—linger here in milder winters.

Another legacy of the Pennsylvanian seas of 300 million years ago, the **Cherokee Lowlands** in southeastern Kansas contain strata of sandstones, shale, and coal, the latter simply the long accumulation of rotting vegetation in the bottom of ancient swamps. In the 1870s, shaft mining for coal began in the region; strip mining followed in the 1950s, and today hundreds of water-filled strip pits dot the area. The **Mined Land Wildlife Areas❖,** with headquarters in Columbus, comprise abandoned coal pits now managed for fishing and wildlife.

deep blue waters of Elk City Reservoir. The cuestas are strata of shale and limestone laid down by shallow seas 300 to 250 million years ago.

A tiny portion of extreme southeastern Kansas, about the size of a thumbprint on the map, is part of the **Ozark Plateau,** which occupies a much larger area in neighboring Missouri. The 24-acre **Schermerhorn Park❖** in the town of Galena provides the best Ozarkian experience in Kansas. Here a typical Ozark forest of white and Shumard's oak, bitternut, and shagbark hickory grows along the steep limestone bluffs that tumble into cold, clear Shoal Creek. Schermerhorn Cave provides a home for bats and cave salamanders.

Also near the Missouri border, about 80 miles farther north on Route 69 south of La Cygne, one of the finest expanses of marsh and swamp in Kansas traces the Marais des Cygnes River. During fall and spring the area is

LEFT: *The barred, or hoot, owl inhabits the flood-plain forests at Marais des Cygnes year-round. The nine-note call of this swamp dweller is one of the most impressive declarations in the bird world.* RIGHT: *Limestone bluffs overlook the glinting waters of Shoal Creek in Schermerhorn Park. With its oak-hickory uplands and giant sycamores, Kansas's bit of the Ozarks is a true birding hot spot in May.*

resplendent with migrating waterfowl; the red-shouldered hawk, a habitué of floodplain forests, is also found here, an indicator of the health of the ecosystem. The 7,140-acre **Marais des Cygnes Wildlife Area❖** provides access to this fascinating region. Although spring migration is a tempting time to visit, summer is equally inviting because of the possibility of spotting such nesting birds as wood ducks, barred owls, pileated woodpeckers, tufted tit-mice, Carolina wrens, wood thrushes, yellow-throated vireos, northern parulas, and Kentucky warblers.

NORTHEAST KANSAS: URBAN ENVIRONS AND MISSOURI RIVER BOTTOMLANDS

In metropolitan Kansas City, three places offer glimpses of natural terrain. On the city's southwestern edge in the suburb of Olathe, on Route 150 six miles west of its intersection with Interstate 35, the 293-acre **Prairie Center❖** provides a fine introduction to the tallgrass prairie and many prairie wildflowers. Also in Olathe, the 113-acre **Ernie Miller Park❖** is on Route 7 about a mile north of its intersection with I-35. The 1,250-acre **Shawnee Mission Park❖** is at 7900 Renner Road in Shawnee.

Just south of the Lawrence city limits, the 573-acre **Baker Wetlands❖** adjoins the Wakarusa River. The threatened northern crawfish frog provided the impetus for the site's protection in 1968. Like many areas created to defend one species, Baker Wetlands now protects many more—225 species of birds, 13 fishes, 35 amphibians and reptiles, 350 plants, and 23 mammals. This preserve also proves that wet, squishy places fit easily into an urban context. Trails and an 850-foot boardwalk keep visitors' feet dry as they wander through a montage of cattails, prairie cordgrass, big bluestem, sedges, cottonwoods, and willows.

Housed in a beautiful Romanesque revival building at the University of

LEFT: *As early as 1804, explorers Lewis and Clark understood that the ubiquitous beaver, prized for its fine pelt, would be a linchpin in the fragile trade alliances with western Native Americans.*

Kansas in Lawrence, the **KU Natural History Museum**❖ displays a panorama of North American plants and animals first shown in 1893 by Lewis Lindsay Dyche, a flamboyant nineteenth-century outdoorsman, naturalist, and taxidermist. About five miles southwest of Lawrence, the 18,856-acre **Clinton Reservoir and Wildlife Area** in 1989 hosted the first successful nesting of bald eagles in Kansas in recent times. Substantial numbers of bald eagles winter here as well.

Of the four major advances of ice that penetrated the continent's midsection, the first barely scraped into northeastern Kansas, whereas the second—known as the Kansan glacier—moved a little farther into the state. Its effects can be seen in the northeastern corner (north of the Kansas River and east of the Blue River) a region of rolling uplands, eroded valleys, meandering streams, and scattered rocks and boulders known as glacial till. The boulders of pink quartzite scattered through the fields and pastures of northeastern Kansas are ancient Precambrian rock plucked by the ice sheets from outcrops in Minnesota and South Dakota and carried southward.

About equidistant from Topeka and Lawrence, **Perry Lake and Wildlife Area**❖ is just east of Route 237 and about three miles north of Perry, which is on Route 24. In this striking valley of the Delaware River, the 31,638-acre preserve is a mosaic of oak-hickory forest, prairie, open water, mudflats, and marsh and a perfect place to become acquainted with this glaciated corner of Kansas.

About 30 miles northeast of Perry, one of the prized natural areas in Kansas, the **Weston Bend Bottomlands**❖, lies in an arc of the Missouri River within the boundaries of Fort Leavenworth. This 5,600-acre expanse of mucky bottomland contains one of the last large floodplain forests on the Missouri. The dank and shadowy stands of cottonwood, elm, pecan, walnut, sycamore, and hackberry look much as they did in 1804, when the

RIGHT: Gangly and a bit awkward, the great blue heron is a picture of grace and concentration when it is stalking a fish. Its silhouette dignifies many a prairie wetland.

expedition led by Meriwether Lewis and William Clark first passed this way in strangling midsummer heat.

Their journals are a remarkable record of the sublime, the miserable, and the ill-mannered; of mosquitoes, ticks, heat; and of the overwhelming beauty of the landscape. On June 29, one member of the corps gets 50 lashes for stealing whiskey, while another receives 100 lashes for being drunk on post and allowing the theft of the hooch. On July 3, the party sees the first sign of beaver. On July 4, the members celebrate by firing a swivel gun and getting an extra issue of whiskey; on that same day, one of their number is bitten by a snake, apparently a rattler.

Established in 1827, Fort Leavenworth is the oldest permanent military installation west of the Missouri, built to protect immigrants on the Santa Fe Trail and to pacify and intimidate Native Americans. Chief Joseph of the Nez Percé was held prisoner in the Weston Bend forest. The fort played an active role in the Mexican and Civil wars, and in 1867 the 10th Cavalry, a regiment of black soldiers, was organized here. In 1895 Leavenworth Penitentiary, a federal civilian prison, was opened next to the fort.

Visitors come to Weston Bend to revel in its history and admire its fine assortment of birds. The old forest, natural sloughs, and swamp of the bottomland proper—along with a perimeter of younger forest and old fields—provide a rich diversity of habitat options. In late April and early May, warbler migration can be excellent. Species nesting here include wood duck, great blue heron, Acadian flycatcher, American redstart, prothonotary warbler, wood thrush, and scarlet tanager. The depth of summer is best for remembering Lewis and Clark and the lesson that nature is both bitter and sweet. Amid the mosquitoes and stinging nettle is the birdsong, the old forest, and, a stone's throw away, the churning, swirling, opaque Missouri going about the infinitesimal business of reshaping the continent.

MISSOURI

MISSOURI:
FROM ROCKS AND RIVERS TO
REMNANTS OF ROLLING PRAIRIE

Missouri is a state of great geological and geographical diversity. Jumbled within its borders are mountains, prairies, swamps, and savannas; caves and sinkholes; thunderous springs, sparkling rivers, and piles of billion-year-old rocks. The climate can be extreme because warm Gulf air and frigid Arctic winds collide over the state, producing blizzards, tornadoes, heat waves, and droughts. The epicenter of the largest earthquake in recorded history to rock North America is here as well, at New Madrid in Missouri's extreme southeastern corner.

Missouri's landscapes are defined by the presence and absence of glaciers. More than half the state—essentially everything south of the Missouri River—lies beyond the grinding and spackling influence of the ice sheets that created the gently undulating plains for which much of the Heartland is famous. Missouri, where glaciers came to a halt some 700,000 years ago, presents a fine opportunity to compare worlds touched and untouched by ice.

The oldest, highest part of Missouri is the Saint François Mountains, a mass of rugged igneous rock about a hundred miles south of Saint Louis. Here the Precambrian granites and other igneous materials are two to three billion years old, the most ancient exposed rocks in the midcontinent. A collection of knobby, conical hills, the Saint François Mountains derive their deeply eroded shapes from the variable rates at which differ-

PRECEDING PAGES: *In the Ozarks, a white oak overhangs the Current River's Blue Spring, aptly called "Spring of the Summer Sky" by Native Americans.*
LEFT: *Silhouettes of American lotus and blazing colors of oaks and hickories enliven this autumnal prospect at Lake of the Ozarks on the Osage.*

ent types of igneous rocks weather. Along streams, water has etched dramatic narrows in the resistant igneous rock, creating picturesque gorges called shut-ins, which feature cascades, potholes, and plunge pools.

In prehistoric times the Saint François Mountains were repeatedly submerged and exposed by the fluctuating warm inland seas that washed the region. The Ozarks, which encircle the Saint François and occupy most of southern Missouri, are also the sum of millions of years of accumulated ocean sediments. Over time, these slabs, which are about 4,000 feet thick, have been uplifted, folded, faulted, and eroded.

The Ozarks lie in a gorgeous heap, providing the most unequivocally scenic terrain in the Heartland: deep forested valleys, hidden hollows, sunbaked glades, crystal streams and rivers, and springs issuing from maws and fissures in the earth. Because sediments from the ancient oceans, predominantly limestones and dolomites, are water soluble, the Ozarks today are honeycombed with caves, sinkholes, aquifers, and artesian springs. (Such riddled terrain is called a karst landscape, a derivation of Kras, the Slavic name for the plateaus along the northeastern coast of the Adriatic Sea between Italy and Croatia that display these classic dissolved-rock features.) Karst landscapes are beautiful, and among the karst areas of the world, Missouri ranks high. Of the more than 5,000 caves cataloged in the Ozarks, some two dozen are open to the public. This part of the state also contains 11 first-magnitude springs (those with flows exceeding 64.6 million gallons daily); Big Spring, near Van Buren, is the third-largest spring in the United States, with an average daily flow of 276 million gallons.

Unlike the prairies, which were forced to relinquish their complex identities to agriculture, the Ozarks retain a sense of their ancient selves. Despite 150 years of intensive logging, mining, overgrazing, fire suppression, and subsistence farming on marginal land, the Ozarks today remain remote, rugged, and mysterious, a rocky island rising above the vast ocean of agriculture, trade, and commerce that surrounds them.

The grasslands that once covered a quarter of Missouri—some 11.6 million acres—were long ago undone by agriculture. Now, amid a latticework of soybeans, corn, and cotton, fewer than 18,000 acres of native prairie remain in the public domain, and the fragmented 40,000 acres in private ownership continue to deteriorate.

Today the last, best prairies in Missouri are found on the Osage Plain, which stretches south of the Missouri River on the northwestern shoulder of the Ozarks. Although it may look uniform to a casual observer, the

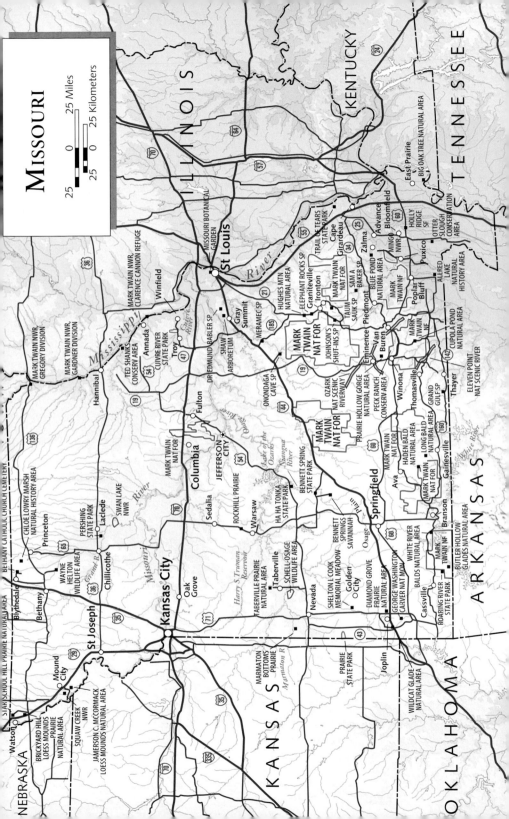

ABOVE: *The secretive Henslow's sparrow frequents wet meadows and fallow fields.* LEFT: *A small spotted fawn is well camouflaged in a meadow of pale purple coneflower.*

Osage Plain possesses a wealth of substrates, different soils that produce a rich biodiversity in its grasslands. The ancient tropical seas that once washed this region left deposits of limestone, sandstone, chert, and dolomite underlying the prairie. The rocky character of these prairie remnants spared them from the plow.

Tufted with little bluestem, these prairies have a distinctive, scruffy appearance. On the upland prairies, eastern meadowlarks, dickcissels, and grasshopper sparrows sing their hearts out in spring and summer. The scissor-tailed flycatcher, one of the most beautiful birds in North America but uncommon in Missouri, can sometimes be spotted on the Osage Plain as well. In swales and floodplains, luxuriant stands of prairie cordgrass, sedges, and cattails provide cover for American bitterns, sora rails, sedge wrens, and western chorus frogs.

Cradled in the arm of the Missouri River, Missouri's other great prairie-scape once covered the northern third of the state atop a subtle dome of deep, fertile soil carried into place by glacial action over a period of two or three million years. In less than a century, European settlement dismantled these grasslands. Today, tiny patches of prairie survive mainly on the precipitous slopes of the loess hills along the Missouri River, in cemeteries, and in a few low spots along the Grand River and its tributaries.

Often called the Bootheel because of its shape, Missouri's southeastern corner is a flat, low-lying plain that was once an inlet of the Gulf of

216

ABOVE: *The eastern blue-bird, Missouri's state bird, nests in the Ozarks.*
LEFT: *The hawthorn, the state flower, announces spring in the woodlands.*

Mexico. As the Gulf waters retreated and the nearby Ozarks uplifted, the Mississippi and Ohio rivers began etching serpentine routes through the mud, sand, and gravel. After 60 million years, what the rivers had not carried away formed ridges known as lost hills. The vast majority of the Bootheel is a murky flood-prone plain that once supported grand expanses of hardwood forest. The trees were cut long ago, a network of drainage canals siphoned off the water, and an orderly patchwork of cotton and soybean fields replaced the forest primeval. Vestiges of the swamp forests are still scattered across the region, their sloughs, oxbows, and sinkhole ponds best explored in a canoe or other small watercraft.

The Bootheel is most famous for a cluster of earthquakes, still unsurpassed on the continent, that jarred the United States and parts of Canada from December 1811 to February 1812. Among thousands that were felt, three of the earthquakes exceeded a magnitude of 8 on the Richter scale. The earthquakes were named for New Madrid, a tiny village on the west bank of the Mississippi River near the epicenter. In *The New Madrid Earthquakes,* James Lal Penick, Jr., recounts the eyewitness story of John Bradbury, a Scottish naturalist studying North American plant life. At 2 A.M. on December 16, 1811, "a most tremendous noise" awoke Bradbury, who was asleep aboard a boat on the Mississippi. "The screaming of the geese, and other wild-fowl, produced an idea that all nature was in a state of dissolution," he later wrote. By daybreak, Bradbury had recorded

217

27 aftershocks. The earthquakes caused widespread flooding and remade great swaths of the Mississippi Valley.

Every landmass is the product of its rivers, and Missouri has been sculpted by some particularly big ones. The longest river in the United States, the 2,465-mile Missouri, forms the borders of Nebraska and northwest Missouri before heading due east at Kansas City for its confluence with the Mississippi at Saint Louis. Two other impressive tributaries—the Illinois and Ohio—flow into the Mississippi on the state's eastern border.

As befits a state at the confluence of mighty waterways, Missouri is famous for its river literature. Travelers in search of natural Missouri will certainly benefit from reading two masterpieces, *The Journals of Lewis and Clark* (the first continental expedition departed up the Missouri River from Saint Charles, now a suburb of Saint Louis, on May 21, 1804) and Mark Twain's 1883 *Life on the Mississippi*. Thomas Hart Benton draws another fine portrait of place in *An Artist in America*. Benton was born in 1889 in Neosho, where the western Ozarks blend into the Osage Plain, into a family of ardent politicians and raconteurs. Now national treasures, his paintings of the Heartland document in part the pioneers' vigorous reworking of the land at the turn of the century. (Anyone in the vicinity of Jefferson City should study the Benton mural in the State Capitol for proof of this transformation.) Benton once described the powerful impact of the landscapes he painted. "For me the Great Plains have a releasing effect," he wrote. "They make me want to run and shout at the top of my voice. I like their endlessness. I like the way they make human beings appear as the little bugs they really are."

This chapter's journey begins south of Saint Louis and moves west through the splendors of the Ozark Mountains. After visiting southwestern Missouri and the Osage Plain, it travels north to the loess hills of the Missouri River and turns east across northern Missouri. Finally, the itinerary heads south through Saint Louis to conclude in the state's southeastern corner, an area called the Bootheel.

THE NORTHERN OZARKS

The Missouri Ozarks have attained a beauty that comes only with age. Time, gravity, water, and intermittent uplift have had their way with the

---

RIGHT: *One of the best-known American regional painters, Thomas Hart Benton (1889–1975) celebrated rural life and landscape in his native Missouri. July Hay (1943) is typical of his rich representational style.*

219

land, and the results are diverse and splendid. The wild-and-woolly look of the land can be deceiving, however. Like the prairies, the Ozarks have a troubled history of resource exploitation. The advent of timber-hauling railroads in the Ozarks in the late 1850s launched a logging bonanza that lasted until the early twentieth century, when the last marketable trees were removed. The timber companies left behind a depleted landscape and a jobless populace, some of whom then attempted to eke out livelihoods as farmers. When many went bankrupt, their tax-delinquent lands were purchased to form a cluster of state and federal forests, wildlife areas, and scenic river corridors.

Interwoven throughout the Ozark forests were expansive oak barrens and savannas teeming with grasses and wildflowers. For a few decades this luxuriant growth provided ready forage for livestock. Continuous grazing, combined with the fire-suppression policies of the Smokey the Bear forest-management era, doomed the barrens and savannas, and most have now been swallowed up by forest. In many ways, the tourism and passive recreation that support the Ozark economy today are the most appropriate economic trends this rugged but fragile landscape has ever entertained. Visitors could spend happy lifetimes seeking out and rediscovering the many nooks and crannies on the more than two million acres of public land in the Ozarks. Some of these places are barely removed from the exhaust fumes of Interstate 44; others can be reached only by canoeing, then hiking over rugged terrain.

An appropriate launching place is atop Taum Sauk Mountain, which at 1,772 feet is the highest elevation in Missouri and like much of the **Saint François Mountains** is composed of igneous rocks more than a billion years old. West off Route 21 about three miles south of Ironton, 6,888-acre **Taum Sauk Mountain State Park**❖ provides a picnic area near the summit. A three-mile-long trail southwest of Taum Sauk's crest leads to **Mina Sauk Falls,** a 132-foot plunge that is the highest waterfall in the state. Be sure to visit during a wet spell because the falls do not flow in dry periods.

In his delightful book *Geologic Wonders and Curiosities of Missouri,* Thomas Beveridge devotes an entire chapter to shut-ins. The Missouri Ozarks are famous for these gorgeous, tortuous gorges that water has cut through igneous rock. The most accessible, and among the most beautiful, are the gorges in the 8,679-acre **Johnson's Shut-Ins State Park**❖ (southwest of Taum Sauk on Route N, 12.5 miles south of its intersection with Route 21). Here the East Fork of the Black River has chiseled a path through a rainbow of pink, purple, blue, gray, and brown rock. The erosive action of swirling water and scouring sand and gravel has formed a dramatic system of chutes, cascades, plunge pools, and potholes. A 2.5-mile trail, with scenic overlooks, passes the main shut-in. Because the shut-ins attract many bathers on summer weekends, lines can be long; the park also regulates the number of visitors to avoid overburdening the landscape.

Some 5,000 acres within Johnson's Shut-Ins State Park have been designated the **Goggins Mountain Wild Area,** which features a range of igneous knobs on the extreme western flank of the Saint François Mountains. This remote and gorgeous expanse of woodlands, glades, savannas, and rock barrens provides a superb glimpse of presettlement Ozarkian landscape. The wilderness quotient of Goggins Mountain is enhanced by its next-door neighbor, the 9,000-acre **Bell Mountain Wilderness❖** in **Mark Twain National Forest❖.**

The trails winding through the Missouri Ozarks are a joy to visitors. In this area, the **Taum Sauk Trail,** a 30-mile hiking path, stretches from Claybaugh Creek Trailhead on Route 21 over the top of Taum Sauk Mountain to Johnson's Shut-Ins State Park and the Goggins and Bell mountains. The Taum Sauk Trail is a section of the 300-mile **Ozark Trail❖,** which will eventually connect Saint Louis with the Ozarks Highland Trail in Arkansas.

Noted on topographic maps as Lower Rock Creek, **Dark Hollow,** in the Fredericktown Unit of the Poposi-Fredericktown Ranger District of the **Mark Twain National Forest,** has been nicknamed "Cathedral Canyon" by admiring hikers. The hollow presents an opportunity to walk through the sheer-walled chasm cut into the Saint François Mountains along Lower Rock Creek. With a gradient of 100 feet per mile, the stream tumbles and roars through cathedral-like bluffs and rock terraces. The five-mile round-trip hike is strenuous and unmarked, requiring both detailed maps and expert map-reading skills. As Thomas Beveridge notes in *Geologic Wonders and Curiosities of Missouri,* "No one should venture into the canyon without a topographic map, because frequent stopping to study the map gives much better insights into the topography details, and allows one to rest while appearing very scholarly."

Igneous magma, the chief ingredient of the Saint François Mountains, assumes yet another form at **Elephant Rocks State Park❖,** just north of the

---

OVERLEAF: *In Johnson's Shut-Ins State Park, the East Fork of the Black River cuts a path through rhyolite porphyry and other igneous rocks. This resistant volcanic material was deposited two billion years ago.*

town of Graniteville. Here a herd of vaguely pachyderm-shaped boulders, the result of 1.2 billion years of weathering, rise from a hillside of granite. A one-mile trail, with signs in Braille, meanders among the huge rocks.

About ten miles northeast of Elephant Rocks on the slopes of Hughes Mountain, little bluestem, prickly pear cactus, and other semi-arid plants grow amid a bizarre rock garden called the **Devil's Honeycomb** (in the 430-acre **Hughes Mountain Natural Area❖,** which is about three miles southwest of Irondale). Encrusted with lichens, salmon-pink igneous rock has split into polygonal columns about four feet in length and ten inches in diameter. A number of resident invertebrates, such as the lichen grasshopper, are camouflaged to match the mottled pastels of their surroundings. Along the fringes of these rocky glades are stunted woodlands of oak, hickory, and redcedar.

Between Saint Louis and Springfield, I-44 provides swift entry into classic Ozark landscapes. Take Exit 226 at Oak Grove and head south on Route 185 to the 6,734-acre **Meramec State Park❖,** named for the lovely river that slices through several hundred of feet of dolomite here and contains the richest assortment of aquatic species in the state. The park encompasses shady old-growth forests, high bluffs, hollows, and more than 30 caves, some of which harbor endangered gray and Indiana bats. A 12-mile network of scenic trails traverses the park, including the 461-acre **Meramec Upland Forest Natural Area,** home to a mature forest of oaks, hickories, basswood, and walnut above a rich understory of flowering dogwood, serviceberry, and papaw. Scattered through the woods, rock outcrops support sunny glades where puccoon, Indian paintbrush, and other prairie wildflowers

ABOVE: *With its rosy cravat and bright song, the male rose-breasted grosbeak enlivens spring woodlands.*

LEFT: *Ghostly by moonlight, the rounded boulders at Elephant Rocks State Park are pink prisms of granite sculpted by erosion.*

BELOW: *The male prothonotary warbler resembles a glint of sunlight in Missouri's shadowy forests as he flits near streams, ponds, and swamplands.*

225

ABOVE: *The wily red fox is the essence of stealth. This secretive opportunist eats anything it can catch, from insects to rabbits.*

RIGHT: *Onondaga Cave offers a window on the karst landscape, where limestone deposits are etched with caverns and sinkholes.*

BELOW: *A pair of young raccoon huddle together along a tree limb, probably chased up out of harm's way by their protective mother.*

bloom. Excellent natural history exhibits at the visitor center include an aquarium devoted to the Meramec River's special inhabitants.

Upstream on the Meramec, **Onondaga Cave State Park❖** borders Route H just south of I-44's Exit 214. First opened for tours in 1897, the cave became popular as a stop for travelers visiting the 1904 Saint Louis World's Fair. Onondaga Cave is noted for its fine assortment of stalagmites, stalactites, flowstones, and other subterranean statuary formed by the slow deposition of calcium carbonate. Regular tours are conducted from March through October. About seven miles downriver from the cave, a 300-acre section of the park contains **Vilander Bluff Natural Area,** a spectacular dolomite cliff overlooking the Meramec River.

THE OZARKS' SOUTHERN TIER: RIVERS, CAVES, AND FOREST

About 75 miles southeast of Onondaga Cave, the 5,168-acre **Sam A. Baker State Park❖** (4 miles north of Route 34 about 12 miles northeast of Piedmont) straddles Mudlick Mountain, another big igneous knob in the Saint François Mountains. Within the park, the 1,370-acre **Mudlick Mountain Natural Area** preserves one of the finest remaining old-growth forests in the Ozarks. Shading a forest floor carpeted with jagged igneous rocks and an understory bright with flowering dogwood, white and black oaks spread across the eastern slope of the mountain. Big Creek cleaves the northern slope to form one of Missouri's deepest gorges, complete with shut-ins, glades, talus slopes, and sheer bluffs.

In 1933 the federal government began buying logged-over, farmed-out properties in the Ozarks, and today these lands form the 1.5-million-acre **Mark Twain National Forest❖.** Eight units of the forest are scattered across the southern tier of Missouri south of I-44, and one unit occupies the eastern outskirts of Columbia. To people in pursuit of natural landscapes, Mark Twain National Forest presents a dithering array of possibilities, including the 44-mile-long section of the **Eleven Point National Scenic River;** seven wilderness areas, together totaling more than 63,000 acres; 18 natural areas totaling 5,824 acres; and several of the largest springs in Missouri. Large portions of the **Ozark Trail❖** traverse national forest land as well. (District offices can provide maps, brochures, and information; Ava and Fulton offer the largest selection of literature.)

Greer Springs❖, 19 miles south of Winona on Route 19, ranks among the most conspicuously beautiful places in Missouri. A one-mile trail descends by switchbacks through a forest of oak, pine, and dogwood, where in late spring and early summer wood thrushes sing their slow, sad songs, and Carolina wrens trill their frenzied, cheery notes. As the steep trail drops into the narrow gorge, the sound of roaring water predominates, although one bird, the Louisiana waterthrush, has evolved the vocal capacity to be heard above the din. Listen in May and June for its piercing, fifelike song. The second-largest spring in Missouri with an average daily output of 214 million gallons, Greer Springs feeds into the Eleven Point

228

LEFT: *Cupola Pond is a limestone sinkhole tucked away in the Mark Twain National Forest. Splashed with sun, the water-filled basin supports towering tupelos; this natural area is one of only two places in the Ozarks where this swamp tree grows.*

RIGHT: *Surrounded by white oaks, a creamy flowering dogwood brightens a woodland in the 16,500-acre Irish Wilderness. The gossamer blossoms on Missouri's state tree are a sign of spring's arrival.*

River, augmenting its flow by roughly 50 percent.

About 15 miles east of Greer Springs via spectacular back roads is the 160-acre **Cupola Pond Natural Area**❖ (take Forest Road 4823, which is off Route J about 8 miles north of Route 160). Cupola Pond is a sinkhole formed by the collapse of a limestone cave, and the shallow bowl of land contains an unexpected swatch of swamp. To walk through an upland forest of oaks and hickories and suddenly behold the bulbous buttresses of water tupelo, a tree native to southern lowlands, rising from the still waters of Cupola Pond is astonishing indeed. In spring, the swamp resounds with the choruses of spring peepers. Cupola Pond is one of 18 designated natural areas—which also include fens, glades, shut-ins, headwater streams, and cliffs—scattered through Mark Twain National Forest. Finding these out-of-the-way places requires both an above-average interest in the oddities of karst topography and maps of the national forest.

Squiggling around the small towns of Van Buren and Eminence, the **Ozark National Scenic Riverways**❖ encompass 134 river miles of the **Current** and its tributary, the **Jacks Fork.** Administered by the National Park Service, this 126-square-mile mosaic of public lands and waterways affords yet another way to explore the landscapes of the Ozarks. Headquarters in Van Buren offers a wide selection of literature on Ozarkian geology, flora, and fauna. About 30 miles south is the **Eleven Point National Scenic River**❖, which traverses a portion of Mark Twain National

229

LEFT: *A grove of box elder flanks a lush meadow of spotted Saint-John's-wort on the Ozark National Scenic Riverways.*

RIGHT: *Now reappearing in its former range, the once rare wild turkey forages in open woodlands and at forest edges.*

Forest between Thomasville and Route 142 and is managed by the U.S. Forest Service district office in Winona.

Part of a system of streams and rivers pouring off the southeastern rim of the Ozark Plateau, the Jacks Fork, Current, and Eleven Point ultimately join the White River in Arkansas. Each river presents its own particular challenges (the Eleven Point demands skilled canoeists), and each leads to remote places. For example, **Jam Up Cave Natural Area❖**, on the Jacks Fork River between Blue Spring and Rymer Spring, is a pile of collapsed rock forming a natural architecture of cliffs, caves, sinkholes, and waterfalls. Jam Up Cave is virtually unreachable except by river, and even then the trek is demanding.

Some four miles southeast of Van Buren just off Route 103 lies one of the state's most thrilling and accessible sites, **Big Spring❖**, the largest spring in Missouri and the largest single-outlet spring in the United States. Issuing from a ragged maw in the face of a dolomite cliff, Big Spring feeds a daily average of 276 million gallons of water into the nearby Current River. Maximum flows, during times of flood, are estimated to be *840 million gallons a day.* So commanding is this performance that visitors can ignore the surrounding hypermanicured grounds of the **Big Spring Historic District,** which includes a lodge and cabins built in the 1930s by the Civilian Conservation Corps.

Upriver from Big Spring, numerous other springs occupy wilder settings, some accessible only by canoe. One of these, **Blue Spring,** situated in a scenic 300-foot-deep hollow, is the sixth-largest spring in Missouri. Secluded in a lovely canyon, **Pulltite Spring,** with rather modest average discharges of 20 million gallons a day, is considered by many observers the most beautiful spring on the Current River. Also on the Current, just below its confluence with the Jacks Fork, the 74-acre **Prairie Hollow Gorge Natural Area❖** presents a diverse and precipitous landscape of sunny glades, shady

ABOVE: *Prairie Hollow Gorge Natural Area is a secret place of sun-baked glades, shadowy woods, crystal streams, rugged precipices, and rocky defiles. Tricky to find, it amply rewards those who make the effort.*

upland forest, sheer cliffs, and shut-ins. The trailhead at the top of the gorge is east of Route V, .7 miles south of Two Rivers Campground.

The forested hills and hollows within the 23,000-acre **Peck Ranch Conservation Area❖,** north of Route 60 between Winona and Van Buren, have withstood a series of boom-and-bust episodes, including efforts to establish a low-grade iron ore mill fueled by cordwood from the forest and a short-lived post-Prohibition enterprise to supply staves for white-oak barrels. In 1945, the state purchased Peck Ranch to manage it for wild turkeys; today many miles of primitive roads weave through the area, and a portion of the Ozark Trail crosses it. Five state natural areas within Peck Ranch protect such special landscapes as the aquatic communities along **Rogers Creek,** one of the most pristine spring-fed streams in the Ozarks, and the forests atop **Stegal Mountain,** the highest point in Peck Ranch.

The 322-acre **Grand Gulf State Park❖,** six miles west of Thayer near the Arkansas line, contains the pièce de résistance of karst topography. In prehistoric times a cave system here collapsed and created a canyon three-quarters of a mile long with 120-foot walls; a surviving portion of the cave roof now forms a 200-foot-long natural bridge across the chasm. Connected by openings to Mammoth Spring, nine miles to the south in Arkansas, Grand Gulf undergoes an incredible transformation during

ABOVE: *One of Missouri's most dramatic illustrations of karst, Grand Gorge is actually a collapsed cave. Because of poor drainage, high water can quickly transform the picturesque canyon into a deep lake.*

heavy rains: Filling with water, sometimes 100 feet or more, the dramatic chasm becomes a placid lake. This metamorphosis occurs because the single small cave that drains 27 square miles above Grand Gulf cannot move the great volume of water fast enough.

THE WESTERN EDGE OF THE OZARKS: SPRINGS, GLADES, AND KNOBS

The northwest shoulder of the Ozarks, south of Jefferson City and Sedalia, is dominated by Lake of the Ozarks and Harry S. Truman Reservoir, two huge serpentine bodies of water formed by damming the Osage River and its tributaries. A spectacular microcosm of the Ozarks, the 2,993-acre **Ha Ha Tonka State Park❖,** on an arm of Lake of the Ozarks formed by the Niangua River, contains Missouri's greatest concentration of karst features. A grand staircase boardwalk winds through the collapsed cave system, which contains a large spring, a natural bridge, and sinkholes. In addition, the 1,000-acre **Ha Ha Tonka Savanna Natural Area** is the state's best ex-

OVERLEAF: *Autumn-tinged trees—maples, hickories, oaks—complement the blue waters of Ha Ha Tonka Spring. Here the collapse of a cavern created one of Missouri's best and most accessible karst regions.*

ABOVE: *In autumn the starkly beautiful White River Balds provide sweeping vistas of the surrounding Ozark plateau. The thin-soiled, rocky balds are barren hilltops with grassy glades along their slopes.*

ample of the once vast mosaic of parklike oak savannas that stretched south across the plains from Minnesota to Texas.

South or upstream from Ha Ha Tonka on the winding Niangua River off Route 64, the 3,000-acre **Bennett Spring State Park❖** embraces Missouri's fourth-largest spring. Unlike such loud, explosive springs as Big and Greer, Bennett Spring, stocked daily with rainbow trout, quietly wells up from fissures to form a still pool. Five miles south of the park on Route OO is the 160-acre **Bennett Spring Savanna,** which is small in size but rich in grasses and wildflowers.

Extreme southwestern Missouri is noted for its glades. These semiarid, thin-soiled areas, also called balds, were once frequented by "baldknobbers," vigilantes who roamed southwest Missouri after the Civil War. Because the view was long and bonfires ominously prominent, glades provided a handy spot to convene meetings. Although glades and balds are synonymous in the vernacular, they are ecologically distinct: A bald is a glade where the hilltop is barren. Glades are variations on prairie habitat. A typical grassland mix of little bluestem, Indian grass, side-oats grama, and

ABOVE RIGHT: *A member of the whiptail family, the six-lined racerunner hunts insects and basks on Missouri's sun-drenched balds on warm mornings; at night it buries itself in the sandy soils to avoid the cold.*

big bluestem generally dominates, along with many plants and animals that live in semiarid habitats. Throughout the summer, characteristic wildflowers include yellow coneflowers, blazing stars, Missouri primroses, silky asters, slender heliotrope, and fringed poppy mallow.

The glades owe their sparse, scruffy appearance to both periodic fire, suppressed for a century but now reintroduced in controlled circumstances, and to patches of exposed bedrock, which in this part of Missouri is most often dolomite. These hot rock surfaces are favored basking spots for a number of herps, including eastern collared lizards, fence lizards, pygmy rattlesnakes, six-lined racerunners, and ground snakes.

The byways of southwest Missouri offer memorable adventures for glade aficionados. Notable examples include **Wildcat Glade Natural Area❖,** in **Wildcat Park,** on the southwest edge of Joplin; **White River Balds Natural Area❖,** in the **Ruth and Paul Henning State Forest,** four miles northwest of Branson on Route 76; **Haden Bald Natural Area❖,** in the **Mark Twain National Forest,** about ten miles south of Ava; **Long Bald Natural Area❖,** in the **Caney Mountain Wildlife Area,** about six

ABOVE: *A regal fritillary (left) perches on a pale purple coneflower, and a buckeye (top right) feeds on goldenrod. Birds rarely prey on the spicebush swallowtail (bottom right) because of its unpleasant taste.*

miles north of Gainesville; and **Butler Hollow Glades Natural Area❖**, near the Sugar Camp Lookout Tower in the **Mark Twain National Forest,** about ten miles south of Cassville.

On the western edge of Mark Twain National Forest about six miles south of Cassville, the 3,354-acre **Roaring River State Park❖** flanks the gorges of the Roaring River, a tributary of the White River. Along this stretch of the Missouri-Arkansas border, much of the White River basin has been impounded to form a series of reservoirs. Most of the ten miles of trails in the park lead to **Roaring River Spring** (which pumps out 20 million gallons daily), shady glens (such as **Ketchem Hollow**), rock shelters (such as **Devil's Kitchen**), and the 120-acre **Roaring River Cove Hardwood Natural Area,** an old-growth oak-hickory forest clutching the steep, rocky ridges. The park also contains an excellent glade, easily accessible from the road. Black bears are known to roam the wildest reaches of these hills.

In southwestern Missouri, around Joplin and Springfield, the Ozarks converge with a high plateau, and the shadowy niches and crevices so typical of karst begin to give way to the big skies of the Osage Plain. A prelude of prairies to come, **Diamond Grove Prairie Natural Area❖**, four miles west of the town of Diamond off Route V, encompasses a 611-acre remnant of upland tallgrass that spreads across the flat to rolling landscape. In spring, greater prairie chickens congregate here amid superb wildflower displays. About three miles southeast off Route V, at the **George Washington Carver National Monument✣**, a streamside woodland and restored prairie approximate the landscape where Carver was born into slavery in the 1860s.

OUT ON THE OSAGE

Prairie devotees could make a career of visiting the prairie patches of the Osage. On lateral side trips from Route 71 between Joplin and Nevada, inveterate grasslanders can find at least 30 prairies. Too numerous to include here, all are listed in *Public Prairies of Missouri,* a booklet available from the Missouri Department of Conservation in Jefferson City. Midsummer mowing, a management tool at many smaller prairie sites, benefits the prairie by mimicking fire in places where burning is inadvisable, providing income when the grass is sold as forage, and supplying grass and wildflower seeds for prairie restoration projects. For visitors, however, finding what looks like a hayed pasture instead of head-high native grasses can be disappointing. Because mowing schedules are often spur-of-the-moment decisions based on weather and equipment availability, prairie enthusiasts should simply anticipate encountering a few shorn grasslands in the course of a lifetime.

West of Route 43 about 30 miles north of Joplin, 3,600-acre **Prairie State Park✣** preserves a premier natural landscape, a last hurrah of tallgrass that is unsurpassed—at least for these times—in Missouri and much of the Heartland. On any of the three trails that loop through the park, a latter-day hiker can imagine the bygone sea of grass that once covered 15 million acres of Missouri. A succession of prairie wildflowers blooms from spring through late summer, and in autumn the stands of grasses turn spectacular shades of gold. Bison and elk roam the park, and people must check the whereabouts of the bison herd at the visitor center before setting off on a walk.

Three portions of the park are designated high-quality prairie ecosystems—320-acre **Regal Prairie,** 160-acre **Tzi-Sho Prairie,** and 160-acre **Hunkah Prairie.** Regal is named for the quintessential butterfly of prairies, the regal fritillary, which in midsummer wafts among butterfly milkweed, common milkweed, and pale purple coneflower. Tzi-Sho and Hunkah are named, respectively, for the Sky People and the Earth People, two divisions of the Osage. **East Drywood Creek Natural Area** encompasses the headwaters of a pristine prairie stream.

Two miles northwest of Golden City on Route U, the 280-acre **Shel-**

ton L. Cook Memorial Meadow❖ protects a prairie-woodland landscape that is a classic, and now rare, example of the convergence of the western Ozarks and Osage Plain. From the preserve sign on the road that skirts the western edge of the prairie, gorgeous long vistas extend across the rolling hills. Cook Meadow harbors a particularly rich diversity of plants. More than 300 species have been identified on the site, including a rare sedge named Harvey's beak rush and a prairie grass called nutrush. Although uncommon throughout their wide range, upland sandpipers, among the most elegant birds of the Great Plains, breed on Osage prairies such as Cook Meadow. Market hunting in the late nineteenth century and conversion of grasslands to row crops throughout the twentieth have kept upland sandpiper numbers precariously low.

ABOVE: *The elegiac upland sandpiper, once a summer staple of the Missouri prairie, now breeds only rarely on scattered remnants of the Osage grasslands.*

The largest remnant of wet prairie in southern Missouri, **Marmaton Bottoms Prairie❖,** three miles northwest of Nevada on Route W, lies in the floodplain of the Marmaton River. About a third of the preserve's 584 acres are dominated by cordgrass, the primary grass of wet prairies. Cordgrass is often called ripgut because its razor-sharp edges cut the bellies of horses and cattle. The prairie is intermixed with a bottomland forest of pin oak, red ash, and pecan.

LEFT: *Bands of vermilion Indian paintbrush and yellow lousewort sweep across Taberville Prairie, a broad expanse of tallgrass.*

BELOW: *The marsh-loving pied-billed grebe is at home on the Osage prairies. When startled, it sinks underwater, resurfacing only in the safety of the reeds.*

Spread across rolling uplands notched with sandstone outcrops, the 1,680-acre **Taberville Prairie Natural Area❖,** on Route H about three miles north of the town of Taberville, shelters another of Missouri's last large expanses of tallgrass and is a highlight of the Osage Plain. The prairie, noted for the variety of its wildflowers, also supports a population of greater prairie chickens.

Just a few miles southwest of Taberville Prairie on Route Y is the 8,633-acre **Schell-Osage Wildlife Area❖,** one of Missouri's birding hot spots. During

241

LEFT: *A common, if seldom seen, Missouri summer resident, the green heron skulks amid camouflaging vegetation near wetlands.* RIGHT: *Supporting cottonwoods, floating American lotus, and water plantain, the Squaw Creek wildlife refuge is cacophonous in fall when snow and Canada geese pass through.*

spring and fall migration, the wetland complex, created by the impoundment the Osage River, offers excellent viewing of geese, ducks, white pelicans, herons, and other shorebirds.

To the northeast, **Rockhill Prairie❖** is five miles north of Warsaw on the east side of Route 65 south of Route BB. Situated on a small rise, the 68-acre preserve is a prairie on dry cherty soil that supports many showy wildflowers, including an impressive population of blazing star, with its purple wandlike flower stalks that typically bloom in mid-June to mid-July.

NORTHWEST MISSOURI: LOESS HILLS AND PRAIRIE REMNANTS

The extreme northwestern wedge of Missouri above Kansas City and Saint Joseph contains two loess hill prairies, the 125-acre **Brickyard Hill Loess Mounds Prairie Natural Area❖** (just east of I-29's Exit 116 at Watson), and the 70-acre **Star School Hill Prairie Natural Area❖** (another six miles north on Route 275, which more or less parallels I-29 on the east). The natural areas share the advantage of easy access from the interstate and the curse of the pervasive murmur of highway traffic. As part of the spine of windblown deposits called loess that border the river from Sioux City, Iowa, to Mound City, Missouri, they provide a glimpse of a ragged, rugged landscape, as well as winsome vistas of the Missouri River valley.

A bit farther south, 40 miles north of Saint Joseph just west of I-29, **Squaw Creek National Wildlife Refuge❖** encompasses a 7,178-acre expanse of wetlands in the broad palm of the Missouri Valley. In the background, a gathering of loess hills resembles a congregation of recumbent brontosauruses. In fall these marshes are jam-packed with snow geese, Canada geese, and various species of ducks migrating south down the Missouri Valley. Lurking majestically in the leafless trees and on mudflats

and muskrat mounds are bald eagles, which accompany large waterfowl assemblages to feed on the dead and dying. In late November, when numbers peak, visitations of 300,000 snow geese and 200 to 300 bald eagles are not unusual. On the road that circles the refuge, traffic can be bumper-to-bumper on the last two weekends in November. Walking is permitted (and preferable at high-traffic times) along the roadway and on the several dikes that crisscross the marsh.

On the loess hills at the southern end of Squaw Creek, the **Jamerson C. McCormack Loess Mounds Natural Area**❖ (about five miles south of Mound City off Route 159) encloses a 67-acre slice of prairie and forest. When waterfowl are pouring into the marshes, these sensuous hills glow in a brilliant patchwork of gold, copper, and burgundy.

The grasslands that once swept across the rolling glacial plain of northern Missouri are all but gone. Near the Iowa border, three tiny fragments survive on a maze of gravel roads within a rectangle formed by the border, I-35, and Routes 136 and 65. A speck of tallgrass prairie, no more than a couple of acres, frames weathered tombstones in the **Bethany Catholic Church Cemetery.** This poignant setting, quiet and deeply rural, lies far off the beaten path just south of the Iowa border. (From Blythedale, just east of I-35, follow Route T 4 miles north, Route UU about 4 miles east, then Route O 1.5 miles north. Turn east on the gravel road that intersects Route O; Bethany Cemetery is tucked into the northeast corner of the intersection.) The best times to visit are late August and September, when in good years the big bluestem reaches heights of six to eight feet.

About 20 miles south, the **Helton Prairie Natural Area** comprises a 30-acre parcel of exquisite native grasses and wildflowers in the northwest corner of the 2,560-acre **Wayne Helton Wildlife Area**❖. (Follow Route 136 about nine miles east of the town of Bethany and Route CC three miles south. Take a gravel road west around the northern perimeter of the wildlife area for 1.75 miles; when the road turns south, the prairie is to the southeast. A map of the wildlife area available from the Missouri Department of Conservation in Jefferson City will expedite the search.) After going to the trouble of finding this or any other prairie, be sure to walk on it. Helton is rich and woolly, full of many different flowering prairie plants, including Indian plantain, leadplant, yellow coneflower, tall coreopsis, black-eyed Susan, compass plant, and blazing star.

To the northeast about another 20 miles on Route 136, near the town of Princeton, the 115-acre **Chloe Lowry Marsh Natural Area**❖ lies in the floodplain of the Grand River. (Take Route FF north one mile, then, following the signs, a gravel road that veers northwest off FF for another two miles.) Wetlands such as Lowry Marsh once laced low spots of the Great Plains—the river and stream valleys, swales, and potholes. Most have been drained—in Missouri, more than 87 percent. Today Lowry is one of the best remaining freshwater marshes in the state.

Nature's marshes are quite different in aspect from the more common wetlands, where water levels are manipulated seasonally to accommodate migratory waterfowl. By late summer, a natural marsh, thick with cattails and bulrushes, has turned a distinctive greenish-black, like a big black eye on the landscape. At Lowry Marsh, zones of vegetation adapt to fluctuations in the water level. The soggy middle of bur reed, bulrush, and cattail shifts to a perimeter of wet prairie dominated by big bluestem and prairie cord-grass. From June through September, a succession of wildflowers blossoms. Among the rare or endangered plants and animals appearing at Lowry Marsh are the northern leopard frog and tufted loosestrife. Bobolinks and sedge wrens, two birds wedded to wet prairie, are still found here. An abandoned railroad bed provides a dryland path across the marsh, but rubber boots are recommended for those who want to explore further.

Pershing State Park❖—in north-central Missouri, about 18 miles east of Chillicothe and just south of Route 36—is named for General John J. Pershing, commander of American troops in Europe during World War I, who was born in nearby Laclede in 1860. In the heart of the park, the 330-acre **Locust Creek Natural Area** is an exceptional outdoor textbook, a shrine to the much-altered riverine landscapes of northern Missouri. Starting on a bridge across Locust Creek, a 1.5-mile boardwalk winds through a shadowy floodplain forest of old-growth hickory, cottonwood, and various oaks, then across a sun-drenched slough, wet prairie, and savanna. The satiny, chocolate-pudding-colored soils of the forest indicate that the ground is regularly awash, making this area one of the rare places where visitors can still see how a river consorts with its floodplain. In spring and summer, the boardwalk is a fine perch for birding; the prothonotary warbler, classic bird of bottomland forests, nests along Locust Creek. Mosquitoes are prevalent throughout the summer.

Just south of Pershing State Park and about 30 miles southeast of Chillicothe, levee roads at the 10,795-acre **Swan Lake National Wildlife Refuge**❖ provide birding vantages for migratory ducks and geese (peaks are in March and November), shorebirds (late April and May), and white pelicans (September and October). The refuge is the primary wintering area for the eastern prairie population of Canada geese.

LEFT: *Near Saint Louis, winged pig-weed grows along a sandbar on Pelican Island, one of the last wild islands in the Missouri River.*

RIGHT: *A consummate swimmer, the muskrat can remain submerged for long periods of time and travels great distances underwater.*

NORTHEAST MISSOURI: SAINT LOUIS AND THE MISSISSIPPI

On Shaw Boulevard in the heart of Saint Louis, the **Missouri Botanical Garden❖** is the legacy of merchant-capitalist Henry Shaw, who came to Saint Louis from England in 1819 and made a fortune dealing in real estate and importing cutlery, hardware, and dry goods. At the age of 40, he turned his business over to his sister and spent the rest of his life designing and building one of the world's finest botanical gardens. Nature seekers can justify a visit to this man-made garden on a number of grounds. Its bookstore is a fabulous marketplace for natural history books on many subjects, including many specific to Missouri. Its exhibits reflect the ethos of an institution that for decades has been at the forefront of research and conservation in tropical ecosystems, especially the besieged forests of Latin America. And finally, the grounds are full of gorgeous specimen trees, which from late April through the first ten days of May form an urban route for migrating warblers and other songbirds.

North of the Saint Louis suburb of Florissant, where the Missouri River bends around the metropolis, is the 2,279-acre **Pelican Island Natural Area.** With its sloughs, mudflats, bottomland forest, and swath of prairie, it is right out of Lewis and Clark—a classic, and now rare, big island in the Big Muddy. It can be seen from the mainland at Sioux Passage County Park (with entrances on Old Jamestown and Kings Drive). The island is accessible by boat or on foot when the river is low.

About 30 miles west, just south of I-44 near the town of Gray Summit, an outlier of the Missouri Botanical Garden, the 2,400-acre **Shaw Arboretum❖,** is designed to show the presettlement landscapes of east-central Missouri in a more natural setting. Restoration efforts here are bringing back examples of dolomite limestone glades, tallgrass prairie, marsh, swamp, oak savanna, and oak-hickory woodland.

An exceptionally fine old-growth upland forest of white oak and sugar maple thrives at **Dr. Edmund A. Babler State Park❖,** about 20 miles west of Saint Louis on Route 109. The 2,400-acre park lies along the narrow valley slopes of the northerly flowing Wild Horse Creek, near its confluence with the Missouri.

Northwest of Saint Louis, **Cuivre River State Park❖** (north of Route 47 about three miles east of Troy) covers more than 6,000 acres in the Lincoln Hills, an Ozarklike landscape on the glaciated plains about ten miles from the west bank of the Mississippi River. This sliver of hills, which extends only from around Troy and Winfield to Hannibal, has terrain and flora that resemble those of southern Missouri's Ozarks. The park encompasses the headwaters of Big Sugar Creek, a tributary of the Cuivre River. Throughout the park small remnants of prairies, glades, savannas, sinkholes, caves, and springs are scattered among the oak woodlands.

The 6,636-acre **Ted Shanks Conservation Area❖,** about 18 miles south of Hannibal, is one of Missouri's top birding locales. Fronting almost seven miles of Mississippi River, this preserve is a matrix of marsh, mudflats, and bottomland hardwood forest. In the marshes, ducks and geese peak in March and November; shorebirds occur on the mudflats from March to May and again from August to October; in the forest, warbler migration is best in late April and early May, when the birds are in high breeding plumage. (In fall, the drab warblers are more challenging to identify.)

Three public-access units of the **Mark Twain National Wildlife Refuge❖** lie along the Mississippi River above Saint Louis: the **Gregory Landing Division,** a 1,519-acre strip of bottomland near Alexandria in extreme northeastern Missouri; the **Gardner Division,** several islands within Lock and Dam 21 that attract many wintering bald eagles; and the 3,751-acre **Clarence Cannon Refuge,** near Annada.

About 100 miles south of Saint Louis on the Mississippi River is **Tower Rock Natural Area** (go 12 miles south of Perryville on Route 61 and take Route A to the gravel road heading south just before the village of Wittenberg). Constituting a 31-acre island accessible only in times of low water, the oak-hickory forest preserve is named for its small tower of limestone, visible from the banks of the river.

RIGHT: Sunrise silhouettes Tower Rock, a distinctive limestone outcrop in the Mississippi River. Fringed with pines and oaks, this small but stalwart island has resisted the mighty erosional forces of the current.

ABOVE: *Giant platterlike leaves of American lotus colonize the quiet waters at Otter Slough, a swampy vestige of almost impenetrable bottomland forests that once set the Bootheel apart from the rest of Missouri.*

SOUTHEAST MISSOURI:
THE BOOTHEEL AND LOST HILLS

On the Mississippi River ten miles north of Cape Girardeau, **Trail of Tears State Park**❖ straddles a portion of the exodus route of 13,000 Cherokee removed to Oklahoma from their homelands in North Carolina in the winter of 1838–39. Within the park, the 1,300-acre **Indian Creek Wild Area** and the 300-acre **Vancill Hollow Natural Area** contain splendid stands of mature hardwood forest. Here American beech, tulip, and cucumber magnolia—trees of Appalachian and southern forests—reach the western edge of their range. Visiting the **Blue Pond Natural Area**❖ in **Castor River State Forest** satisfies those with a predilection for eccentric landforms. This sinkhole, the sheerest and deepest (approximately 66 feet) in Missouri, may have formed during the 1811–12 New Madrid earthquakes. Visitors need a topographic map to locate the 15-acre site, which lies about six miles northwest of the town of Zalma.

A fragment of the vast tupelo–bald cypress swamps that once covered the Bootheel survives at the 22,000-acre **Mingo National Wildlife Refuge**❖ and the nearby 6,190-acre **Duck Creek Conservation Area**❖,

both old channels of the Mississippi River. Mingo lies west of Route 51 just north of Puxico; the entrance to Duck Creek is another seven miles north. Both are prime locations for watching birds. A boardwalk at Mingo that extends into the fringes of the swamp provides a great vantage point for spotting migrating warblers in April. Barred owls and red-shouldered hawks—two swamp-haunting raptors—often appear at Mingo and Duck Creek. In 1982 trumpeter swans were reintroduced at Mingo, and bald eagles now nest at both refuges. Listen for the weird, raspy caws of the fish crow, a predominantly coastal species that moves inland along waterways.

The Bootheel's murky, shadowy swamps are home to two showy southern flowers. The spider lily (above), an amaryllis, bears its gauzy white flowers as early as March. The copper, or red, iris (below) blooms in May and June.

Crowley's Ridge, the most impressive of the lost hills that survived the erosional influences of the Mississippi and Ohio rivers, has not weathered so well the effects of human habitation. Stretching 200 miles from Cape Girardeau to Helena, Arkansas, the ridge extends down the Bootheel like a 300-foot-high 3-to-12-mile-wide spinal column. To Native Americans, Crowley's Ridge offered high ground above the murky, impenetrable swamps and marshes of the Bootheel. The Shawnee, Delaware, and Osage, who lived on the ridge until the early 1800s, maintained a system of paths, most notably the Shawnee Trail. The full-scale development that began in the late 1800s, however, soon turned Crowley's Ridge into a patchwork of orchards, pastures, towns, and small farms.

Visitors driving Route 25 south from Advance to Dexter can still see and appreciate the geology of this long serpentine hill, but glimpsing the natural fabric—including

a number of unusual plants, animals, and fish—of this isolated corridor is much more difficult. A formidable problem is invasive honeysuckle, which is overtaking the native vegetation.

Holly Ridge State Forest❖, east of Route 25 about three miles south of Bloomfield, harbors examples of the dry sand forests and moist seeps that once characterized Crowley's Ridge. Within the state forest, the best places to see such mostly vanished terrain are the 84-acre **Holly Ridge Natural Area** and the 35-acre **Beech Spring Natural Area,** where forests of oaks, hickories, beech, yellow poplar, alder, American holly, and farkle-berry play across a roller-coaster landscape of sandy ridges.

Down from the lost hills, the Mississippi alluvial plain contains three echoes of the vast labyrinth of swamps, sloughs, oxbows, and bottomland forest that composed the Bootheel: the 4,863-acre **Otter Slough Conservation Area❖,** 8 miles southwest of Dexter; the 160-acre **Allred Lake Natural Area❖,** about 15 miles south of Poplar Bluff; and the **Big Oak Tree Natural Area❖,** about 10 miles south of East Prairie.

In these last forests primeval, characteristic trees, which display a high tolerance for standing in water, include bald cypress, swamp tupelo, sweet gum, water locust, pecan, willow, and numerous oaks (swamp chestnut, overcup, and water). Buttonbush is a common swamp shrub, and among muck-loving flowers are copper irises and spider lilies, which typically bloom in May. Swimming in the sloughs and ponds are populations of rare fish (the swamp darter and taillight shiner at Allred Lake; the pugnose minnow and bantam sunfish at Otter Slough).

At Allred Lake, restricted to nonmotorized watercraft and considered the most pristine bald-cypress pond in Missouri, the rare Nuttall's oak grows at the northern extent of its range. A one-mile boardwalk at the heartbreakingly beautiful Big Oak Tree Natural Area winds through an 80-acre stand of virgin Mississippi bottomland forest. In the rich, mucky alluvial soil, giant oaks and hickories form an umbrella canopy averaging 120 feet above the forest floor. No fewer than nine state and national champion trees populate this forest, including a bur oak that is 142 feet tall. The giant trees are speechless but in their dwindled ranks have much to say about the Heartland's long-lost forests and prairies and all of us who used them up. In abundance, these places inspired mostly insouciance. In their virtual absence, they now arouse a kind of Druid's adulation.

RIGHT: *The pink and lavender light of dawn complements the tranquillity of a bald cypress swamp at the Otter Slough Conservation Area.*

FURTHER READING ABOUT THE HEARTLAND

AMBROSE, STEPHEN E. *Undaunted Courage: Meriwether Lewis, Thomas Jefferson, and the Opening of the American West.* New York: Simon & Schuster, 1996. A triumph of historical narrative.

BROWN, LAUREN. *Grasslands. The Audubon Society Nature Guide.* New York: Knopf, 1985. All prairies are not alike; this excellent guide summarizes the major prairie types and the characteristic flora and fauna of each.

BUCHANAN, REX. *Kansas Geology: An Introduction to Landscapes, Rocks, Minerals, and Fossils.* Lawrence: University Press of Kansas, 1984. A perfect book to accompany the geologically curious traveler in Kansas.

CATHER, WILLA. *My Ántonía.* 1918. Boston: Houghton Mifflin Company, 1988. What distinguishes Cather as a novelist are her descriptions of the larger landscapes her characters inhabit, and the first four chapters in *My Ántonía* contain some of the most evocative descriptions of the prairie ever written.

————. *O Pioneers!* 1913. Boston: Houghton Mifflin Company, 1988. This great American novel is about two overarching topics: love and "the last struggle of a wild soil against the encroaching plowshare."

DEVOTO, BERNARD, ED. *The Journals of Lewis and Clark.* 1953. Boston: Houghton Mifflin Company. Reprinted by American Heritage Library. Lewis and Clark's journal accounts are the benchmark for comparing 200 years of landscape changes throughout the vast watershed of the Missouri River.

FRAZIER, IAN. *Great Plains.* New York: Farrar, Straus and Giroux, 1989. The author has a wonderful, whimsical eye for the details of life and culture in Middle America.

GRESS, BOB, AND GEORGE POTTS. *Watching Kansas Wildlife: A Guide to 101 Sites.* University Press of Kansas, 1993. This concise survey of some of the best natural landscapes in Kansas helps travelers find and identify wildlife.

HEITZMAN, J. RICHARD, AND JOAN E. HEITZMAN. *Butterflies and Moths of Missouri.* Missouri Department of Conservation, 1987. This is the best lepidopteran handbook for Illinois, Iowa, Kansas, Missouri, and Nebraska.

HUNT, DAVID C., AND MARSHA V. GALLAGHER. *Karl Bodmer's America.* Lincoln, NE: Joslyn Art Museum and University of Nebraska Press, 1984. Bodmer's remarkable paintings and sketches of the Missouri River country, made in the early 1830s, can help modern readers begin to understand what the heart of America looked like before European settlers overhauled it.

JOHNSGARD, PAUL A. *This Fragile Land: A Natural History of the Nebraska Sandhills.* Lincoln: University of Nebraska Press, 1995. The largest expanse of sand dunes in the Western Hemisphere is lovingly scrutinized by a biologist and artist whose customary subject is birds.

Further Reading

LADD, DOUG. *Tallgrass Prairie Wildflowers.* Helena, MT: Falcon Press, 1995. Ladd, an authority on restoring prairies, savannas, and glades, shares his knowledge about the many flowering plants and grasses of the tallgrass prairie. Most of the picturess are by noted prairie photographer Frank Oberle.

MADSON, JOHN. *Where the Sky Began, Land of the Tallgrass Prairie.* Houghton Mifflin & Co., 1982. Long after it was gone, but before much of the world took note, Madson wrote this classic lament for a bygone ecosystem.

MCFALL, DON, ED. *A Directory of Illinois Nature Preserves.* Illinois Department of Conservation, Division of Natural Heritage, 1991. For finding every natural nook and cranny in Illinois, this book is essential.

MUTEL, CORNELIA F. *Fragile Giants: A Natural History of the Loess Hills.* Iowa City: University of Iowa Press, 1989. An excellent introduction to one of the most peculiar and lovely landforms in the Heartland.

PRIOR, JEAN C. *Landforms of Iowa.* Iowa City: University of Iowa Press, 1991. Prior deftly leads her readers across Iowa's wonderfully undulating landscapes.

RUNKEL, SYLVAN T., AND DEAN M. ROOSA. *Wildflowers of the Tallgrass Prairie: The Upper Midwest.* Ames: Iowa State University Press, 1989. Prairie visitors will find this handy book full of information, including the culinary and medicinal uses of the plants.

SANDOZ, MARI. *Love Song to the Plains.* Harper & Bros., 1961. Sandoz's account of Nebraska is one of dozens of books she wrote about the Great Plains. Others include *Old Jules* (about her crusty father homesteading in the Nebraska Sandhills), *Crazy Horse*, and *The Buffalo Hunters*.

STUBBENDIECK, JAMES L., STEPHAN L. HATCH, AND KATHIE J. KJAR. *North American Range Plants.* Lincoln: University of Nebraska Press, 1981. Fine line drawings and range maps make this the best all-purpose prairie handbook available.

THOM, RICHARD H. *Directory of Missouri Natural Areas.* Missouri Department of Conservation and Department of Natural Resources, and Missouri Natural Areas Committee, 1985. This book will get the dedicated naturalist deep into some of the best hidden corners of Missouri.

WEAVER, J. E. *North American Prairie.* Lincoln, NE: Johnsen Publishing Co. 1954. The classic grassland ecology text, written by a pioneer in the field of prairie research, includes photographs and line drawings of the incredible roots and rhizomes of prairie plants.

WEBB, WALTER PRESCOTT. *The Great Plains.* 1931. Lincoln: University of Nebraska Press, 1981. The first book to critically consider "what happened in American civilization when in its westward progress it emerged from the woods and essayed life on the Plains" is a classic.

'

GLOSSARY

aquifer underground layer of porous, water-bearing rock, sand, or gravel

bluff cliff, or steep wall of rock or soil bordering a river or floodplain

bog wetland, formed in glacial kettle holes in cool climates; its acidic nature produces large quantities of peat moss

butte tall, steep-sided tower of rock formed from an eroded plateau

dolomite limestone-like rock

escarpment cliff or steep rock face separating two comparatively level land surfaces

fen any lowland covered wholly or partly with water

floodplain flat area along the course of a stream subject to periodic flooding

flowstone calcite mineral deposited by a thin sheet of flowing water along the floor or walls of a cave

glacial till unsorted rock debris, usually of a wide range of sizes, deposited directly from the ice without reworking by streams

grassland inland region where grass is the naturally dominant vegetation

kame cone-shaped hill of rock debris deposited by glacial meltwater

karst area of land lying over limestone that is dotted with sinkholes, underground streams, and caves formed by the erosion of the limestone by rainwater

kettle hole glacial depression that often evolves into a bog or pond

loess windblown layer of fine, mineral-rich dust and silt that may slowly accumulate into a landform

moraine debris (rock, sand, gravel, silt, and clay) carried by a glacier and left along its sides or terminus wher-ever it pauses or retreats

oxbow lake that forms where a meandering river overflows and creates a crescent-shaped body of water

pothole bowl-shaped depression left by a chunk of glacial ice buried in soil; when ice melts, water fills the pothole creating a lake or a marsh

prairie temperate grassland supporting an extensive variety of grasses; occurs in areas where there are distinct seasonal variations in climate

ravine narrow, steep-sided valley eroded by running water

savanna grassland with clumps of grasses and widely scattered tree growth; occurs in areas where a prolonged dry season alternates with a rainy season

sedge family of grasslike plants found in brackish swamps and marshes

sinkhole funnel-shaped hole where water has collected in the cracks of limestone, dissolved the rock, and carried it away; also formed when roofs of caves collapse

slough swampy, backwater area, river inlet, marshy creek, or tidal flat

stalactite icicle-shaped piece of dripstone formed from a cave ceiling when limestone-rich water drips and evaporates, leaving a mineral formation

stalagmite spire formed when water drips onto a cave floor and deposits dissolved minerals

swale moist, low area in a tract of land; usually more dense in vegetation than the surrounding areas

wetland area of land covered or saturated with groundwater; includes swamps, marshes, and bogs

LAND MANAGEMENT RESOURCES

The following public and private organizations are among the important administrators of the preserved and protected areas described in this volume. Brief explanations of the various legal and legislative designations of these areas follow.

MANAGING ORGANIZATIONS

Illinois Department of Natural Resources
Administers 409,290 acres in 62 state parks, 58 wildlife management areas, and 112 state nature preserves. Issues state hunting and fishing licenses.

Iowa Fish and Wildlife Division
Manages 300,000 acres in 360 wildlife management areas. Issues state hunting and fishing licenses. Part of the Department of Natural Resources.

Iowa Forests and Forestry Division
Manages 33,000 acres in nine state forests for recreation and timber production. Part of the Department of Natural Resources.

Iowa Parks, Recreation and Preserves Division
Maintains approximately 60,000 acres in 70 state parks and 8,900 acres in 84 state preserves. Part of the Department of Natural Resources.

Kansas Parks Division
Manages 29,535 acres in 24 state parks. Part of the Department of Wildlife and Parks.

Kansas Fisheries, Wildlife and Public Lands Division
Manages 24,774 acres in 37 state fishing lakes and wildlife management areas and 205,658 acres in leased properties. State hunting and fishing licenses issued by administrative services office. Part of the Department of Wildlife and Parks.

Missouri Division of State Parks
Manages 134,496 acres in 47 state parks and 32 state historic sites. Part of the Department of Natural Resources.

Missouri Forestry, Wildlife and Natural History Divisions
Manages more than 900,000 acres including 86 natural areas and 835 conservation areas. Issues state hunting and fishing licenses. Part of the Department of Conservation.

National Park Service (NPS) Department of the Interior
Regulates the use of national parks, monuments, and preserves. Resources are managed to protect the landscape, natural and historic artifacts, and wildlife. Administers historic and national landmarks, national seashores and lakeshores, wild and scenic rivers, and the national trail system.

Nebraska Game and Parks Commission
Manages 136,363 acres of land and water in 88 state parks, historic parks, recreation areas, and one state recreation trail as well as 150,000 acres in 213 wildlife management areas. Responsible for issuing state hunting and fishing licenses.

The Nature Conservancy (TNC) Private organization
International nonprofit organization that owns the largest private system of nature sanctuaries in the world, some 1,300 preserves. Aims to preserve significant and diverse plants, animals, and natural communities. Some areas are managed by other private or public conservation groups, some by the Conservancy itself.

U.S. Fish and Wildlife Service (USFWS) Department of the Interior
Principal federal agency responsible for conserving, protecting, and enhancing the country's fish and wildlife and their habitats. Manages national wildlife refuges and fish hatcheries as well as programs for migratory birds and endangered and threatened species.

U.S. Forest Service (USFS) Department of Agriculture
Administers more than 190 million acres in the national forests and national grasslands and is responsible for the management of their resources. Determines how best to combine commercial uses such as grazing, mining, and logging with conservation needs.

DESIGNATIONS

Conservation Area
Area set aside to protect specific environments. May be used for recreation, research, or other specific purposes. Managed by individual states.

National Grassland
Federal land where more than 80 percent of the canopy cover is dominated by grasses or grasslike plants. May encompass private holdings. Managed by the USFS.

National Forest
Large acreage managed for the use of forests, watersheds, wildlife, and recreation by the public and private sectors. Managed by the USFS.

National Historic Site
Land area, building, or object preserved for its national historic importance. Managed by the NPS.

National Monument
Nationally significant landmark, structure, object, or area of scientific or historic significance. Managed by the NPS.

National Wildlife Refuge
Public land set aside for wild animals; protects migratory waterfowl, endangered and threatened species, and native plants. Managed by the USFWS.

Natural Area
Area designated and preserved in its natural state for its exceptional value in showing the natural history of its region. Managed by individual states.

Nature Preserve
Tract of land protecting specific natural resources and high-quality ecosys-

tems such as old-growth forests and prairies. Managed by individual states' Departments of Natural Resources and county forest preserve districts.

Recreation Area
Natural area for recreation; hunting, fishing, camping, powerboats, dirt and mountain bikes, and ORVs allowed with restrictions. Managed by the NPS or individual states.

Wild and Scenic River System
National program set up to preserve selected rivers in their natural free-flowing condition. Stretches are classified as wild, scenic, or recreational, depending on the degree of development on the river, shoreline, or adjacent lands. Management shared by the BLM, NPS, and USFWS.

Wilderness Area
Area with particular ecological, geological, scientific, scenic, or historic value that has been set aside in its natural condition to be preserved as wild land; limited recreational use is permitted. Managed by USFWS and USFS

Wildlife Area
State land managed to protect wildlife. Hunting, fishing, and public access are allowed, with seasonal restrictions. Managed by individual states.

Wildlife Management Area
Natural area owned and maintained for recreation; hunting, fishing, trapping, and cross-country skiing permitted. Managed by individual states.

ABOVE: *About 1886, a family of homesteaders paused to pose for a photographer beside their covered wagon in Nebraska's Loup River valley.*

NATURE TRAVEL

The following is a selection of national and local organizations that sponsor nature-related travel activities or can provide specialized regional travel information.

NATIONAL

National Audubon Society
700 Broadway
New York, NY 10003
(212) 979-3000
Offers a wide range of ecological field studies, tours, and cruises throughout the United States

National Wildlife Federation
1400 16th St. NW
Washington, D.C. 20036
(703) 790-4363
Offers training in environmental education, wildlife camp and teen adventures, conservation summits with nature walks, field trips, and classes

The Nature Conservancy
1815 North Lynn St.
Arlington, VA 22209
(703) 841-5300
Offers a variety of excursions from regional and state offices. May include hiking, backpacking, canoeing, horseback riding. Call to locate state offices

Sierra Club Outings
85 2nd St., 2nd Fl.
San Francisco, CA 94105
(415) 977-5630
Offers tours of different lengths for all ages throughout the United States. Outings may include backpacking, hiking, biking, skiing, and water excursions

Smithsonian Study Tours and Seminars
1100 Jefferson Dr. SW
MRC 702
Washington, DC 20560
(202) 357-4700
Offers extended tours, cruises, research expeditions, and seminars throughout the United States

REGIONAL

Illinois Bureau of Tourism
100 W. Randolph St., Ste. 300-400
Chicago, IL 60602
(800) 226-6632
http://www.enjoyillinois.com
Call to request visitors' guide and calendar of events

Iowa Division of Tourism
200 E. Grand Ave.
Des Moines, IA 50309
(800) 345-4692
http://www.state.ia.us
Call to request state travel guide, calendar of events, map, and camping/outdoors guide or for specific information

Kansas Travel and Tourism Development Division
700 S.W. Harrison St., Ste. 1300
Topeka, KS 66603
(800) 252-6727
(913) 296-2009
Call to ask specific travel questions or to request information packet and map

Missouri Division of Tourism
PO Box 1055
Jefferson City, MO 65102
(800) 877-1234
(573) 751-4133
Call for specific travel information or to request state travel guide, highway map, and calendar of events

Nebraska Department of Travel and Tourism
PO Box 94666
Lincoln, NE 68509
(800) 228-4307
gmiller@ded2.bed.state.ne.us
Call to order travel packet, maps, accommodation guide, or to ask specific travel-related questions

HOW TO USE THIS SITE GUIDE

The following site information guide will assist you in planning your tour of the natural areas of Illinois, Iowa, Kansas, Missouri, and Nebraska. Sites set in boldface and followed by the symbol ❖ in the text are here organized alphabetically by state. Each entry is followed by the mailing address (sometimes different from the street address) and phone number of the immediate managing office, plus brief notes and a list of facilities and activities available. (A key appears on each page.)

Information on hours of operation, seasonal closings, and fees is often not listed, as these vary from season to season and year to year. Please bear in mind that responsibility for the management of some sites may change. Call well in advance to obtain maps, brochures, and pertinent, up-to-date information that will help you plan your adventures in the Heartland.

Each site entry in the guide includes the address and phone number of its immediate managing agency. Many of these sites are under the stewardship of a forest or park ranger or supervised from a small nearby office. Hence, in many cases, those sites will be difficult to contact directly, and it is preferable to call the managing agency.

The following umbrella organizations can provide general information for individual natural sites, as well as the area as a whole:

REGIONAL
National Park Service (Midwest)
1709 Jackson Street
Omaha, NE 68102
(402) 221-3431

U.S. Fish and Wildlife Service
Region 3 (IA, IL, MO)
1 Federal Drive
Federal Building
Fort Snelling, MN 55111
(612) 725-3563

Region 6 (KS, NE)
PO Box 25486
Denver, CO 80225
(303) 236-7920

U.S. Forest Service
Region 9 (IA, IL, MO)
310 W. Wisconsin Ave.
Room 500
Milwaukee, WI 52303
(414) 297-3600

Region 2 (KS NE)
740 Sims Street
Lakewood, CO 80225
(303) 275-5450

ILLINOIS
Illinois Department of Natural Resources
524 South 2nd Street,
Room 400 LTP
Springfield, IL 62701
(217) 785-0075

IOWA
Iowa Department of Natural Resources
Fish and Wildlife;
Forests and Forestry;
Parks, Recreation, and
Preserves Divisions
Wallace Building
East 9th Street
Des Moines, IA 50319
(515) 281-5918

KANSAS
Kansas Department of Wildlife and Parks
Parks Division; Fisheries,
Wildlife, and Public Lands
Divisions
900 SW Jackson Street
Topeka, KS 66612-1233
(913) 296-2281

MISSOURI
Missouri Department of Natural Resources
Division of State Parks
PO Box 176
Jefferson City, MO 65102
(573) 751-2479

Missouri Department of Conservation
Forestry; Natural History;
and Wildlife Divisions
PO Box 180
Jefferson City, MO 65102
(573) 751-4115

NEBRASKA
Nebraska Game and Parks Commission
2200 North 33rd Street
PO Box 30370
Lincoln, NE 68503-0370
(402) 471-0641

ILLINOIS

APPLE RIVER CANYON STATE PARK
Illinois Dept. of Natural Resources
8763 E. Canyon Rd.
Apple River, IL 61001
(815) 745-3302
BW, C, F, GS, H, I, MT, PA, T

AYERS SAND PRAIRIE NATURE PRESERVE
c/o Mississippi Palisades State Park
16327A Rte. 84
Savanna, IL 61074
(815) 273-2731   BW, H

BARBARA KEY PARK
Village of Lake in the Hills
1115 Crystal Lake Rd.
Lake in the Hills, IL 60102
(847) 669-4100
Tours by prearrangement
BT, BW, F, H, MT, PA, T, TG

BAY CREEK WILDERNESS
Shawnee National Forest
901 S. Commercial St.
Harrisburg, IL 62946
(800) 699-6637; (618) 658-2111
BW, C, H, HR, MT

BEALL WOODS NATURE PRESERVE
c/o Beall Woods State Park
RR 2, Mt. Carmel, IL 62863
(618) 298-2441
BW, H, I, MT, PA, RA, T

BELL SMITH SPRINGS RECREATION AREA
Shawnee National Forest
901 S. Commercial St.
Harrisburg, IL 62946
(800) 699-6637; (618) 658-2111
BW, C, H, HR, MT, PA, T

BLACK PARTRIDGE WOODS
Forest Preserve District of Cook County
536 North Harlem Ave.
River Forest, IL 60305
(708) 771-1330
BT, BW, H, MB, PA, T

BLUFF SPRING FEN NATURE PRESERVE
The Nature Conservancy
8 S. Michigan Ave., Ste. 900
Chicago, IL 60603
(312) 346-8166
No pets   BW, H, MT

BRAIDWOOD DUNES AND SAVANNA NATURE PRESERVE
Forest Preserve District of Will County
22606 S. Cherry Hill Rd.
Joliet, IL 60433
(815) 727-8700   H

BURDEN FALLS WILDERNESS
Shawnee National Forest
901 S. Commercial St.
Harrisburg, IL 62946
(800) 699-6637; (618) 658-2111
BW, C, H, HR, MT

CACHE RIVER STATE NATURAL AREA
Illinois Dept. of Natural Resources
930 Sunflower Lane
Belknap, IL 62908
(618) 634-9678
BW, CK, F, H, I, MT, RA, T, TG

CASTLE ROCK STATE PARK
Illinois Dept. of Natural Resources
1365 W. Castle Rd.
Oregon, IL 61061
(815) 732-7329
Includes George B. Fell Nature Preserve;
primitive camping accessible by boat
BW, C, CK, F, H, MT, PA, T, XC

CHAUNCEY MARSH NATURE PRESERVE
c/o Red Hills State Park
RR 2, Box 252A, Sumner, IL 62466
(618) 936-2469   BW, H

CHAUTAUQUA NATIONAL WILDLIFE REFUGE
U.S. Fish and Wildlife Service
19031 E. County Rd. 2105N
Ilavanna, IL 62644
(309) 535-2290
BW, CK, F, H, I, MT, PA, RA, T, XC

COLORED SANDS FOREST PRESERVE
Winnebago County Forest Preserve District
5500 Northrock Dr.
Rockford, IL 61103
(815) 877-6100
Sand bluff bird-banding station open
spring and fall   BW, F, H, MT, PA, T

CRETACEOUS HILLS NATURE PRESERVE
Illinois Dept. of Natural Resources
c/o Fort Massac State Park
1308 E. 5th St.

BT	Bike Trails	**CK**	Canoeing, Kayaking	**F**	Fishing	**HR**	Horseback Riding
BW	Bird-watching			**GS**	Gift Shop		
C	Camping	**DS**	Downhill Skiing	**H**	Hiking	**I**	Information Center

Metropolis, IL 62960
(618) 524-4712   **BW**

CYPRESS CREEK
NATIONAL WILDLIFE REFUGE
U.S. Fish and Wildlife Service
Rte. 1, Box 53D
Ullin, IL 62992
(618) 634-2231   **BW, CK, F, H, RA, T, TG**

DEAN CEMETERY BARRENS PRESERVE
Shawnee National Forest
901 S. Commercial St.
Harrisburg, IL 62946
(800) 699-6637   **BW, H**

FERMILAB PRAIRIE
U.S. Dept. of Energy
PO Box 500, Batavia, IL 60510
(708) 840-3351
                    BT, BW, F, H, I, MT, T, TG

FERNE CLYFFE STATE PARK
Illinois Dept. of Natural Resources
PO Box 10, Goreville, IL 62939
(618) 995-2411
    Includes Round Bluff Nature Preserve
                    BW, C, F, H, HR, MT, PA, T

FRANKLIN CREEK STATE NATURAL AREA
Illinois Dept. of Natural Resources
1872 Twist Rd.
Franklin Grove, IL 61031
(815) 456-2878
            BW, F, H, HR, MT, PA, T, XC

FULTS HILL PRAIRIE NATURE PRESERVE
c/o Randolph State Fish and Wildlife Area
4301 South Lakeside Dr.
Chester, IL 62233
(618) 826-2706
    Trail is very steep   **BW, MT, PA**

GARDEN OF THE GODS
Shawnee National Forest
Elizabethtown Ranger District
Rte. 2, Box 4, Elizabethtown, IL 62931
(618) 287-2201   **BW, C, H, MT, T**

GIANT CITY STATE PARK
Illinois Dept. of Natural Resources
336 South Church Rd.
Makanda, IL 62958
(618) 457-4836
    Cabins available
            BW, C, F, GS, H, HR, L, MT, PA, RC, T

GLACIAL PARK
McHenry County
Conservation District
6512 Harts Rd.
Ringwood, IL 60072
(815) 678-4431
            BW, C, CK, F, H, HR, MT, PA, T, XC

GOOSE LAKE PRAIRIE
Illinois Dept. of Natural Resources
5010 North Jugtown Rd.
Morris, IL 60450
(815) 942-2899
    Includes state natural area within state
    park   **BW, I, MT, T, TG, XC**

GRANT CREEK PRAIRIE
NATURE PRESERVE
Illinois Dept. of Natural Resources
c/o Des Plaines Conservation Area
24621 N. River Rd.
Wilmington, IL 60481
(815) 423-5326
(815) 423-6370   **BW**

HANOVER BLUFF NATURE PRESERVE
c/o Apple River Canyon
State Park
8763 E. Canyon Rd.
Apple River, IL 61001
(815) 745-3302; (815) 244-3655
    No trail system; hiking rated as difficult
                                        BW, H

HARLEM HILLS NATURE PRESERVE
Illinois Dept. of Natural Resources
c/o Rock Cut State Park
7318 Harlem Rd.
Loves Park, IL 61111
(815) 885-3612   **BW, H, MT**

HOOPER BRANCH SAVANNA
NATURE PRESERVE
Illinois Dept. of Natural Resources
Iroquois County Conservation Area
PO Box 151
Beaverville, IL 60912
(815) 435-2218   **BW, H, I, MT, PA, T**

HORSESHOE LAKE
STATE CONSERVATION AREA
Illinois Dept. of Natural Resources
PO Box 85
Miller City, IL 62962
(618) 776-5689
                            BW, C, F, PA, T

L	Lodging	**PA**	Picnic Areas	**RC**	Rock Climbing	**TG**	Tours, Guides
MB	Mountain Biking	**RA**	Ranger-led Activities	**S**	Swimming	**XC**	Cross-country Skiing
MT	Marked Trails			**T**	Toilets		

263

ILLINOIS BEACH NATURE PRESERVE
Illinois Beach State Park
Lake Front, Zion, IL 60099
(847) 662-4811; (847) 662-4828
Includes nature center; southern unit
closed for all activities except scientific
study **BW, H, I, MT, T**

ILLINOIS BEACH STATE PARK
Illinois Dept. of Natural Resources
Lake Front, Zion, IL 60099
(847) 662-4811; (847) 662-4828
BT, BW, C, F, GS, H, I, L, MB, MT, PA, RA, S, T, TG, XC

INDIAN BOUNDARY PRAIRIES
Biology Dept., Northeastern
Illinois University
5500 N. St. Louis Ave.
Chicago, IL 60625
(773) 583-4050 **BW, H, MT**

KANKAKEE RIVER STATE PARK
Illinois Dept. of Natural Resources
PO Box 37, Bourbonnais, IL 60914
(815) 933-1383
BT, C, CK, F, H, HR, I, MT, PA, T, TG, XC

LARUE–PINE HILLS/OTTER POND RESEARCH NATURAL AREA
Shawnee National Forest
Jonesboro Ranger District
521 N. Main St.
Jonesboro, IL 62952
(618) 833-8576; (618) 833-3693 (TTY)
Camping adjacent to nature area
BW, C, CK, F, H, MT, PA, T

LIMEKILN SPRINGS PRESERVE
The Nature Conservancy
Rte. 1, Box 53E, Ullin, IL 62992
(618) 634-2524 **BW, MT**

LODA CEMETERY PRAIRIE NATURE PRESERVE
The Nature Conservancy
8 S. Michigan Ave., Ste. 900
Chicago, IL 60603
(312) 346-8166

LUSK CREEK CANYON NATURE PRESERVE
Illinois Dept. of Natural Resources
85 Glen O. Jones Rd.
Equality, IL 62934
(618) 276-4405 **BW, CK, H, HR, MT, T**

MERWIN NATURE PRESERVE
ParkLands Foundation
PO Box 3132
Bloomington, IL 61702-3132
BW, CK, H, MT, PA, TG

MIDDLE FORK WOODS NATURE PRESERVE
c/o Kickapoo State Park
10906 Kickapoo Park Rd.
Oakwood, IL 61858
(217) 442-4915
Recreational facilities at park **BW, H**

MISSISSIPPI PALISADES STATE PARK
Illinois Dept. of Natural Resources
16327A Rte. 84, Savanna, IL 61074
(815) 273-2731
Most facilities are handicapped-accessible
BW, C, CK, F, H, MT, PA, RC, T, XC

MOMENCE WETLANDS NATURE PRESERVE
Illinois Dept. of Natural Resources
Iroquois County Conservation Area
PO Box 15
Beaverville, IL 60912
(815) 435-2218
Undeveloped area **BW**

MORAINE HILLS STATE PARK
Illinois Dept. of Natural Resources
914 South River Rd., McHenry, IL 60050
(815) 385-1624
BT, BW, F, H, I, MT, PA, T, XC

MORTON ARBORETUM
Rte. 53, Lisle, IL 60532-1293
(630) 719-2465
(630) 719-2400 (24-hr. taped message)
Admission fee
BW, GS, H, I, MT, PA, T, TG

NACHUSA GRASSLANDS
The Nature Conservancy
2055 Lowden Rd.
Franklin Grove, IL 61031
(815) 456-2340 **BW, H**

PECATONICA BOTTOMS NATURE PRESERVE
Winnebago County Forest Preserve District
5500 Northrock Dr., Rockford, IL 61103
(815) 877-6100
Fully operational in 1998
BW, CK, F, HR

BT	Bike Trails	**CK**	Canoeing, Kayaking	**F**	Fishing	**HR**	Horseback Riding
BW	Bird-watching			**GS**	Gift Shop		
C	Camping	**DS**	Downhill Skiing	**H**	Hiking	**I**	Information Center

PERE MARQUETTE STATE PARK
Illinois Dept. of Natural Resources
PO Box 158, Grafton, IL 62037
(618) 786-3323
**BT, BW, C, CK, F, GS, H, HR, I, L, MT,
PA, RA, RC, T, TG**

**PROSPECT CEMETERY PRAIRIE
NATURE PRESERVE**
Paxton Twp. Cemetery Association
Paxton, IL 60957
(217) 379-2676   **BW, H**

REVIS SPRINGS HILL NATURE PRESERVE
c/o Sand Ridge State Forest
PO Box 111, Forest City, IL 61532
(309) 597-2212
Tours by prearrangement
                              BW, H, TG

ROBERT ALLERTON PARK
University of Illinois
515 Old Timber Rd.
Monticello, IL 61856
(217) 762-2721
Tours by prearrangement
          BW, GS, H, I, MT, PA, T, TG, XC

RYERSON WOODS
Lake County Forest Preserves
21950 N. Riverwoods Rd.
Deerfield, IL 60015
(847) 948-7750
          BW, H, I, MT, RA, T, TG, XC

**SAND PRAIRIE-SCRUB OAK
NATURE PRESERVE**
c/o Sand Ridge State Forest
PO Box 111, Forest City, IL 61532
(309) 597-2212
Tours by prearrangement   **BW, H, TG**

SAND RIDGE NATURE CENTER
Forest Preserve District of Cook County
15890 Paxton Ave.
South Holland, IL 60473
(708) 868-0606
          BW, GS, H, I, MT, RA, T, TG

SAND RIDGE STATE FOREST
PO Box 111
Forest City, IL 61532
(309) 597-2212
Tours by prearrangement
          BW, C, H, HR, MT, PA, RA, T, TG, XC

SEARLS PARK PRAIRIE NATURE PRESERVE
Rockford Park District
1401 N. 2nd St.
Rockford, IL 61107
(815) 987-8800   **BW**

**SHAWNEE HILLS ON THE OHIO NATIONAL
FOREST SCENIC BYWAY**
Shawnee National Forest
901 S. Commercial St.
Harrisburg, IL 62946
(800) 699-6637; (618) 287-2201
          **BT, BW, C, F, H, HR,
          L, MB, MT, PA, RA, S, T, TG**

SHAWNEE NATIONAL FOREST
U.S. Forest Service
901 S. Commercial St.
Harrisburg, IL 62946
(800) 699-6637; (618) 287-2201;
(618) 658-2111
          BW, C, CK, F, H, HR, MB, MT, PA, T

SOMME PRAIRIE NATURE PRESERVE
Forest Preserve District of Cook County
536 N. Harlem Ave.
River Forest, IL 60305
(708) 771-1330   **BW, H, PA, T**

SPITLER WOODS STATE NATURAL AREA
Illinois Dept. of Natural Resources
705 Spitler Park Dr.
Mt. Zion, IL 62549
(217) 864-3121   **BW, H, I, MT, PA, T**

STARVED ROCK STATE PARK
Illinois Dept. of Natural Resources
PO Box 509, Utica, IL 61373
(815) 667-4726
          **BW, C, CK, F, GS, H, HR, I,
          L, MT, PA, RA, T, XC**

SUGAR RIVER FOREST PRESERVE
Winnebago County Forest
Preserve District
5500 Northrock Dr., Rockford, IL 61103
(815) 877-6100
          BW, C, CK, F, H, HR, MT, PA, T

**UPPER EMBARRAS WOODS
NATURE PRESERVE**
Illinois Dept. of Natural Resources
RR 2, Box 108
Charleston, IL 61920
(217) 345-2420   **BW, H, MT**

L Lodging   **PA** Picnic Areas   **RC** Rock Climbing   **TG** Tours, Guides
MB Mountain   **RA** Ranger-led   **S** Swimming   **XC** Cross-country
Biking   Activities   **T** Toilets   Skiing   **265**
MT Marked Trails

Site Guide

VOLO BOG STATE NATURAL AREA
Illinois Dept. of Natural Resources
28478 W. Brandenburg Rd.
Ingleside, IL 60041
(815) 344-1294
BW, GS, H, I, MT, PA, RA, T, TG, XC

WESTON CEMETERY PRAIRIE
Illinois State University
Dept. of Biolgical Sciences
Campus Box 4120
Normal, IL 61790-4120
(309) 438-3800 **BW, H**

WILDCAT BLUFF–LITTLE BLACK SLOUGH NATURE PRESERVE
Illinois Dept. of Natural Resources
c/o Cache River State Natural Area
930 Sunflower Lane
Belknap, IL 62908
(618) 634-9678
Includes Heron Pond
BW, CK, H, MT

WILMINGTON SHRUB PRAIRIE NATURE PRESERVE
Illinois Dept. of Natural Resources
Natural Heritage Biologist
PO Box 88, Wilmington, IL 60481
(815) 423-6370
No developed access; call before visiting

WOLF ROAD PRAIRIE
Forest Preserve District of Cook County
536 N. Harlem Ave.
River Forest, IL 60305
(708) 771-1330 **BW, H, MT, PA, T**

IOWA

ANDERSON PRAIRIE STATE PRESERVE
Iowa Parks, Recreation and Preserves Div.
Wallace Bldg.
900 E. Grand Ave.
Des Moines, IA 50319-0034
(515) 281-3891 **BW, H**

BACKBONE STATE PARK
Iowa Parks, Recreation and Preserves Div.
1282 120th St.
Strawberry Pt., IA 52076
(319) 924-2527
BW, C, CK, F, GS, H, HR, I, L, MT, RC, S, T, TG, XC

BIXBY STATE PARK
Iowa Parks, Recreation and Preserves Div.
Wallace Bldg., 900 E. Grand Ave.
Des Moines, IA 50313-0034
(515) 281-3891 **BW, H, MT, PA, T**

BLUFFTON FIR STAND STATE PRESERVE
Iowa Parks, Recreation and Preserves Div.
Wallace Bldg., 900 E. Grand Ave.
Des Moines, IA 50319-0034
(515) 281-3891 **BW, H**

BROKEN KETTLE GRASSLANDS PRESERVE
The Nature Conservancy, Iowa Chapter
431 E. Locust St., Ste. 200
Des Moines, IA 50309
(515) 244-5044 **BW, H**

CAYLER PRAIRIE STATE PRESERVE
Iowa Parks, Recreation and Preserves Div.
Wallace Bldg., 900 E. Grand Ave.
Des Moines, IA 50319-0034
(515) 281-3891 **BW, H**

CEDAR HILLS SAND PRAIRIE PRESERVE
The Nature Conservancy, Iowa Chapter
431 E. Locust St., Ste. 200
Des Moines, IA 50309
(515) 244-5044 **BW, H**

DESOTO NATIONAL WILDLIFE REFUGE
U.S. Fish and Wildlife Service
1434 316th Lane
Missouri Valley, IA 51555
(712) 642-4121
Vehicle entrance fee; camping nearby
BW, CK, F, GS, H, I, MT, PA, T

EFFIGY MOUNDS NATIONAL MONUMENT
National Park Service
151 Rte. 76, Harpers Ferry, IA 52146
(319) 873-3491 **BW, I, MT, RA, T, TG**

FEN VALLEY WILDLIFE AREA
Iowa Fish and Wildlife Div.
Wallace Bldg., 900 E. Grand Ave.
Des Moines, IA 50319-0034
(515) 281-3891 **BW, H**

FIVE RIDGE PRAIRIE PRESERVE
Plymouth County Conservation Board
25601 County Rd. 60, Hinton, IA 51024
(712) 947-4270
Foot traffic only; carry water
BW, F, H, RA

BT Bike Trails
BW Bird-watching
C Camping
CK Canoeing, Kayaking
DS Downhill Skiing
F Fishing
GS Gift Shop
H Hiking
HR Horseback Riding
I Information Center

FLOYD MONUMENT PARK
Sioux City Parks and Recreation Dept.
520 Pierce St.
Sioux City, IA 51102-0447
(712) 279-6126
(712) 279-6115   **BW, T**

**FREDA HAFFNER KETTLEHOLE
STATE PRESERVE**
The Nature Conservancy, Iowa Chapter
431 E. Locust St., Ste. 200
Des Moines, IA 50309
(515) 244-5044   **BW, H**

GITCHIE MANITOU STATE PRESERVE
Iowa Parks, Recreation and Preserves Div.
Wallace Bldg., 900 E. Grand Ave.
Des Moines, IA 50319-0034
(515) 281-3891   **BW, H**

HAYDEN PRAIRIE STATE PRESERVE
Iowa Parks, Recreation and Preserves Div.
Wallace Bldg., 900 E. Grand Ave.
Des Moines, IA 50313-0034
(515) 281-3891   **BW, H**

HERON BEND CONSERVATION AREA
Lee County Conservation Board
PO Box 218, Montrose, IA 52639
(319) 463-7673
    Tours by prearrangement
            BW, CK, F, H, I, PA, T, TG

HITCHCOCK NATURE AREA
Pottawattamie County Conservation Board
27792 Ski Hill Loop
Honey Creek, IA 51542
(712) 545-3283
    Primitive camping; annual summer sol-
    stice weekend event
        BW, C, GS, H, I, MT, PA, T, TG

IOWA LAKESIDE LABORATORY
Iowa State University
1838 Rte. 86, Milford, IA 51351
(712) 337-3669
    Must check in with resident manager
                    BW, F, L, T

IOWA PRAIRIE NETWORK
PO Box 516
Mason City, IA 50402-0516
(402) 571-6230
    Organization produces newsletter and
    plans 40-50 field trips per year

KALSOW PRAIRIE STATE PRESERVE
Iowa Parks, Recreation and Preserves Div.
Wallace Bldg., 900 E. Grand Ave.
Des Moines, IA 50319-0034
(515) 281-3891   **BW, H**

LACEY KEOSAUQUA STATE PARK
Iowa Parks, Recreation and Preserves Div.
PO Box 398, Keosauqua, IA 52565
(319) 293-3502
    Cabins available seasonally
            BW, C, CK, F, H, L, MT, PA, S, T

LEDGES STATE PARK
Iowa Parks, Recreation and Preserves Div.
1519 250th St.
Madrid, IA 50156
(515) 432-1852
            BW, C, H, MT, PA, RA, T, XC

LOESS HILLS WILDLIFE AREA
Iowa Fish and Wildlife Div.
RR 2, Box 15A, Onawa, IA 51040
(712) 423-2426
    Primitive camping   **BW, C, H, MT, XC**

**MARK TWAIN
NATIONAL WILDLIFE REFUGE**
U.S. Fish and Wildlife Service
10728 C.R. X61
Wapello, IA 52653
(319) 523-6982
    Refuge closed September 15–February 1;
    trail around refuge open year-round
            BW, CK, F, H, I, MB, MT

MAQUOKETA CAVES STATE PARK
Iowa Parks, Recreation and Preserves Div.
10970 98th St.
Maquoketa, IA 52060
(319) 652-5833   **BW, C, H, I, MT, PA, T**

**MINES OF SPAIN
STATE RECREATION AREA**
Iowa Parks, Recreation and Preserves Div.
8999 Bellevue Heights
Dubuque, IA 52003-9214
(319) 556-0620
        BW, CK, F, H, I, MT, PA, RA, TG, XC

OCHEYEDAN MOUND STATE PRESERVE
Osceola County Conservation Board
5945 Rte. 9
Ocheyedan, IA 51354
(712) 758-3709   **BW, H**

L	Lodging	**PA**	Picnic Areas	**RC** Rock Climbing **TG** Tours, Guides
MB	Mountain Biking	**RA**	Ranger-led Activities	**S** Swimming **XC** Cross-country Skiing
MT	Marked Trails			**T** Toilets

267

PALISADES-KEPLER STATE PARK
Iowa Parks, Recreation and Preserves Div.
700 Kepler Dr., Mt. Vernon, IA 52314
(319) 895-6039
BW, C, CK, F, H, MT, PA, RC, T

PIKES PEAK STATE PARK
Iowa Parks, Recreation and Preserves Div.
15316 Great River Rd.
McGregor, IA 52159-8558
(319) 873-2341
BT, BW, C, GS, H, MB, MT, PA, T, XC

PILOT KNOB STATE PARK
Iowa Parks, Recreation and Preserves Div.
2148 340th St.
Forest City, IA 50436
(515) 581-4835
Tours by prearrangement
BT, BW, C, CK, F, H, HR, I, MB, MT, PA, RA, T, TG, XC

PREPARATION CANYON STATE PARK
c/o Lewis and Clark State Park
Rte. 1, Box 104, Onawa, IA 51040
(712) 423-2829
Hike-in camping only
BW, C, H, PA, T, XC

RIVERTON WILDLIFE AREA
Iowa Fish and Wildlife Div.
PO Box 490
Sidney, IA 51652
(712) 374-3133; (712) 387-2791
Primitive camping; tours by prearrangement
BW, C, F, H, I, T

SHEEDER PRAIRIE STATE PRESERVE
Iowa Parks, Recreation and Preserves Div.
Wallace Bldg., 900 E. Grand Ave.
Des Moines, IA 50319-0034
(515) 281-3891
BW, H

SHIMEK STATE FOREST
Iowa Forests and Forestry Div.
RR 1, Box 95
Farmington, IA 52626
(319) 878-3811
BW, C, F, H, HR, MT, PA, T, XC

SILVER LAKE FEN STATE PRESERVE
Iowa Parks, Recreation and Preserves Div.
Wallace Bldg., 900 E. Grand Ave.
Des Moines, IA 50319-0034
(515) 281-3891
BW

STARR'S CAVE STATE PRESERVE
Des Moines County Conservation Board
11627 Starr's Cave Rd.
Burlington, IA 52601
(319) 753-5808
BW, H, I, MT, PA, RA, T, XC

STEELE PRAIRIE STATE PRESERVE
Cherokee County Conservation Board
629 River Rd.
Cherokee, IA 51012
(712) 225-6709
C, F, MT, RA, T, XC

STEPHENS STATE FOREST
Iowa Forests and Forestry Div.
RR 3, Box 31
Chariton, IA 50049
(515) 774-4559; (515) 774-5632
(camping information)
BT, BW, C, F, H, HR, MB, MT, PA, T, XC

STONE STATE PARK
Iowa Parks, Recreation and Preserves Div.
5001 Talbot Rd.
Sioux City, IA 51103
(712) 255-4698
Includes the Loess Ridge Nature Center
(one mile south) and Mt. Talbot State Preserve; vehicle travel restricted through
park roads in winter; snowmobiling
BT, BW, C, F, GS, H, HR, I, MT, PA, RA, T, TG, XC

TURIN LOESS HILLS STATE PRESERVE
Iowa Fish and Wildlife Div.
RR 2, Box 15A
Onawa, IA 51040
(712) 423-2426
Primitive camping
BW, C, H, MT, XC

**UNION SLOUGH
NATIONAL WILDLIFE REFUGE**
U.S. Fish and Wildlife Service
1710 360th St.
Titonka, IA 50480
(515) 928-2523
BW

**UPPER MISSISSIPPI RIVER NATIONAL
WILDLIFE AND FISH REFUGE**
U.S. Fish and Wildlife Service
PO Box 460
McGregor, IA 52157
(319) 873-3423
BW, C, CK, F, H, I, MT, S, T, XC

BT	Bike Trails	**CK**	Canoeing, Kayaking	**F**	Fishing	**HR**	Horseback Riding
BW	Bird-watching			**GS**	Gift Shop		
C	Camping	**DS**	Downhill Skiing	**H**	Hiking	**I**	Information Center

WALNUT CREEK NATIONAL WILDLIFE REFUGE AND PRAIRIE LEARNING CENTER
U.S. Fish and Wildlife Service
PO Box 399
Prairie City, IA 50228
(515) 994-2415
Auto-tour route
BW, H, I, MT, PA, RA, T, TG

WHITE PINE HOLLOW STATE PRESERVE
Iowa Parks, Recreation and Preserves Div.
Wallace Bldg., 900 E. Grand Ave.
Des Moines, IA 50319-0034
(515) 281-3891 **BW, H**

WILLIAMS PRAIRIE
The Nature Conservancy, Iowa Chapter
431 E. Locust St., Ste. 200
Des Moines, IA 50309
(515) 244-5044 **BW, H**

YELLOW RIVER STATE FOREST
Iowa Forests and Forestry Div.
729 State Forest Rd.
Harpers Ferry, IA 52146
(319) 586-2254; (319) 586-2548
BW, C, F, H, HR, MT, PA, XC

KANSAS

BAKER WETLANDS
Baker University
PO Box 65
Baldwin City, KS 66006
(913) 594-6451 (B.U. Biology Dept.)
(913) 865-4411 (Lawrence C&V Bureau)
BT, BW, H, I, MT, TG

BYRON WALKER WILDLIFE AREA
Kansas Fisheries, Wildlife
and Public Lands Div.
8685 W. Rte. 54
Cunningham, KS 67035
(316) 532-3242
No motorized vehicles
BW, C, CK, F, H, I, MB, MT, PA, T

CEDAR BLUFF RESERVOIR AND STATE PARK
Kansas Parks Div.
RR 2, Box 76A
Ellis, KS 67637
(913) 726-3212; (913) 628-8614
Two primitive cabins available
BW, C, F, H, I, L, MB, PA, S, T

CHAPLIN NATURE CENTER
Wichita Audubon Society
Rte. 1, Box 216
Arkansas City, KS 67005
(316) 442-4133
BW, GS, H, I, MT, PA, RA, T, TG

CHASE STATE FISHING LAKE WILDLIFE AREA
Kansas Fisheries, Wildlife
and Public Lands Div.
RR 1, Box 195
Council Grove, KS 66846
(316) 767-5900
Horses allowed on roads only
BW, C, CK, F, H, HR, PA

CHEYENNE BOTTOMS WILDLIFE AREA
Kansas Fisheries, Wildlife
and Public Lands Div.
Rte. 3, Box 301, Great Bend, KS 67530
(316) 793-7730; (316) 793-3066 **BW**

CIMARRON NATIONAL GRASSLAND
U.S. Forest Service
PO Box 300, Elkhart, KS 67950
(316) 697-4621
Includes portion of National Historic
Sante Fe Trail; gravel roads hazardous in
wet weather; bring drinking water; some
facilities for handicapped
BT, BW, C, F, GS, H, HR, MB, MT, PA, T

DILLON NATURE CENTER
Hutchinson Recreation Commission
3002 East 30th Ave.
Hutchinson, KS 67502
(316) 663-7411
Day use area
BW, F, GS, H, I, MT, PA, RA, T, TG

ELK CITY RESERVOIR AND WILDLIFE AREA
Kansas Fisheries, Wildlife
and Public Lands Div.
PO Box 945, Independence, KS 67301
(316) 331-6295
BW, C, CK, F, H, HR, I, MB, MT, PA, RC, S, T

ERNIE MILLER PARK
Johnson County Park and Recreation District
909 Rte. 7 North, Olathe, KS 66061
(913) 764-7759
BW, GS, H, MT, RA, T, TG

L	Lodging	**PA**	Picnic Areas	**RC**	Rock Climbing	**TG**	Tours, Guides
MB	Mountain Biking	**RA**	Ranger-led Activities	**S**	Swimming	**XC**	Cross-country Skiing
MT	Marked Trails			**T**	Toilets		

FICK FOSSIL AND HISTORY MUSEUM
700 West 3rd, Oakley, KS 67748
(913) 672-4839
Museum donation requested   **GS, TG**

FINNEY GAME REFUGE
Kansas Fisheries, Wildlife,
and Public Lands Divs.
785 S. Rte 83, Garden City, KS 67846
(316) 276-8886   **BW**

FLINT HILLS NATIONAL WILDLIFE REFUGE
U.S. Fish and Wildlife Service
PO Box 128
Hartford, KS 66854
(316) 392-5553
BW, C, CK, F, H, HR, I, MT

GREAT PLAINS NATURE CENTER
Chisholm Creek Park
6232 East 29th St. N.
Wichita, KS 67114
(316) 683-5499
Handicapped-accessible
BW, F, GS, H, I, MT, PA, RA, T, TG

KANOPOLIS LAKE AND STATE PARK
Kansas Parks Div.
200 Horsethief Rd.
Marquette, KS 67464
(913) 546-2565
Horses and bikes allowed on trails only
**BT, BW, C, CK, F, GS, H, HR,
I, MB, MT, PA, RA, S, T, XC**

KIRWIN NATIONAL WILDLIFE REFUGE
U.S. Fish and Wildlife Service
RR 1, Box 103
Kirwin, KS 67644
(913) 543-6673
BW, C, CK, F, H, I, MT, PA, T

KONZA PRAIRIE
Kansas State University
Div. of Biology, Ackert Hall
Manhattan, KS 66506
(913) 539-1961; (913) 532-6620
BW, H, MT

KU NATURAL HISTORY MUSEUM
University of Kansas
Dyche Hall
Lawrence, KS 66045
(913) 864-4450
(913) 864-4540   **GS, T**

**LAKE SCOTT STATE PARK
AND WILDLIFE AREA**
Kansas Parks and Fisheries, Wildlife and
Public Lands Divs.
520 West Scott Lake Dr.
Scott City, KS 67871
(316) 872-2061
Fishing boats only
**BT, BW, C, F, H, HR, I,
MB, MT, PA, RC, S, T**

LAND INSTITUTE
2440 E. Water Well Rd.
Salina, KS 67401
(913) 823-5376
Self-guided tours, no charge; one-week
advance notice for guided tours
BW, GS, I, PA, TG

MARAIS DES CYGNES WILDLIFE AREA
Kansas Parks Div.
Rte. 2, Box 186A
Pleasanton, KS 66075
(913) 352-8941   **BW, C**

MAXWELL WILDLIFE REFUGE
Kansas Fisheries, Wildlife and
Public Lands Div.
2577 Pueblo Rd., Canton, KS 67428
(316) 628-4592
Fee for tours to see buffalo and elk in
native prairie; observation tower
BW, I, TG

MCPHERSON STATE FISHING LAKE
Kansas Fisheries, Wildlife
and Public Lands Div.
2577 Pueblo Rd., Canton, KS 67428
(316) 628-4592
BW, C, CK, F, H, MT, PA, T

MUSHROOM ROCKS STATE PARK
Kansas Parks Div.
c/o Kanopolis State Park
200 Horsethief Rd., Marquette, KS 67464
(913) 546-2565   **BW, H, PA, T**

PERRY LAKE AND WILDLIFE AREA
Army Corps of Engineers,
Perry Project Office
10419 Perry Park Dr.
Perry, KS 66073-9717
(913) 597-5144
(913) 246-3449 (Perry State Park)
BW, C, F, H, HR, I, MB, MT, PA, S, T

BT	Bike Trails	**CK**	Canoeing, Kayaking	**F**	Fishing	
BW	Bird-watching			**GS**	Gift Shop	**HR** Horseback Riding
C	Camping	**DS**	Downhill Skiing	**H**	Hiking	**I** Information Center

PRAIRIE CENTER
Kansas Parks Div.
26001 West 255th St., Paola, KS 66071
(913) 783-4507
Primitive facilities only   **BW, F, H**

QUIVIRA NATIONAL WILDLIFE REFUGE
U.S. Fish and Wildlife Service
RR 3, Box 48A
Stafford, KS 67578
(316) 486-2393   **BW, F, H, I, MT, T**

ROCK CITY
c/o Kanopolis State Park
200 Horsethief Rd.
Marquette, KS 67464
(913) 546-2575   **BW, PA, T**

SAND HILLS STATE PARK
Kansas Parks Div.
c/o Cheney State Park
16000 N.E. 50th St.
Cheney, KS 67025-8487
(316) 542-3664   **BW, H, MT**

SCHERMERHORN PARK
City of Galena
315 West 7th St., Galena, KS 66739
(316) 783-5265
      BW, CK, F, H, MT, PA, S, T

SHAWNEE MISSION PARK
Johnson County Park
and Recreation District
6501 Antioch Rd.
Shawnee Mission, KS 66202
(913) 831-3355   **BT, BW, F, GS, H, HR, I,
MT, PA, RA, S, T, TG, XC**

**STERNBERG MUSEUM
OF NATURAL HISTORY**
Fort Hays State University
600 Park St., Hays, KS 67601
(913) 628-4286
Admission fee; closed during renovation, call for opening date
      BW, GS, MT, T, TG

TORONTO LAKE AND WILDLIFE AREA
Kansas Fisheries, Wildlife
and Public Lands Div.
Rte. 1, Box 88
Severy, KS 67137
(316) 583-6783; (316) 637-2213
      BW, C, F, H, MT, PA, S, T

WESTON BEND BOTTOMLANDS
Forestry Dept.
Office of the Garrison Commander
Fort Leavenworth, KS 66027
(913) 684-2749   **BW, H**

WILSON LAKE
U.S. Army Corps of Engineers
Rte. 1, Box 241, Sylvan Grove, KS 67481
(913) 658-2551
      BW, C, CK, F, H, I, MT, PA, RA, S, T, TG

WILSON STATE PARK
Kansas Parks Div.
RR 1, Box 181
Sylvan Grove, KS 67481
(913) 658-2465
Dakota Trail provides hilltop view of
Wilson Lake
      **BT, BW, C, CK, F, H, I,
MB, MT, PA, RA, S, T**

**WOODSON STATE FISHING LAKE AND
WILDLIFE AREA**
Kansas Fisheries, Wildlife
and Public Lands Div.
RR 1, Box 123
Toronto, KS 66777
(316) 637-2748; (316) 637-2213
Primitive camping
      BW, C, F, H, PA, T

Z BAR/SPRINGHILL RANCH
National Park Trust
Rte. 1, Box 14
Strong City, KS 66869
(316) 273-8247   **BW, H, MT, T, TG**

MISSOURI

ALLRED LAKE NATURAL AREA
c/o Otter Slough Conservation Area
7001 C.R. 675
Dexter, MO 63841
(513) 624-5821
Boardwalk   **BW, CK, H**

BELL MOUNTAIN WILDERNESS
Mark Twain National Forest
Potosi-Fredericktown Ranger District
PO Box 188
Potosi, MO 63664
(573) 438-5427
Foot travel only beyond gate
      BW, C, H, HR

L Lodging	**PA** Picnic Areas	**RC** Rock Climbing	**TG** Tours, Guides
MB Mountain Biking	**RA** Ranger-led Activities	**S** Swimming	**XC** Cross-country Skiing
MT Marked Trails		**T** Toilets	**271**

BENNETT SPRING STATE PARK
Missouri Div. of State Parks
26250 Rte. 64A
Lebanon, MO 65536
(417) 532-4338
Information on Bennett Spring Savanna
available here
BW, C, CK, F, GS, H, I, L,
MT, PA, RA, S, T, TG

BIG OAK TREE NATURAL AREA
c/o Big Oak Tree State Park
13640 S. Rte. 102
East Prairie, MO 63845
(573) 649-3149
Half-mile-long boardwalk
BW, H, MT

BIG SPRING
National Park Service
PO Box 490, Van Buren, MO 63965
(573) 323-4236
BW, C, CK, F, H, L, MT, PA, S, T

BLUE POND NATURAL AREA
Castor River State Forest
2302 County Park Dr.
Cape Girardeau, MO 63701-1842
(573) 290-5730; (573) 238-2321
Primitive camping
BW, C, H, MT

**BRICKYARD HILL LOESS MOUNDS
PRAIRIE NATURAL AREA**
Missouri Wildlife Div.
701 NE College Dr.
St. Joseph, MO 64506
(813) 271-3100
BW, C, F, H, PA, T

BUTLER HOLLOW GLADES NATURAL AREA
Mark Twain National Forest
Cassville Ranger District
PO Box 188, Ava, MO 65608
(417) 683-4428
BW

CHLOE LOWRY MARSH NATURAL AREA
Missouri Wildlife Div.
Rte. 2, Box 162, Princeton, MO 64673
(813) 748-3820; (816) 646-6122
BW, H, MT

CUIVRE RIVER STATE PARK
Missouri Div. of State Parks
Rte. 1, Box 25, Troy, MO 63379
(314) 528-7247
BW, C, F, H, HR, I, MT, PA, RA, S, T

CUPOLA POND NATURAL AREA
Mark Twain National Forest
Doniphan Ranger District
1104 Walnut St., Doniphan, MO 63936
(573) 996-2153
Information available at ranger district
BW, H, HR, I, MT

**DIAMOND GROVE PRAIRIE
NATURAL AREA**
Missouri Wildlife Div.
2630 North Mayfair
Springfield, MO 65803
(417) 895-6880
BW

DR. EDMUND A. BABLER STATE PARK
Missouri Div. of State Parks
88 Guy Park Dr.
Chesterfield, MO 63005
(314) 458-3813
BT, BW, C, GS, H, HR,
I, MT, RA, S, T, TG, XC

DUCK CREEK CONSERVATION AREA
Missouri Wildlife Div.
RR 1
Puxico, MO 63960
(573) 222-3337
BW, C, F, PA, T

ELEPHANT ROCKS STATE PARK
Missouri Div. of State Parks
PO Box 509
Pilot Knob, MO 63663
(573) 546-3454
BW, H, MT, PA, RC, T

**ELEVEN POINT NATIONAL
SCENIC RIVER**
Mark Twain National Forest
Eleven Point Ranger District
Rte. 1, Box 1908
Winona, MO 65588
(573) 325-4233
BW, C, CK, F, H, I, MT, S, T

GEORGE WASHINGTON CARVER NATIONAL MONUMENT
National Park Service
5646 Carver Rd.
Diamond, MO 64840
(417) 325-4151
BW, GS, I, MT, PA, RA, T, TG

GRAND GULF STATE PARK
Missouri Div. of State Parks
PO Box 176, Jefferson City, MO 65102
(417) 264-7600
BW, H, MT, PA, T

BT Bike Trails	**CK** Canoeing, Kayaking	**F** Fishing	**HR** Horseback Riding
BW Bird-watching		**GS** Gift Shop	
C Camping	**DS** Downhill Skiing	**H** Hiking	**I** Information Center

GREER SPRINGS
Mark Twain National Forest
Eleven Point Ranger District
Rte. 1, Box 1908
Winona, MO 65588
(573) 325-4233   **BW, H, T**

HADEN BALD NATURAL AREA
Mark Twain National Forest
Ava Ranger District
PO Box 188, Ava, MO 65608
(417) 683-4428   **BW**

HA HA TONKA STATE PARK
Missouri Div. of State Parks
Rte. 1, Box 658
Camdenton, MO 65020
(573) 346-2986; (800) 334-6946
                 BW, F, H, I, MT, PA, RA, T, TG

HOLLY RIDGE STATE FOREST
Missouri Forestry Div.
2302 County Dr.
Cape Girardeau, MO 63701-1842
(573) 290-5730; (573) 624-7483
      Primitive camping   **BW, C, H, HR, MT**

HUGHES MOUNTAIN NATURAL AREA
Missouri Forestry and Natural History Divs.
PO Box 248, Sullivan, MO 63080
(573) 468-3335   **BW, H**

**JAMERSON C. McCORMACK LOESS
MOUNDS NATURAL AREA**
Missouri Wildlife Div.
701 N.E. College Dr., St. Joseph, MO 64507
(816) 271-3100   **BW**

JAM UP CAVE NATURAL AREA
National Park Service
Van Buren, MO 63965
(573) 323-4236
      Access by canoe only   **BW, CK, F, S**

JOHNSON'S SHUT-INS STATE PARK
Missouri Div. of State Parks
HCR 1, Box 126
Middlebrook, MO 63656
(800) 334-6946; (573) 546-2450
      Includes Goggins Mountain Wild Area;
      ranger-led activities summer only; rock
      climbing September–May; hiking trails
      are rugged
                          **BW, C, F, GS, H,
                      MT, PA, RA, RC, S, T**

LONG BALD NATURAL AREA
Missouri Wildlife Div.
PO Box 138, West Plains, MO 65775
(417) 256-7161; (417) 679-4218
      No collecting allowed   **BW, H**

MARK TWAIN NATIONAL FOREST
U.S. Forest Service
401 Fairgrounds Rd., Rolla, MO 65401
(573) 364-4621
      Permission required for hiking or fishing
      on private lands   **BT, BW, C, CK, F, H,
                          HR, MB, MT, PA, S, T**

MARK TWAIN NATIONAL WILDLIFE REFUGE
U.S. Fish and Wildlife Service
PO Box 88, Annada, MO 63330
(573) 847-2333
      Fishing allowed in limited areas
                                   BW, F, I, T

MARMATON BOTTOMS PRAIRIE
The Nature Conservancy of Missouri
2800 S. Brentwood Blvd., St. Louis, MO 63144
(314) 968-1105   **BW, H**

MERAMEC STATE PARK
Missouri Div. of State Parks
2800 S. Rte. 185, Sullivan, MO 63080
(573) 468-6072; (573) 468-6519
      **BW, C, CK, F, GS, H, I, L, MT, PA, RA,
                                 RC, S, T, TG**

MINGO NATIONAL WILDLIFE REFUGE
U.S. Fish and Wildlife Service
24279 Rte. 51, Puxico, MO 63960
(573) 222-3589
                 BW, CK, F, H, I, MT, PA, T

MISSOURI BOTANICAL GARDEN
PO Box 299, St. Louis, MO 63166-0299
(314) 577-5100
      Admission fee   **BW, GS, T, TG**

ONONDAGA CAVE STATE PARK
Missouri Div. of State Parks
Rte. 1, Box 115, Leasburg, MO 65535
(573) 245-6576   **BW, C, CK, F, GS, H, I,
                          MT, PA, RA, S, T, TG**

OTTER SLOUGH CONSERVATION AREA
Missouri Wildlife Div.
7001 C.R. 675, Dexter, MO 63841
(573) 624-5821
      Boardwalk   **BW, C, CK, F, H, I, PA, T**

L	Lodging	**PA**	Picnic Areas	**RC**	Rock Climbing	**TG**	Tours, Guides	
MB	Mountain Biking	**RA**	Ranger-led Activities	**S**	Swimming	**XC**	Cross-country Skiing	**273**
MT	Marked Trails			**T**	Toilets			

OZARK NATIONAL SCENIC RIVERWAYS
National Park Service
PO Box 490, Van Buren, MO 63965
(573) 323-4236   **BW, C, CK, F, GS, H, HR, I, L, MT, PA, RA, S, T**

OZARK TRAIL
Missouri Dept. of Natural Resources
Ozark Trail Coordinator
PO Box 176, Jefferson City, MO 65102
(800) 334-6946; (573) 751-2479
    BW, C, H, HR, MT

PECK RANCH CONSERVATION AREA
Missouri Wildlife Div.
Rte. 1, Box 1395, Winona, MO 65588
(573) 323-4249   **BW, C, H, HR, MT**

PERSHING STATE PARK
Missouri Div. of State Parks
29277 Rte. 130, Laclede, MO 64651
(816) 963-2299
    BW, C, CK, F, H, MT, PA, RA, T, TG

PRAIRIE HOLLOW GORGE NATURAL AREA
National Park Service
PO Box 490, Van Buren, MO 63965
(573) 323-4236   **BW, H**

PRAIRIE STATE PARK
Missouri Div. of State Parks
PO Box 97, Liberal, MO 64762
(417) 843-6711
    BW, GS, H, I, MT, PA, RA, T

ROARING RIVER STATE PARK
Missouri Div. of State Parks
Rte. 2, Box 2530, Cassville, MO 65625
(417) 847-2539 (park office)
(417) 847-3742 (nature center)
    Cabins available   **BW, C, F, GS, H, HR, I, L, MT, PA, RA, S, T, TG**

ROCKHILL PRAIRIE
The Nature Conservancy of Missouri
2800 S. Brentwood Blvd.
St. Louis, MO 63144
(314) 968-1105   **BW, H**

SAM A. BAKER STATE PARK
Missouri Div. of State Parks
Rte. 1, Box 114, Patterson, MO 63956
(573) 856-4411
    BW, C, CK, F, GS, H, I, L, MT, PA, RA, S, T

SCHELL-OSAGE CONSERVATION AREA
Missouri Wildlife Div.
PO Box 106, El Dorado Springs, MO 64744
(417) 876-5226   **BW, C, F, H, PA, T**

SHAW ARBORETUM
Missouri Botanical Garden
PO Box 38, Gray Summit, MO 63039
(314) 451-3512
    Service roads used as bike trails
    BT, BW, H, I, MB, MT, PA, T, TG, XC

SHELTON L. COOK MEMORIAL MEADOW
The Nature Conservancy of Missouri
St. Louis, MO 63144
(314) 968-1105   **BW, H**

SQUAW CREEK
NATIONAL WILDLIFE REFUGE
U.S. Fish and Wildlife Service
PO Box 158, Mound City, MO 64470
(816) 442-3187
    Horses and bikes allowed on auto-tour
    route   **BW, F, GS, H, HR, I, MB, MT, PA, T**

STAR SCHOOL HILL PRAIRIE
NATURAL AREA
Missouri Wildlife Div.
701 N.E. College Dr., St. Joseph, MO 64507
(816) 271-3100   **BW, C, H**

SWAN LAKE NATIONAL WILDLIFE REFUGE
U.S. Fish and Wildlife Service
Rte. 1, Box 29A, Sumner, MO 64681
(816) 856-3323   **BW, F, I, T**

TABERVILLE PRAIRIE NATURAL AREA
Missouri Wildlife Div.
PO Box 106, El Dorado Springs, MO 64744
(417) 876-5226   **BW, H**

TAUM SAUK MOUNTAIN STATE PARK
Missouri Div. of State Parks
PO Box 176, Jefferson City, MO 65101
(800) 334-6946; (573) 546-3454
    Primitive camping; no office at park
    BW, C, H, MT, PA, T

TED SHANKS CONSERVATION AREA
Missouri Wildlife Div.
PO Box 13, Ashburn, MO 63433
(573) 754-6171
    Tours for groups only by appointment
    BW, C, CK, F, H, I, PA, T, TG

BT	Bike Trails	**CK**	Canoeing, Kayaking	**F**	Fishing	**HR**	Horseback Riding
BW	Bird-watching			**GS**	Gift Shop		
C	Camping	**DS**	Downhill Skiing	**H**	Hiking	**I**	Information Center

TRAIL OF TEARS STATE PARK
Missouri Div. of State Parks
PO Box 176, Jefferson City, MO 65102
(573) 334-1711
    BW, C, CK, F, GS, H, I, MT, PA, RA, S, T

WAYNE HELTON CONSERVATION AREA
Missouri Wildlife Div.
c/o Lake Paho Conservation Area
Rte. 2, Box 162, Princeton, MO 64673
(816) 748-3820
(816) 646-6128   **BW, C, F, H**

WHITE RIVER BALDS NATURAL AREA
Missouri Forestry Div.
Springfield District Forester
2630 N. Mayfair St., Springfield, MO 65803
(417) 895-6880
    No wheeled vehicles; collecting of
    plants prohibited   **BW, H, MT, T**

WILDCAT GLADE NATURAL AREA
Joplin Parks and Recreation Dept.
212 W. 8th St., Joplin, MO 64801
(417) 624-0820, ext. 571   **BW**

NEBRASKA

AGATE FOSSIL BEDS NATIONAL MONUMENT
National Park Service
301 River Rd., Harrison, NE 69346
(308) 668-2211
    Collecting of fossils, rocks or plants pro-
    hibited; watch for rattlesnakes
        BW, H, I, MT, T

ARBOR LAKE WILDLIFE MANAGEMENT AREA
Nebraska Game and Parks Commission
2200 N. 33rd St., Lincoln, NE 68503
(402) 471-0641   **BW**

**ASHFALL FOSSIL BEDS
STATE HISTORICAL PARK**
Nebraska Game and Parks Commission
University of Nebraska at Lincoln
PO Box 66, Royal, NE 68773
(402) 893-2000   **BW, GS, I, RA, T**

BAUERMEISTER PRAIRIE
Omaha Parks, Recreation
and Public Property Dept.
1819 Farnam St., Ste. 701
Omaha, NE 68183
(402) 444-5941
    BT, BW, CK, F, H, MT, PA, T

BESSEY RANGER DISTRICT
Nebraska National Forest
PO Box 38, Halsey, NE 69142-0038
(308) 533-2257; (308) 432-0300
    BW, C, CK, F, H, HR, MT, PA, RA, S, T

**BURCHARD LAKE
WILDLIFE MANAGEMENT AREA**
Nebraska Game and Parks Commission
RR 3, Box 102, Tecumseh, NE 68450
(402) 335-2534
    BW, C, CK, F, H, HR, MT, PA, T

CHADRON STATE PARK
Nebraska Game and Parks Commission
15951 Rte. 385, Chadron, NE 69337-7353
(308) 432-6167
    Vehicle entrance fee
    **BT, BW, C, F, GS, H, HR, I, L, MB, MT,
    PA, S, T**

**CHIMNEY ROCK
NATIONAL HISTORICAL SITE**
Nebraska State Historical Society
PO Box F, Bayard, NE 69334
(308) 586-2581
    Admission fee to visitor center
        BW, I, T

COURTHOUSE AND JAIL ROCKS
Nebraska State Historical Society
PO Box F, Bayard, NE 69334
(308) 586-2581   **H**

**CRESCENT LAKE
NATIONAL WILDLIFE REFUGE**
U.S. Fish and Wildlife Service
HC 68, Box 21, Ellsworth, NE 69340
(308) 635-7851
    4WD vehicle necessary to see most of
    refuge   **BW, F**

CUMING CITY CEMETERY PRAIRIE
Dana College Biology Dept., Blair, NE 68008
(402) 426-7261   **BW, H**

**FONTENELLE FOREST
AND NEALE WOODS NATURE CENTERS**
Fontenelle Forest Association
1111 N. Bellevue Blvd.
Bellevue, NE 68005
(402) 731-3140 (forest office)
(402) 453-5615 (Neale Woods)
    Tours by prearrangement; trail admis-
    sion fee   **BW, GS, H, MT, PA, RA, T, TG**

L	Lodging	**PA**	Picnic Areas	**RC**	Rock Climbing
MB	Mountain Biking	**RA**	Ranger-led Activities	**S**	Swimming
MT	Marked Trails			**T**	Toilets

TG	Tours, Guides	
XC	Cross-country Skiing	

FORT KEARNY STATE HISTORICAL PARK
Nebraska Game and Parks Commission
Rte. 4, Kearney, NE 68847
(308) 865-5305
    Vehicle entrance fee   **I, T, TG**

FORT NIOBRARA NATIONAL WILDLIFE REFUGE
U.S. Fish and Wildlife Service
HC 14, Box 67
Valentine, NE 69201
(402) 376-3789
    Tours by prearrangement
        BW, CK, F, GS, H, HR, I, MT, PA, RA, T, TG

FORT ROBINSON STATE PARK
Nebraska Game and Parks Commission
PO Box 392
Crawford, NE 69339-0392
(402) 471-5498; (308) 665-2900
    Vehicle entrance fee
        BT, BW, C, F, GS, H, HR, I, L, MB, MT, PA, RA, S, T, TG, XC

HARVARD MARSH
U.S. Fish and Wildlife Service
PO Box 1686, Kearney, NE 68848
(308) 236-5015   **BW, H, I, MT**

HOMESTEAD NATIONAL MONUMENT
National Park Service
Rte. 3, Box 47, Beatrice, NE 68310
(402) 223-3514   **BW, H, I, MT, PA, T, XC**

INDIAN CAVE STATE PARK
Nebraska Game and Parks Commission
Rte. 1, Box 30, Shubert, NE 68437
(402) 883-2575
    Vehicle entrance fee
        BT, BW, C, F, GS, H, HR, MB, MT, PA, T, XC

LAKE McCONAUGHY
Lake McConaughy State Recreation Area
1500 Rte. 61N
Ogallala, NE 69153
(308) 284-3542
        BT, BW, C, F, H, MT, PA, S, T

MALLARD HAVEN MARSH
U.S. Fish and Wildlife Service
PO Box 1686, Kearney, NE 68848
(308) 236-5015   **BW, I**

MISSOURI NATIONAL RECREATIONAL RIVERS
National Park Service
PO Box 591, O'Neill, NE 68763
(402) 336-3970
    Strong winds can cause good-size waves; private lands border most of the river   **BW, CK, F**

NINE MILE PRAIRIE
School of Biological Sciences
348 Manten Hall
University of Nebraska
Lincoln, NE 68588-0118
(402) 472-2720   **BW**

NIOBRARA NATIONAL SCENIC RIVER
National Park Service
PO Box 491, O'Neill, NE 68763
(402) 336-3970
(402) 376-3789 (Fort Niobrara NWR)
    Camping in state parks only
        BW, C, CK, I

NIOBRARA STATE PARK
Nebraska Game and Parks Commission
PO Box 226
Niobrara, NE 68760
(402) 857-3373
    Includes portion of Lewis and Clark National Historic Trail; cabins available; handicapped-accessible hike/bike trail with fishing bridge; vehicle entrance fee
        BT, BW, C, CK, F, GS, H, HR, I, L, MB, MT, PA, RA, S, T

NIOBRARA VALLEY PRESERVE
The Nature Conservancy
1722 St. Mary's Ave., #403
Omaha, NE 68102
(402) 342-0282   **BW, H, I, MT, T**

NIOBRARA WILDERNESS AREA
U.S. Fish and Wildlife Service
HC 14, Box 67
Valentine, NE 69201
(402) 376-3789
    Day use only
        BW, H

OGLALA NATIONAL GRASSLAND
U.S. Forest Service
Pine Ridge Ranger District
16524 Rte. 385, Chadron, NE 69337
(308) 432-4475   **BW, H, HR, MT**

BT	Bike Trails	**CK**	Canoeing, Kayaking	**F**	Fishing	**HR**	Horseback Riding
BW	Bird-watching			**GS**	Gift Shop		
C	Camping	**DS**	Downhill Skiing	**H**	Hiking	**I**	Information Center

PAWNEE PRAIRIE
WILDLIFE MANAGEMENT AREA
Nebraska Game and Parks Commission
RR 3, Box 102, Tecumseh, NE 68450
(402) 335-2534 **BW, F**

PINE RIDGE NATIONAL RECREATION AREA
Nebraska National Forest
Pine Ridge Ranger District
16524 Rte. 385, Chadron, NE 69337-7364
(308) 432-4475; (308) 432-0300
No motorized travel except wheelchairs
BT, BW, C, H, HR, MB, MT, PA, T

PONCA STATE PARK
Nebraska Game and Parks Commission
PO Box 688, Ponca, NE 68770
(402) 755-2284
Vehicle entry fee; cabins available during summer **BW, C, F, GS, H, HR, I, L, MT, PA, S, T, XC**

RAINWATER BASIN WETLAND DISTRICT
U.S. Fish and Wildlife Service
PO Box 1686, Kearney, NE 68848
(308) 236-5015 **BT, BW, C, CK, H, I, L, MT, PA, T, TG**

ROCK CREEK STATION
HISTORICAL PARK
Nebraska Game and Parks Commission
57425 710th Rd.
Fairbury, NE 68352
(402) 729-5777
Vehicle entrance fee
BT, BW, C, H, HR, I, MT, PA, T, TG

SAMUEL R. MCKELVIE NATIONAL FOREST
U.S. Forest Service
HC 74, Box 10,
Nenzel, NE 69219
(402) 823-4154 **BW, C, F, H, HR, MT, T**

SCOTTS BLUFF NATIONAL MONUMENT
National Park Service
PO Box 27, Gering, NE 69341
(308) 436-4340 **BT, BW, H, I, MT**

SMITH FALLS STATE PARK
Nebraska Game and Parks Commission
HC 13, Box 38, Sparks, NE 69220
(402) 376-1306
Vehicle entrance fee; tours by prearrangement **BW, C, CK, F, GS, H, HR, I, MT, PA, RA, S, T, TG**

SOLDIER CREEK WILDERNESS
Nebraska National Forest
Pine Ridge District
16524 Rte. 385
Chadron, NE 69337-7364
(308) 432-4475; (308) 432-0300
No motorized travel except wheelchairs
BW, C, F, H, HR, MT, PA, T

STOLLEY PRAIRIE
Omaha Parks, Recreation
and Public Property Dept.
1819 Farnam St., Ste. 701
Omaha, NE 68183
(402) 444-5941 **BW, H**

TOADSTOOL GEOLOGIC PARK
U.S. Forest Service
Pine Ridge Ranger District
16524 Rte. 385
Chadron, NE 69337
(308) 432-4475 **BW, C, H, MT, PA, T**

VALENTINE NATIONAL WILDLIFE REFUGE
U.S. Fish and Wildlife Service
HC 14, Box 67
Valentine, NE 69201
(402) 376-3789
Tours by prearrangement
BW, CK, F, H, HR, RA, T, TG

WILDCAT HILLS STATE RECREATION AREA
Nebraska Game and Parks Commission
PO Box 65, Gering, NE 69341-0065
(308) 436-3777
Vehicle entrance fee
BT, BW, C, GS, H, I, MB, MT, PA, RA, T

WILLA CATHER MEMORIAL PRAIRIE
The Nature Conservancy
1722 St. Mary's Ave., #403
Omaha, NE 68102
(402) 342-0282 **BW, H**

L	Lodging	**PA**	Picnic Areas	**RC**	Rock Climbing	**TG**	Tours, Guides
MB	Mountain Biking	**RA**	Ranger-led Activities	**S**	Swimming	**XC**	Cross-country Skiing
MT	Marked Trails			**T**	Toilets		

INDEX

Index

283

ACKNOWLEDGMENTS

The editors gratefully acknowledge the professional assistance of Susan Kirby and Patricia Woodruff. We also wish to thank those site managers and naturalists whose time and commitment contributed to this guide. The following consultants also helped in the preparation of this volume: Dallas Rhodes, Professor and Chair of Geology, Whittier College, and Keith P. Tomlinson, Principal Naturalist, Biogeographic, Inc. Suzanne Winckler wishes to thank Mary Clausen, John Fleckenstein, Mike Fritz, Yvonne Hardy, Doug Ladd, Robert Mohlenbrock, Paul Nelson, John Pearson, Jean Prior, Lynda Richards, David Smith, Gerry Steinauer, Tim Vogt, and Gerould Wilhelm.

PHOTOGRAPHY CREDITS